TUCSON
A Drama in Time

John Warnock

Tucson: A Drama in Time

Copyright © 2019 John Warnock. All rights reserved. No part of this book may be reproduced or retransmitted in any form or by any means without the written permission of the publisher.

Published by Wheatmark®
2030 East Speedway Boulevard, Suite 106
Tucson, Arizona 85719 USA
www.wheatmark.com

ISBN: 978-1-62787-706-0 (paperback)
ISBN: 978-1-62787-707-7 (ebook)
LCCN: 2019940370

Bulk ordering discounts are available through Wheatmark, Inc. For more information, email orders@wheatmark.com or call 1-888-934-0888.

rev201901

[A] city is more than a place in space, it is a drama in time.
                                            Sir Patrick Geddes[*]

[O]ne place comprehended can make us understand other places better.
                                                    Eudora Welty[**]

---

[*] Sir Patrick Geddes (1854-1932) was a Scot, a professor of civics and sociology, and a pioneering town planner.

[**] Eudora Welty (1909-2001) won the Pulitzer Prize for fiction among many awards. She was born in Jackson, Mississippi and set much of her fiction in the South.

Contents

Maps and Photographs Index		vii
Introduction		ix
1	Before People Appear	1
2	People Arrive	4
3	The Europeans Arrive	9
4	Father Kino in the Santa Cruz Valley	14
5	After Kino: The Santa Cruz Valley in New Spain and Mexico	23
6	The Americans Arrive	46
7	Tucson in the Arizona Territory	61
8	Tucson in the State of Arizona	175
9	To Be Continued	436
Acknowledgments and Thanks		439
Selected Documents and Stories by Those Who Came Before		445
Resources on the Web		453

Maps and Photographs Index

1701	Padre Kino's map of the Pimería Alta, 21
1862	Fergusson map of Tucson, 59
1864	Union army map of Arizona, 67
1871	First Pima County Courthouse (construction started in 1868), Muybridge photograph, 80
1871	Map of Tucson area by S. W. Foreman, 83
1876	J. F. White map of agricultural plots along the Santa Cruz, 94
1883	Second Pima County Courthouse (construction started in 1881) and other buildings in Tucson, Buehman photograph, 112
1886	Sanborn fire insurance map of central Tucson, 124
1899	Pima County Board of Supervisors topographic map of Tucson region, 141
1905	Tucson in earliest US Geological Survey quadrangle map of the region, 161

1913	Good Roads Association maps of Tucson's attractions and route to Florence, 182 and 183
1919	Sanborn map of downtown Tucson, 197
1926	Official City of Tucson street map, 218
1929	Third Pima County Courthouse (completed 1929, photograph taken 1934), 230
1936	Pima County map of downtown Tucson area, 258
1956	Gousha road map of Tucson in modern road-map style, 311
1974	Fourth Pima County Courthouse (completed 1974, photograph taken 2013) with the third (1929) in the foreground, 356
1983	US Geological Survey topographic map of central Tucson, 379
1995	Digitally designed general overview map of Tucson, 399
2013	Fifth Pima County Courthouse under construction, 418
2014	Central Tucson screen shot map, 422

Introduction

One day we go for a walk. After a while, we sit on a rock to rest. Looking down idly between our feet, we see nothing much at first, and then spot some flakes of flint. Even if we know little about what we are seeing, we know now that another person sat on that rock at a time and in a place different from our own, and yet maybe not so different in human terms. On another day, someone sat there, right there, and worked at making something useful or beautiful or both, as we also may have done that day. We know now that the place we are in has a human story and that, however incidentally, we are now included in it.

Wherever we find ourselves, we know, don't we, that we stand at the end of a story, a long one, longer than we could know. Not just one story either, but many stories, with stories inside those stories that overlap and are entangled and that work sometimes at cross-purposes. As in a drama.

Stories are what make a *location* into a *place*. If we do not find ourselves *in place* where we are—anywhere in America, anywhere in the world—it may be because we don't know the stories of that place or don't know how to include ourselves in those stories. We may not want to make the effort because the places we find ourselves in can seem not so interesting. However, they may only appear uninteresting because we don't know the stories.

We dwell in stories. Stories can add texture and interest and meaning to our lives whether they are stories about something that actually happened or not. From some of our stories, we don't ask more than what interests and delights us in them. The stories that follow here, though, are about what actually happened in and around the place called Tucson. That is, this account is, as far as I have been able to take it, factually and historically accurate. Sometimes we want that. Sometimes that matters.

This account doesn't tell the whole story—no account could do that—and in some ways it isn't even *a* story. It is more like the threads of many stories, offered in the hope that readers will be moved to make something of it for themselves. It offers but one selection of the possible threads. The selecting has been done, the colors and textures chosen, the weaving begun, to provide some of what the language philosopher Kenneth Burke calls "equipment for living" in Tucson. In the simplest terms, I hope this account will make Tucson *more* of a place for readers than it might have been before.

The entries are in chronological order, which makes it possible for stories of different kinds to run alongside each other in the larger story. The juxtapositions that result create places where readers may be moved to make their own connections and contributions. I am hoping that this account will open conversation about the stories that make this place called Tucson, not close it down.

I was born in Tucson and grew up there in the 1940s and 1950s. Maybe I should have felt in place in Tucson, but I didn't. I graduated from Tucson High School in 1959 and left Tucson for college back East, returning almost thirty years later to take a job in the English Department at the University of Arizona, surprised to find myself back in town and surprised at how good it felt to be back.

I soon began to discover all that I hadn't learned growing up in Tucson, and still didn't know, about its stories, stories I thought I would need to know if I were to feel in place there. Much of what follows is what has helped me toward that end.

Readers who aren't looking to make Tucson home will nonetheless find in these pages a place of variety and interest to dwell in imaginatively and relate to their own histories in ways that might enrich what home is for them.

Readers can feel free to start their journey in time wherever they like, with the emergence of Sentinel Peak in deep time, or with the advent of humans, or with the advent of Europeans, or with the period that began with the U.S. War with Mexico and extended through territorial times, or with statehood for Arizona in 1912, or with any of the decades that followed, going forward or backward from there. Readers who read the whole work will find that some threads reappear, as do streams that go underground and reappear downriver. Streams like, once upon a time, the Santa Cruz River.

Readers will find few specific citations to sources along the way. I hope this will allow those who take this voyage to participate more fully in the unfolding of the stories. Here at the outset, however, to help readers relax into this kind of reading, I will offer a general account of the resources I have relied on. Readers already relaxed on this score can go right to the account. Specific citations to more of the resources that have been used to produce this account will be found in the bibliography at the end.

For geology and water, the Arizona Geological Society website was useful as were books by Michael Logan (*The Lessening Stream*, 2002) and Robert Webb et al. (*Requiem for the Santa Cruz*, 2014). Also useful were the resources available on the websites of Climate Assessment for the Southwest (CLIMAS), Tucson Water, and the Arizona Water Resources Research Center.

For stories of the peoples here before the Europeans arrived, resources available through the Archaeology Southwest website were useful, as was work by Edward Spicer (e.g., *Cycles of Conquest*, 1962) and Emil Haury (e.g., *Prehistory of the American Southwest*, 1986). William Doelle, the president and CEO of Archaeology Southwest, generously answered a number of key questions.

For Spanish Colonial history, basic works are Herbert Bolton, *Rim of Christendom* (1936); Henry Dobyns, *Spanish Colonial Tucson* (1976); Oakah Jones, *Los Paisanos: Spanish Settlers on the Northern Frontier of New Spain* (1979); John Kessell, *Spain in the Southwest* (2002); Kieran McCarty, *Desert Documentary* (1976); Charles Poltzer S.J., *Kino, a Legacy: His life, His Works, His Missions, His Monuments* (1998).

For territorial times and early statehood, material has come from William Kalt, *Tucson Was a Railroad Town* (2007); Bettina Lyons, *Zeckendorfs and Steinfelds* (2008); Thomas Sheridan, *Los Tucsonenses* (1986) and *Landscapes of Fraud* (2006); Jay Wagoner, *Arizona Territory, 1863–1912* (1970); articles in the *Journal of Arizona History* and the *Journal of the Southwest* about particular periods, structures, and figures. A rich source of information about this period can be found in the applications for Historic District status that are on file with the City of Tucson at http://oip.tucsonaz.gov/preservation/national-register-historic-districts.

Early population numbers come from reports written by priests, soldiers, and visitors. For various reasons they may not be exact but are usually given as reported. U.S. Census data are identified. Information is gleaned from Tucson City Directories for the period in which they were published (1881–1997). Tucson Unified School District (TUSD) school enrollments and history are taken from James F. Cooper, *TUSD District History: First Hundred Years*, supplemented by information provided by TUSD's Department of Accountability and Research. For Pima Community College (PCC), information came from the Student Reports section under the About Pima tab on the PCC website. The Office of Institutional Research at the University of Arizona (UA) and Douglas Martin's *The Lamp in the Desert* (1960) provided information about the university's growth. Information about other institutions and businesses has come from City of Tucson records and the organizations' websites, unless there is reason to doubt the claims that appear there.

Newspaper accounts have provided information, including excellent acts of place-making like David Leighton's "Street Smarts" columns in the *Arizona Daily Star*. For autobiographical and eyewitness accounts, the writer will be named and the source will be found under that name in the bibliography at the end. Interviews and correspondence with principals have also provided material.

When I was growing up in Tucson in the 1940s and 1950s, a number of primary historical documents were available but not much history had been written. Today, there's a lot to look at and readers are invited to go from this account to where their interests take them. A visit with the excellent and helpful librarians at the archives of the Arizona Historical Society and the University of Arizona's Special Collections would be a good place to start.

We should not expect the kinds of resolutions from our stories of place that we tend to ask for in our myths. Readers can expect to find drama in this account, and tension, and interesting turns of events. A kind of heroism makes an appearance; also, perhaps, villainy. But if there are tragic and comic and farcical moments, the account does not offer in the end only tragedy, or comedy, or farce. While this account is not a standard history that "explains" things, it is much more than a chronology. Call it, then, as Joe Wilder, editor of the *Journal of the Southwest*, has, a *crónica*.

Why does this account end in 2014? Well, it had to end sometime.

With *crónicas*, a good ending is "To be continued."

With thanks to those who came before, in Tucson's history and in the telling of it.

Buen viaje.

Before People Appear

(~1,000,000 to ~20,000 years ago)

About 1,000,000 years ago

A volcanic extrusion produces Sentinel Peak. The lava cools and darkens. Just to the north, Tumamoc Hill is produced, and an area within what are now the Tucson Mountains that has come to be called "the Chaos." Several miles south, a hill now known as Martinez Hill appears. Already in place about 40 miles south is a version of the low Sierrita Mountains, which in 2014 are the site of two large open-pit mines. Also in place farther away are versions of the taller mountains that today surround the Tucson Basin: the Santa Catalina Mountains (20 miles northeast of Sentinel Peak), the Rincon Mountains (27 miles to the east—the north end of these mountains forms a kind of corner with the east end of the Catalinas and *rincón* means "inside corner" in Spanish), and the Santa Rita Mountains (50 miles to the southeast). "Sentinel Peak" was so-called by early Anglo residents of Tucson because it provided a place from which they might try to spot hostile Apaches approaching from the east. It is no higher than Tumamoc Hill next to it but it has commonly been called Sentinel *Peak,* perhaps because of its conical shape. To many current residents of Tucson, it is known as "'A' Mountain" because of the big white "A" that appears on its east face, the story of which is told later (see 1915). "Tumamoc" is the O'odham word for what English-speaking residents call the "horned lizard" or "horny toad," a lizard the size and shape of a small oblong pancake with a crown of thorns that was common in the Tucson Basin when the author was a boy.

About 500,000 years ago

The proto-Santa Cruz River runs through the Tucson Basin, flowing from south to north. In the Tucson Basin, a floodplain is created by layers of alluvium that are deposited over time, flooded, downcut by arroyos, and built up again by new deposits.

About 20,000 years ago

Nearing the end of the last Ice Age, the Santa Cruz River in the Tucson Basin is a braided stream flowing across bottomlands that are 20–30 feet below the current land surface of the banks along the river. Groundwater levels are high, though they fluctuate over time. When groundwater pumping begins in the Santa Cruz Valley in the late 19th century, the alluvium above depths of 1,200 feet is estimated to have contained about 70,000,000 acre-feet of water. An acre-foot of water, the amount that would cover one acre to a depth of one foot, equals 325,851 gallons. In his book on the Santa Cruz, Michael Logan offers the following visualization: "One acre-foot of water would cover a football field, including both end zones, nine inches deep.... [If 70,000,000 acre-feet could be piled in a column on top of that football field, it] would constitute a pillar of water 10,000 miles high." A lot, but not an infinite amount.

People Arrive

(~ 15,000 years ago to AD 1450)

About 15,000 to 20,000 years ago

The Tucson Basin, also known today as the middle Santa Cruz River Valley, has become grassy, sometimes marshy, plains that are surrounded by high mountains covered with oaks and conifers. The plains support large grazing animals—among them huge ground sloths, camels, horses (the smaller North American ones), bison, mammoths, mastodons—and saber-toothed cats. Humans appear in the valley, Paleo-Indian big-game hunters, likely descended from the people thought by archaeologists to have been "the first Americans"—people who, during the Ice Age, came east from what is now Asia to what is now Alaska via Beringia, a land bridge that at the time connected Asia to North America. Significant archaeological evidence of the presence of Paleo-Indian hunters has been found east of Tucson in the San Pedro River Valley, including Clovis spear points found in a mammoth skeleton near Naco, Arizona, in 1952. As of 2014 no evidence of these Paleo-Indian hunters has been found in the valley of the Santa Cruz River. Many archaeologists believe that people were present even pre-Clovis but evidence for them has proved elusive. Ventana Cave—some 75 miles southwest of Tucson on the Tohono O'odham Reservation, excavated by Univerity of Arizona (UA) archaeologists Emil Haury and Julian Hayden in 1941–42 and designated a National Historic Landmark in 1964—offers an unbroken stratigraphic record of human occupation in southern Arizona from the mammoth hunters of the late Pleistocene (which ended about 11,700 years ago) to the present day.

About 7,000 years ago

As warmer and drier conditions set in, many animal species in the region go extinct. The Paleo-Indian hunters are not among them. "Pleistocene overkill" by these hunters has been proposed as a contributing cause of these extinctions, along with climate change. The Paleo-Indian hunters are succeeded by hunter-gatherers now called the Cochise People of the Archaic or Desert Culture, who hunt the small game that is still available and gather mesquite beans and other wild desert plant foods.

2100 BC to AD 50

Incipient agriculture begins and more "sedentary" human groups emerge. The nomadic Desert Culture people are slowly supplanted by groups benefiting from two major technological innovations likely to have been developed in what is now Mexico and Central America: domesticated plants, including maize (or "corn"), a crop that had been developed from a grass and improved over many generations, and, several hundred years later, ceramic pottery (the nomadic Desert Culture people had only baskets and skins) to store and cook food in. The oldest fired pottery yet found in the American Southwest is found at the base of Sentinel Hill, along with the pit-houses that give evidence of continuous human occupation that goes back more than 4,000 years from the present, which gives this area a serious claim to being the longest continuously inhabited spot in the United States. Evidence of canals here and elsewhere in the Tucson Basin goes back 3,500 years. In 2002, this area begins to be referred to as the Birthplace of Tucson.

AD 50

The Hohokam (an O'odham word meaning "they are gone/all used up" or "those who have perished"), who may have come from the south, arrive and begin to farm on the floodplain of the Santa Cruz River. The first ceramic pottery comes with them. The Early Ceramic Period extends from AD 50-500.

- In the 1930s, Hohokam settlements in the Phoenix Basin along the Salt and Gila Rivers will begin to be excavated by archaeologists. They had been known to exist since the 19th century and long were thought to be limited to that area.

- Soon afterward, significant sites in the Tucson Basin are located, among them the Jaynes and Hodges sites in northwest Tucson, sites to the east at Fort Lowell and Indian Ridge, and sites to the south where Valencia Road joins the Santa Cruz. Evidence of canals is found at some but not all sites. A major Hohokam site (AD 750-1150) is excavated at Julian Wash before construction of the I-10/I-19 freeway exchange. Almost 17 acres of it have been preserved inside the exchange.

- At the top of Tumamoc Hill low stone walls are still to be found that were built 500–300 BC, thought to be for defense and called *trincheras*. Later the Hohokam scratch and chip petroglyphs into the dark rocks on the hill. In the mid-1970s over 450 petroglyphs will be catalogued here by UA archaeologist Alan Ferg and members of the Arizona Archaeological and Historical Society. In 2014, many of these petroglyphs are still to be seen on the rocks, along with more recent less compelling contributions.

- Around AD 800, the Hohokam in the Tucson Basin begin to build sunken ballcourts in their settlements. In the 1100s, this practice is supplanted by the building of platform mounds on which other structures are built. Six mounds have been found in villages in the Tucson Basin, built sometime around 1275-1300.

- The peak population of Hohokam in the Tucson Basin is reached in about AD 1000, during what is called the Classic Period. Estimates range from about 6,000 to 7,000 on the low end to more than 40,000 on the high end. Agave cultivation is widespread in the Classic Period.

- Around 1275, native cultures from the north begin to migrate into Hohokam regions as evidenced by changes in pottery.

- Not long after 1300, Hohokam culture begins a steady decline. By AD 1450, the Hohokam culture has disintegrated. Why it did so is not yet confidently understood, though changes in climate and environmental degradation are suspected to have played a significant part.

The Europeans Arrive

(1536–1681)

Note: Italics indicate entries related to, but not strictly local to, Tucson.

1536

The first Europeans in what is now the American Southwest are a group that includes Alvar Nuñez Cabeza de Vaca, a Spanish colonizer who had been shipwrecked eight years earlier on the northern coast of the Gulf of Mexico and captured and enslaved by coastal Indians. Eventually, Cabeza de Vaca escaped with a small party of survivors and headed west overland, hoping to reach the "Christians," as he referred to them, that he knew to be to the south in Mexico. The four surviving members of the party made their way into what is now southern New Mexico (it is now believed) and finally into what is now the Mexican state of Sonora. One of the four surviving castaways is a black Moroccan slave named Estévan who in the survivors' travels back to the Christians had proven himself useful as a shaman (in Tucson, Estevan Park, just south of Speedway and east of Main Avenue, is named for him). The survivors' first encounter with Christians, about 100 miles north of the town of Culiacán, is with a group of Spanish slave-catchers who, operating under the authority of the Spanish governor, Nuño de Guzmán, have been terrorizing the indigenous population. In the encounter with Guzmán's soldiers, the castaways side with the Indians, eventually taking their case to the new viceroy in Mexico City, Antonio Mendoza.

1539

In April, Estévan comes back into what today is southeastern Arizona with a party of Europeans that includes the Franciscan Marcos de Niza, in search of substantial settlements to the north that the Cabeza de Vaca party had heard about. Estévan and some Indians from villages in the San Pedro Valley who are traveling with him go north ahead of Marcos into the village of Zuñi in what is now northern New Mexico. Estévan and many of the Indians with him are killed there by the residents. Fray Marcos, having heard this news, continues north until he comes within sight of the pueblos at Zuñi and then retreats, bringing tales of the large settlements he has seen, called Cíbola.

1540

A large expedition of soldiers, priests, Africans, and "Indian allies," mounted and led by the governor of Nueva Galicia (what is now northwest Mexico), Francisco Vasquez de Coronado, comes up from the south in search of Cíbola. The investors supporting the expedition include Viceroy Mendoza. In mid-June they enter present-day Arizona going north, downstream, along the San Pedro River. At the *approximate location of present-day Fort Huachuca, they turn northeast, pass through Sulphur Springs Valley, cross over Apache Pass, and then work their way into the high country of what is present-day New Mexico. In July, they come to the plains of Hawikuh where Indians from the nearby Zuñi Pueblo come out to confront them and the first battle between Europeans and Native Americans takes place in what is to become the United States. Though far from home and hungry, the Spanish, with their horses and armor and crossbows and firearms, win the battle and occupy Zuñi, which they now know is not the Cíbola they seek. While recovering there from an arrow wound in his foot, Coronado dispatches Pedro de Tovar to the (Hopi) settlements he had heard about in present-day northern Arizona. The Hopi tell Tovar of a great chasm nearby. Later that year, Coronado dispatches García López de Cárdenas on a mission to find the river responsible for the chasm. Cárdenas comes upon the south rim of the Grand Canyon but is unable to descend to the river and returns to the main party. From Zuñi Coronado's party continues east, commandeering a pueblo on the Rio Grande and wintering near what is now Coronado State Park, not far north of the city of present-day Albuquerque. Later, they move on east over Glorieta Pass into the Pecos River Valley where they come upon what is now known as Pecos Pueblo, a trading center between the nomadic Plains Indians to the east and Indians who have settled in pueblos in the Rio Grande Valley to the west. At this time, Pecos Pueblo, called Cicuye by its inhabitants, is likely the largest settlement in what is to become the United States, but neither is it a city of gold. From Cicuye, the Spanish go on out into the Great Plains to the east, living on the many buffalo there at the time, still searching for cities of gold but now cities that an Indian informant had told them were to be found in a place called Quivira. Their informant later confesses, before being garroted, that he had hoped to lead them away from Pecos and to their deaths in the Plains. Coronado is on an expedition of conquest and religious conversion, not settlement, and in 1542, after he has failed to find the cities and the wealth he is searching for, he and the remaining* members of the disappointed expedition return to Mexico to face their investors.

1598

Fifty-six years after Coronado's departure from northern New Mexico, the Spanish return, led by Juan de Oñate, coming this time up the Rio Grande Valley from El Paso del Norte as colonists who claim the area for New Spain. At a site a few miles north of what is now Santa Fe, New Mexico, Oñate establishes what will be the northernmost provincial capital in New Spain.

1604

Oñate leads an expedition from New Mexico into what is now northern Arizona, traverses it to the Colorado, and travels down along the Colorado River to the Yuma Crossing. He returns the way he came, without penetrating east into what is now southern Arizona.

1610

In northern New Mexico, the second governor, Pedro de Peralta, moves the capital several miles south from its original site to Santa Fe, today the capital of the state of New Mexico. On the east coast of what will become the United States, the British manage this year to establish a permanent colony in Jamestown, Virginia, after failed attempts that had started in 1607. Between these two sites, no European settlement exists in North America.

1680

Indians from the different pueblos in northern New Mexico and Arizona—six different languages are spoken among them—manage to *combine forces and in what is called the Pueblo Revolt drive the Spanish out of Santa Fe and south down the Rio Grande past El Paso del Norte, killing many. The churches of the Spanish, often having been built on sites where the Indians' kivas had been, are destroyed, including a very large mission church that had been built in Pecos Pueblo. From this time onward, Indians will win some battles with Europeans and Americans but this will be the only revolt that succeeds in driving them out of territory they had come to occupy.*

1681

The Jesuit Father Eusebio Kino, age 36 (b. in the Italian Tyrol in 1645), sails from Spain to New Spain, arriving at the port of Veracruz as Cortéz had done 160 years before him. The first Jesuits had arrived 39 years after Cortéz and begun missionary work on the west coast of New Spain.

Father Kino in the Santa Cruz Valley

(1691–1711)

1691

In the ten years since his arrival, Kino has founded several missions in the northwest of New Spain, the area known as the Pimería Alta, home to several groups of Pima-speaking Indians as well as other Indian groups. In 1687, Kino had established a mother mission, Mission Dolores, near Cucurpe in what is now the state of Sonora in Mexico. In the last 24 years of his life Kino will travel extensively throughout the Pimería Alta, founding 24 missions and visitas *(designated sites for occasional visits by priests), and will produce the first maps of the region. This year Kino makes his first penetration into the northern region of the Pimería Alta. Here, in the region that today is northern Sonora, Mexico, and southwestern Arizona, the rivers flow not to the southwest as at Mission Dolores but northward. In the upper basin of the Santa Cruz (a river Kino names the Rio Santa Maria), just north of the current border between Mexico and Arizona, he establishes two prospective mission sites, one at Guevavi and another 12 miles north and downstream at Tumacácori. Significant Indian populations are found at both sites, which is what often decides where missions and visitas get founded. Mission churches will be built later at both sites.*

1692

On a second trip from Mission Dolores into the Santa Cruz River Valley, Kino travels 40 miles farther downstream from Tumacácori into the middle basin of the Santa Cruz River, coming to the large Sobaipuri Indian village of Bac near springs at the base of what is now called Martinez Hill. The largest native population in what becomes southern Arizona is now living in the middle basin of the Santa Cruz. It consists of three groups of Pima-speaking peoples: the Sobaipuri at Bac (Wa:k) with a significant population also in the San Pedro River Valley to the east; a group later called Papago ("bean eaters" or "bean people"), who cultivate the native tepary bean, among other indigenous crops; and a group concentrated in the lower Santa Cruz Valley and along the Gila River. In historical documents, the designation "Pima" is sometimes restricted to the people dwelling and farming along the rivers, and sometimes used more generally, as in "Pimería Alta," for those who speak any dialect of the Pima (now O'odham) language. Today the Papagos survive as the Tohono ("Desert") O'odham, with "Pima" being restricted to the people on the Gila River Reservation in Phoenix, now called the Akimel ("River") O'odham. Members of the Sobaipuri group, who also were River O'odham, survive among the Tohono O'odham at Wa:k. The question of whether O'odham descended from the Hohokam, who had disappeared 250 years before the Europeans arrived in the Santa Cruz Valley, has not been settled. The word "Huhugam" is now used by O'odham people to designate their ancestors, whether thought to be Hohokam in the specific archaeological sense or not.

1692

Five hundred miles northeast of Bac in what is now New Mexico, a Spanish force under Diego de Vargas returns and peacefully re-occupies Santa Fe. The people of the pueblos no longer present a united front of resistance to the Spanish. Santa Fe will remain the northernmost capital of New Spain until the Mexican Revolution.

1692

Kino comes to the Pima village at the foot of Sentinel Hill in Tucson's Birthplace and establishes a visita but it is not clear exactly when. Kino may have visited the site in 1692, the year of his first coming to Bac, but might not have done so until 1694 during his third visit to the valley of Santa Cruz (see next entry). Indians were already settled at the base of Sentinel Hill in any case. In surviving documents, Kino's first reference to Tucson comes in 1698. His maps of 1695 and 1701 both show a village on the west side of the Santa Cruz several miles downstream of Bac that had been given the name San Cosme (later referred to as San Cosme del *Tucsón*). The word the Pima Indians were using for the spot when the Spanish arrived, *S-cuk Son,* which becomes "Tucson," is translated as "at the foot of the black." Kino's maps show another village a few miles downstream from San Cosme, on the east side of the Santa Cruz, named San Agustín (del Oiaur—*oidac* is the O'odham word for "fields"). As to the size of the villages of Bac and Tucson, Kino, who might have been tempted to inflate the figures since he was writing to financial backers, reported later that there were 830 Indians living at the village of Bac in 176 houses (between four and five persons per house), with 758 Indians occupying 177 houses at the village of San Agustín downstream. In the whole of the Tucson Basin, 2,580 persons were living at this time, argue modern archaeologists Czaplicki and Mayberry. Throughout the 50,000 square miles of the Pimería Alta, argues the anthropological historian William B. Kessel, 25,000 Indians were then living.

1694

After his first visit to Bac in 1692, Father Kino had returned to Mission Dolores in the southern part of the Pimería Alta. He now comes back to the Tucson Basin, having heard stories he has found credible of a "casa grande" (big house) that is to be found beyond Bac to the north on a west-flowing river. Departing from Bac to find it, he travels down the Santa Cruz to the Gila River, no doubt passing through San Cosme del Tucsón on the way. In November Kino "discovers" the Casa Grande and guesses that it may be one of the Seven Cities that the Franciscan Marcos de Niza had reported seeing on his travels in 1539 in what is now Arizona. Niza's report is what had motivated Coronado's expedition 154 years before Kino arrived at the site. The "big house" itself, the purpose of which is still not well understood, built by the Hohokam probably in the 1300s, near the end of their run, is made out of *caliche*, a Spanish word for a hardened limestone found widely under the ground in southern Arizona. In 1892, Casa Grande will be the first prehistoric structure to be protected by Congress. Excavation of the 900-acre site begins in 1906 by which time pot and souvenir hunters will have taken much of what was to be found on the surface. In 1918, the Casa Grande will become one of the first National Monuments.

1695

In the lower Pimería Alta, Pima Indians revolt and destroy a number of Kino's missions and visitas. After three months of bloodshed and military reprisals by the Spanish, peace is negotiated by Kino at Santa Rosa.

1697

Kino comes again to Bac, this time with a large drove of livestock—cattle, sheep, goats, some mares. This makes him, it has been said, the father of ranching in the Santa Cruz Valley. He returns to Mission Dolores, then journeys north again, into the San Pedro River Valley, continuing along it to the Gila River and the Casa Grande, returning south along the Santa Cruz. The enthusiastic reception of his party by the Sobaipuris and other Pimas along the way on this journey demonstrates, Kino argues to doubters, the "fine and friendly" spirit of these peoples, as contrasted to that of the "pestiferous" Apaches, Jocomes, Manzos, and Janos to the east, a source of ongoing troubles for all other parties, European and Indian. The "Apaches" inhabiting the area north and west of the Santa Cruz known as the "Apachería" do not refer to themselves with this term, which is of uncertain origin and seems to have been applied to them first by Spanish colonizers. In the Apachería, the "Apaches" comprise at least three different Athabaskan-speaking groups that usually operate separately but the Spanish, Mexicans, and Anglos after them tend to group them and other hostile Indian groups under the single term. These Athabascan-speaking peoples seem to have migrated into the area from the north between the 13th and 16th centuries. "Apache" attacks upon the Spanish seem to have begun in the late 16th century, that is, as soon as the European colonizers arrived in the region.

1698

In the southern San Pedro Valley the Apaches and their allies attack the village of Santa Cruz de Gaybanipitea. At first, the attackers prevail but reinforcements arrive from nearby led by a Sobaipuri captain named El Coro. In a contest of champions that is agreed to by the parties, the attackers are defeated and decimated during their retreat back to the east.

1700 April 26

Kino returns to Bac from Dolores intending to continue on in an effort to discover a land route to California. At the request of Bac's many inhabitants, he remains there and on the 28th begins to lay the foundations for a "muy grande y capaz iglesia y casa" (a very large and spacious church and house), structures that will not, however, be completed in his lifetime. The Spanish and the Pima Indians have benefited by now from ranching the livestock he introduced to the region earlier, as have the raiding Apaches. Kino had earlier introduced agricultural plants like wheat (*trigo*), which can yield a winter crop, and fruits, like the fig (*higo*), pomegranate (*granada*), and quince (*membrillo*). The Indians continue to cultivate the indigenous crops of corn, beans, and squash—today called "the three sisters"—as well as melons and cotton, which is indigenous but not exclusive to the New World, as corn (*maíz*) is. Kino remarks on the year-round availability of water at the site which he considers "una de las mayores y mejores campiñas de toda la Nueva Vizcaya," one of the biggest and best fields in all of northern New Spain.

1700 September

Having returned to Dolores, Kino sets out from there on the expedition that will introduce him to several new Indian nations in what is now southwestern Arizona and finally take him to the Colorado River and the discovery that a land route to Alta California is possible. His map of 1701 will correct the error on his map of 1695 that shows California as an island. Missions have been established in Baja California by now but none yet in Alta California because of the difficulty of the approach from the south by sea or through Baja California.

1700

At this time at least nine large Indian agricultural settlements exist in the lower Santa Cruz Basin. By the end of the century diseases imported by the Europeans will have depopulated all of them.

1701

The first resident priest at San Xavier del Bac is the Jesuit Father Francisco Gonzalvo, but he soon leaves the post, dying in 1702, and San Xavier is again without a resident priest. San Ignacio to the south becomes the principal church

Father Kino map (English language version). Beginning in 1681, the Jesuit Father Eusebio Kino traveled the region of the Pimería Alta (northwest New Spain) on horseback, doing missionary work, and in 1695 produced the first map of the region. Kino's map of 1701 of the same area corrects his initial depiction of California as an island. Kino's maps are not to scale but they identify the major rivers in the region correctly in relation to each other and trace their routes with remarkable accuracy, showing, for example, the south-to-north loop at the origin of the Santa Cruz River. Just north of San Xavier on the "Sta. Maria" (Santa Cruz) River, the place marked 'S. Cosme' appears about where Tucson does today.

(*cabecera*), with Father Agustín del Campo in charge. The first resident missionary priest arrives at Guevavi this year. At this time, Tumacácori is a visita of the mission at Guevavi rather than a mission in its own right.

1711 March 15

Kino dies in Magdalena, Sonora, at age 66, with no church having been built yet at Mission San Xavier del Bac or at San Cosme del Tucsón. Nor had Kino ever served as the resident priest at Mission San Xavier, though he had wished to. Among Kino's other frustrated aspirations is "the reduction and conversion of the neighboring Apachería, which lies northeast and north of us." This, he realized, would open large areas to the east to Spanish colonization.

After Kino: The Santa Cruz Valley in New Spain and Mexico

(1732–1853)

1732

Swiss Jesuit Father Philipp Segesser becomes the resident mission priest at San Xavier for a brief time. Segesser's letters mention no mission church yet at San Xavier, indeed not much of anything beyond the native population, with whom he demonstrates scant sympathy. At Guevavi a major mission complex is finally begun this year, under the direction of

Austrian Father Johann Grazhoffer, who dies, unfortunately, in March of the next year.

1736

At a site a few miles south of the Guevavi mission, large slabs of native silver are discovered on the grounds of a ranch called the Rancho Arizonac, owned by Bernardo de Urrea. Miners and prospectors rush to the area but the silver is claimed finally by the crown as an artificial treasure trove. The area becomes known as Planchas de Plata *(slabs of silver).*

1740s, 1750s, 1760s

In the Pimería Baja, in today's state of Sonora in Mexico, Yaquis, Seris, and lower Pimas revolt against the Spanish. Hostilities with Apaches have been a continuing issue for everyone, other Indian groups as well as the Spanish, and as the Spanish suppress the non-Apache Indians in the Pimería Alta, Apache raids there increase.

1744

Because of Apache attacks, Mission Dolores, Kino's mother mission in Sonora, is abandoned.

1751

A significant Pima Rebellion devastates both Guevavi and Bac, though Indians at Bac join the rebellion belatedly. The Jesuit priest who had just arrived in Bac to reestablish the mission, a native of Bohemia named Franz Bauer, is warned by a Native American resident in time to escape with some soldiers. He reports that at Bac the Indians had destroyed the simple brush ramada (a structure of poles and covering branches provided for shade) that had served as the church, along with his house, vestments, and livestock.

1752

The first Spanish military garrison, or presidio, *in the Santa Cruz Valley is established in Tubac, 47 miles south of Tucson's Birthplace, commanded by Tomás de Velderrain. The Presidio San Ignacio de Tubac (now an Arizona State Historic Park) is the first permanent Spanish settlement in Arizona. In 1757 it is reported to have a population of 411.*

1752

In the first known listing of northern Pima Indians living in Tucson, Captain Joseph Díaz del Carpio gives their number as 154, far fewer than the 758 that had been reported by Kino.

1756

At Bac, recently arrived Jesuit missionary Father Alonso Espinosa touches off a rebellion by Pimas from Bac and other Indians from the north by attempting in fall 1755 to suppress a traditional ceremony. During the Indian assault, 15 soldiers from Tubac arrive, rescue Espinosa, and defeat the Indians after a stiff fight. The governor of Sonora, Juan Antonio de Mendoza, a native of Castilla in Spain, quickly sets out on a punitive expedition that goes all the way down the Santa Cruz to the confluence of the Gila and Salt Rivers. On his way back, he lays at Bac the first brick for a new mission church. The first church, completed in 1763, will be a flat-roofed, hall-shaped adobe building on a site west of the current church. Some of the adobes from that first church will be used later to build the east wing of the current San Xavier Mission church.

1757

The first priest to live at a mission near Sentinel Hill seems to have been the German Jesuit Bernhardt Middendorf (Espinosa has been reinstalled at Bac). Middendorf comes this year to establish a mission at a settlement north of Bac which the record suggests was not San Cosme but the settlement several miles north of Sentinel Hill on the east side of the Santa Cruz that is shown on Kino's maps as San Agustín de Oiaur. About 10 miles north of San Agustín de Oiaur, another mission called Santa Catalina de Cuitabagu may have existed in some form and Middendorf may also have set up a mission there. In any case, there was no church or housing on the site. Middendorf has been in the area for four months or so baptizing and proselytizing when his party is attacked in the night by what he reports to be "about five hundred savages" and he is forced to retreat with his military escort and some Pima families to San Xavier. He does not return to the north. No archaeological evidence of either of these more northerly missions has been found.

1762

The Sobaipuri Indians who had been living in the valley of the San Pedro River are brought by the Spanish to locations in the Santa Cruz Valley, some 250 or so to the base of Sentinel Hill. Their forced relocation removes the first line of defense for Sonora and the Santa Cruz Valley against hostile Apaches.

1763

The commander of the presidio at Tubac is now Juan Bautista de Anza (b. Arizpe, Sonora 1734), a Spanish-Basque criollo *soldier whose father, also named Juan Bautista de Anza, had commanded a presidio to the south at Fronteras and been killed by Indians in 1737. The son had replaced Velderrain as commander at Tubac on the latter's death in 1759. Anza now approves abandoning several* rancherias *(small agricultural settlements) in Sonora because of Apache raids. Also abandoned is the mission at Calabazas, upstream of Tubac on the Santa Cruz (founded after Kino's time).*

1767

The kings of France, Portugal, and Spain expel the Jesuits from New Spain, as well as from France, Portugal, and Sicily, bringing to an end the line of resident Jesuit missionaries at San Xavier del Bac. Kino had been followed by Agustín de Campos, Luis Gallardi, Philipp Segesser, Kaspar Stiger, Ignaz Keller, Franz Bauer, Bernard Middendorf, and Alonso Espinosa. Before Espinosa, only Stiger had stayed more than a few months. The last Jesuit at San Xavier before expulsion was José Neve. The Jesuits' status in the Catholic Church is restored only in 1814, during the Mexican War of Independence.

1768

Juan Bautista de Anza leaves Tubac and goes south to Cerro Prieto near Pitic (present-day Hermosillo) to suppress a revolt of the Seris and lower Pimas.

1768

The line of Franciscan missionaries at San Xavier del Bac begins with Francisco Garcés, who comes this year via Tubac to the missions at Bac and "Tugson," reporting that both are "quiet" and the people "content." The Indians are also glad to learn that the priest will feed himself from his stipend and not force them to labor for him. Garcés finds in Tugson about 60 huts for families, about the same as in Bac, but the population is diminished because the Papagos "have gone to their lands" west of the Santa Cruz. In August Garcés leaves Bac on a trip of exploration and proselytizing to the Gila River. This is the first of many travels Garcés will undertake over the next 12 years. Returning in October from this first trip, he falls violently ill and is removed to Guevavi to recover. While he is gone, the Apaches attack Bac, kill its governor, and carry off two soldiers assigned to Garcés as escorts.

1769

In early 1769, after Garcés has recovered and returned to Bac, the Apaches raid it again. A month later, Garcés is on another journey, this one perhaps to the San Pedro River Valley. The Apaches raid Bac again in April and July of this year.

1769

A difficult land route is established from Baja (lower) to Alta (upper) California (the current state of California) and missions and presidios finally begin to be established there. The first ones are estab-

lished at San Diego in the south and at Monterrey in the north. Baja California has some 16 missions by now, the Pimería Alta has many more, though some have been abandoned because of Indian attacks.

1770

Anza returns from the south to prevent the Sobaipuri refugees from leaving Tucson and moving downstream to the Gila. He directs the Indians at the base of Sentinel Hill to build a breastworks for defense against the Apaches, the first major European-style structure in Tucson. In the structure they build, the inhabitants are able to repel an attack by Apaches in February of the next year.

1771

A chapel is built at the foot of Sentinel Hill for the visitas of the priest at Bac.

1771

Ninety miles south of the current border with Mexico, at Cieneguilla, Spanish soldiers discover placers rich with gold. Mines have been operating in the Pimería Alta before now but sporadically because of pressure from the Apaches. This rich find leads to the establishment of a royal mining settlement, San Idelfonso de Cieneguilla.

1772

Fray Antonio de los Reyes gives what is apparently a secondhand report on the condition of the missions in the upper and lower Pimería Alta, writing that "The village of San Xavier at Bac is situated on open ground with an abundance of water and good land where the Indians cultivate a few small fields of wheat, Indian corn, and other crops. The church is of medium capacity, adorned with two side chapels with paintings in gilded frames." He estimates "270 souls" at San Xavier (far fewer than the 830 Kino had reported 80 years earlier) and, at the site of what he refers to as the visita of San José del Tucsón, using a name that had been bestowed by a military captain 10 years before, "more than two hundred heads of families" (Kino had reported 758 souls there) but reports that "no church or house for the Missionary" has been built.

1772

At the foot of Sentinel Peak, with the support of the Indians and under the direction of Fray Garcés, the first Franciscan missionary priest at San Xavier, work begins on a church building for the mission that Garcés will dedicate to San Agustín. The church will not be completed until 25 years later, more than 14 years after the presidio of Tucson is established.

1773

The mission at Guevavi is permanently abandoned after the most recent Apache attacks.

1774

The Spanish have become concerned about incursions in Alta California by the Russians and the British. With the approval of the king of Spain and the viceroy of New Spain, Juan Bautista de Anza sets out from the presidio at Tubac in January to establish a new land route to northern California. In 1769, a land route had been established up from Baja California but it required a perilous crossing of the Sea of Cortez and was difficult. The sea route up from the south was even more difficult because of contrary currents and prevailing winds. Accompanied by Fray Francisco Garcés and guided by a California Indian he had picked up, Anza passes through the upper Pimería Alta, as had Kino before him, then west down the Gila to its junction with the Colorado River. (In January Garcés leaves the expedition to conduct his own explorations, which will take him the next six months and eventually reach from the Grand Canyon to the Gulf of California and into the Mohave Desert in California.) Anza, after cultivating friendly relations with the Yuma Indians he finds at the Colorado, crosses the river and marches across the interior of California to Mission San Gabriel, just established in the Los Angeles Basin. From there, he travels north, arriving in Monterey, then the capital of Alta California, in April 1774. He quickly turns around and returns to Tubac, arriving by the end of May. The next year, in October, he departs Tubac again, this time with a party of 240 colonists who had been brought north from Sinaloa. This time he goes north down the Santa Cruz past Tucson's Birthplace to where the Santa Cruz joins the Gila River, down the Gila to the Colorado, then through the interior of Alta California to Monterey, arriving in January 1776, after a five-month journey made much more difficult by the large party and the winter weather, but having lost only one colonist, a woman who died in childbirth. From Monterey he heads north with a smaller party, finds a land route from Monterey to San Francisco Bay, and in March 1776, three months before the Declaration of Independence is signed, locates there the sites for the presidio and mission of San Francisco that in June will be occupied by some of the colonists.

1775 August 20

On the east bank of the Santa Cruz, across the river from where the San Agustín Mission Church will be built at the foot of Sentinel Peak, Spanish Commandant Inspector General Hugo O'Conor founds the Presidio "San Agustín de Toixón" as part of a campaign that has been ordered by the viceroy of New Spain to fortify the northern border from the Gulf of California to the Gulf of Mexico. The wood palisades that are erected at first are replaced by adobe walls starting in 1777, a job that is completed in 1783. The walls are 10 to 12 feet high and three feet wide at the base (before the rain erodes them). The walls of the presidio are said to have run along Washington Street on the north, Church Street on the east, Pennington Street on the south, and Main Avenue on the west (current street names). Each side of the presidio will be about 750 feet long, with gates in the west and east walls, about where Alameda Street is now. Inside the presidio along the east wall a church (also named for San Agustín) and cemetery will later be built, with the commandant's house in the center. The interior walls are lined with homes, barracks, stables, and warehouses. In the center of the presidio will be an open space called Plaza de las Armas. By 1779, the *armas* on the post include four bronze cannon for which 66 balls are available and enough powder that the captain could sell some to the settlers. Across the Santa Cruz River to the west, "Indian town" and the mission church that is under construction are connected to the presidio by a bridge. The adobe wall that is built for the presidio will survive until 1918, when the last section is taken down. In 1954, UA archaeologist Emil Haury and students excavate the northeast corner of the presidio, exposing a prehistoric dwelling under the wall. Excavations from 2001 to 2006 locate other sections of the presidio walls, now marked on the sidewalks for passersby. In 2007 the bastion on the northeast corner of the presidio is reconstructed with a life-size mural that depicts the scene in 1775.

1775

The Spanish forces at Tubac are ordered to be transferred to Tucson, which now becomes the center for defense of the Pimería Alta. The settlers who remain in Tubac quickly begin to suffer more raids by Apaches.

1776

In the San Pedro Valley the Presidio Santa Cruz de Terrenate is constructed as is the Presidio San Bernardino just east of present-day Douglas, Arizona. By 1780, attacks by Apaches have caused both to be abandoned.

1776

Friar Juan Bautista Velderrain, a Basque, arrives at San Xavier and begins to raise funds to build a large mission church at Bac. This is the beginning of the church that stands there today.

1776

Spain supports the American Revolution, aligning itself with the Americans against the British, raising money in New Spain, conducting an offensive on the southern seaboard, and operating patrols on the Mississippi to prevent a rearguard action by the British.

1778

Seventy-seven soldiers are now assigned to the Tucson presidio, under the command of Captain Pedro Allande y Saabedra, who had arrived early in 1777. By October, the Apaches have run off the last of the horses and cattle of the settlers in Tubac and are grazing their own animals in Tubac's fields.

1778

East of the San Agustín Church that Gárces and the locals are building at the foot of Sentinel Hill, work begins around this time on a large *casa conventual*, the building later called the Convento, to serve as residences for priests, administrative offices, and a refuge from Apache attacks. It seems to have been substantially added to 20 years later by Father Juan Bautista Llorens after completion of the San Xavier Mission Church (see 1797).

1779 November 6

Allande has recruited Pimas, Papagos, and Gileños to serve as soldiers in campaigns against the Apaches. While the adobe walls of the presidio are being built but before they are finished, the First Battle of Tucson takes place between the presidio's soldiers and Apaches. Not much is known about the battle but it does represent a change in the Apaches' typical practice of raiding. Allande reports in his memoir (speaking in the third person) that on this date "when the palisade was under construction, he pursued 350 Apaches with only fifteen men. He caught up with them after an extended chase. Among the Apaches he killed were the brother of Chief Quilché and another war captain, whose head he cut off before the very eyes of the enemy. Then he charged the Apache line single-handed, with the head stuck on his lance. The maneuver took the enemy off guard and they stampeded."

1781 July

At the Yuma Crossing on the Colorado River, Father Garcés had established two more missions among indigenous Quechan-speaking groups. This year Garcés, his fellow friars, and the Spanish settlers in the area are all killed by the Quechan peoples in what is called the Yuma Uprising. The land route to Alta California closes.

1782 May 1

With the adobe walls not finished, the Second Battle of Tucsón takes place, in which Allande's soldiers defeat an even larger force of Apaches (Allande says 600) who this time come in from the north and surprise the presidio. In a change from their raiding tactics, they make a concerted and almost successful effort to breach the still-open entrance. Allande himself, with few other defenders, manages to fight them off despite a serious wound in his leg. The battle lasts two hours. The Apaches are prevented from attacking the Pima Pueblo across the running river (Father Velderrain is visiting it at the time) by defenders on the bridge. The Apaches, who still have almost no firearms, withdraw after a soldier succeeds in firing one of the presidio's cannons. Though prevented in this battle from overcoming the presidio, the Apaches raid it again in December and make off with the livestock, though the soldiers manage to recover it. Allande, still recovering from his leg wound, and his soldiers are now being assisted by the Spanish civilians who began to settle near the presidio soon after it was established, building houses south of the presidio's walls.

1783

Two years before the founding of the Presidio San Agustín in 1775, the Pima population in Tucsón had been 239. The Native American population of the Tucsón Pueblo is now 189, and that of Bac has fallen to 167 persons, a total of 356 Native Americans in the two settlements. Efforts have begun to encourage in-migration of other northern Pimans, partly for help in fighting the Apaches.

1785

From Presidio San Agustín in Tucsón, Allande has conducted several other campaigns against the Apaches, including the first one by the Spanish into the upper Gila River region. In 1785, he asks to be promoted to a position of less hardship because of wounds and ill health. During his command, he had paid with his own funds for a military chapel to be built in the presidio, a small one, which, like the mission church across the river, is dedicated to San Agustín.

1786

Because the Spanish have been unable to prevent raids by Apaches, the viceroy of New Spain, Bernardo Galvez, institutes the "New Indian Policy" which creates *establecimientos de paz* (peace establishments) to provide the Apaches with "horses, guns, food and ornaments," while keeping up the military pressure in search-and-destroy expeditions from Presidio San Agustín in Tucsón and other presidios. In time, the raids decline. In the Tucson Basin, livestock populations begin to increase, sometimes to the annoyance of the O'odham when the livestock of the Spanish settlers trample their *milpas* (fields). Four entities are now competing for the water in the Tucson Basin: El Pueblito (the Pima village across the river from the presidio), the presidio community, the communal mission lands of San Xavier del Bac, and the individual farms of the Pimas and Papagos.

1787

The Spanish reestablish the presidio at Tubac.

1788

Juan Bautista de Anza, former commander of the presidio at Tubac, is appointed commander of the Presidio San Agustín de Tucsón. Eleven years earlier, after his notable accomplishments in finding a land route from Tubac to Alta California and delivering a party of colonists to Monterey, he had been appointed governor of the province of New Mexico by the viceroy of New Spain. In 1779, while governor, he had discovered a new land route from Santa Fe into Sonora. In August and September of the same year, he had embarked on a campaign against the Plains Indians known as Comanches who, mounted now on the horses that had been introduced by the Spanish, have been raiding and killing the Spanish and Indian inhabitants of northern New Mexico. With a force of about 600 Spanish soldiers and 200 Apache and Ute Indian recruits, he had decisively defeated a large force of Comanches at what becomes known as Greenhorn Creek, killing Cuerno Verde, their principal war chief, his son, and four other chiefs. After other campaigns against the Comanches, he had signed a final peace treaty with them at Pecos Pueblo in 1786. In 1787, he had left the governorship of New Mexico and returned home to Arizpe, Sonora. Before he can leave to take up the new post as commander of the presidio in Tucsón, he dies in Arizpe at age 52.

1789

Not long after his arrival at Bac in 1776, Father Velderrain had raised funds, hired an architect from Mexico, and, with Tohono O'odham and possibly some western Apache labor, begun to build the San Xavier Mission Church that survives today south of Tucson. Bernard Fontana argues that the de facto architect was one Ignacio Gaona, who is referred to as a *maestro albañil* or "master mason."

1793

On January 5, a band of Aravaipa (aka Western) Apaches comes in to settle near the Tucsón presidio. The first Apaches to come in under the New Indian Policy had been the Chiricahuas, who had come in to settle near Arizpe, Sonora, in 1786. Eventually more than 100 Apaches take up residence in Tucsón and even help with the construction of the mission church and convent. They do not, however, take to agriculture. The current mission priest, Father Juan Bautista Llorens, reports that he has some "difficulty" achieving amicable relations between the Apaches and the Pimas but that he manages to "conquer" this. Some raiding by other Apaches continues.

1795

With the Apaches largely at peace, Captain Zuñiga of the Tucsón presidio leads a successful expedition north and east to establish a trade route to the Zuñi Pueblo in New Mexico, perhaps following the route Coronado had taken 255 years earlier. The route goes through the heart of Apache country and, though it is established, it is never much used.

1797

Construction of the San Xavier Mission Church ceases for lack of funds with one church tower unfinished and the building's red bricks exposed, otherwise very nearly complete. Father Velderrain had died at San Xavier in 1789 or 1790, with the body of the new church in place—stone footings, inner and outer walls of burned adobe (fired brick), and an inner core of stone rubble. The completion and decoration of the church had been overseen by Velderrain's successor at San Xavier, Father Juan Bautista Llorens. Llorens now turns his attention to the Mission San Agustín and *convento* at the base of Sentinel Hill. He will add substantially to both. The two-story *convento* will survive longer than the San Agustín Church: Its substantial ruins are clearly visible in early photographs of territorial Tucson though the church is no longer to be seen.

1799

At Tucsón, the population of the "Spanish" *ciudadanos* (civilians), now largely *mestizo* (meaning some combination of European and Indian ancestry), is numbered at 39. Spanish law prohibits them living in Indian villages and most live south of the presidio across the river from the "Pueblito."

1801

A census of the population in Tucsón by Father Llorens counts 246 Native Americans in three tribal designations, Papago, Pima, and Gileño. The Sobaipuris do not appear in this record or henceforth as a separate group. A recent smallpox epidemic had exacerbated the decline of the Native American population. By this time, diseases imported by the Europeans have depopulated all large settlements in the lower Santa Cruz Basin. In the middle Santa Cruz Basin, Tucsón and Bac are the only significant settlements remaining, and their populations are being maintained, at declining levels, by immigration.

1804

In the vicinity of the Tucsón presidio, including at San Xavier del Bac, a census by Commander Zúñiga reports 300 "Spanish" (up from the 77 soldiers in 1777) and a total population (Spanish, mixed, Indian) of 1,014. Tubac reports a population of 164, of which 88 are soldiers and their families. The missions at Guevavi and Calabazas are still abandoned.

1807

The Sonoran government in Arizpe grants the O'odham people land that extends south from Tubac up along the Santa Cruz to near the current Mexican border. The three communities along the river south of Tubac are Tumacácori and Calabazas, both now repopulated, and

Guevavi, which had been permanently abandoned in 1773 because of Apache attacks.

1810

The Mexican War of Independence from Spain begins.

1812

In 1789, Spain had issued a grant of land north of Tubac to Toribio Otero. This year, Augustín Ortíz of Tucsón receives a land grant in Arivaca for a livestock operation.

1815

Father Llorens is killed by Apaches on his way to Santa Cruz. In 1816, another smallpox epidemic sweeps through northern Sonora. By 1818, Bac and the Tucsón mission are in the charge of Friar Juan Vaño.

1819

A group of 67 Pinal Apaches comes to Tucsón to join the other *Apaches de paz* living there.

1820

The sons of Agustín Ortíz, Tomás and Ignacio, petition Sonora for a grant of land along the Santa Cruz north of Tubac to be used for the same purpose as their father's grant in Arivaca. This will become the San Ignacio de Canoa grant, which is twice the size of the grant in Arivaca.

1821

While the Mexican War for Independence is still raging, the Spanish government grants to León Herreros of Tubac land around the settlement of Sonoita for a livestock operation. Kino had founded Los Santos Reyes de Sonoita as a visita of Guevavi in the late 1600s. In 1698 the Sobaipuri population of the San Pedro Valley had concentrated there after a major battle with the Apaches and their allies at Santa Cruz de Gaybanipitea. For the last 50 years, the site had been abandoned.

1821

With the success of the Mexican War of Independence in September, Tucsón, population c. 500, which unfortunately had remained loyal to Spain, ceases to be part of New Spain and becomes part of the new nation of Mexico. The *establecimientos de paz* had begun to decline with the beginning of the War of Independence in 1810. Hostilities with Apaches had resumed at a lower level and finally increased to levels of 30 years earlier.

1828

The Mexican government expels the Spanish priests from Mexico. The first period of resident Franciscan priests at San Xavier del Bac ends three years later when Fray Rafael Díaz, a naturalized Mexican, is asked to leave by Mexican authorities. He goes to Imurís in Sonora, taking many of the church's artifacts with him. Fray Antonio González, born in Guanajuato, Mexico, is later in residence from 1834 to 1837 but he will be San Xavier's last resident priest until 1913, when the then bishop of Tucson, Henry Granjon, reluctantly puts the supervision of San Xavier under the Franciscans. In 2014, the Franciscans continue to administer the mission's affairs.

1834

The Mexican government decrees an end to the mission system, though far to the north in Sonora, some Franciscan missions persist.

1835

In their own attempt to deal with the Apaches, Mexican authorities institute a scalp bounty system. Notable among these scalp hunters is an American, James Kirker, a Northern Ireland-born mountain man and mercenary. In 1835 he becomes a Mexican citizen and contracts with the government of Chihuahua to kill Apaches, with any black-haired scalps being the evidence accepted for bounty payments. Beginning in 1840, he and other scalp hunters produce a good deal of such evidence for the Mexican authorities.

1836–1838

Jose María Martinez serves as acting commandant of Presidio San Agustín in Tucsón. When he retires from the Mexican military in 1838, he is granted land in Tubac by the presidio commander there. Ten years later, when Apaches drive the settlers out of Tubac, he takes up residence at San Xavier and later acquires land there under a law that grants land in Tucsón or San Xavier to residents of Tubac who have been driven out of that town. Martinez's land includes or is adjacent to what is now Martinez Hill. In 1863, while looking after his cattle near San Xavier, he is seriously wounded by Apaches, finally dying of these wounds in 1868.

1837

The last Franciscan in permanent residence at Bac departs.

1838

The landscape of the Santa Cruz watershed, now part of Mexico, has become "a sea of private claims," according to anthropologist and historian Tom Sheridan's *Landscapes of Fraud*.

1840s

Mission San Agustín and its *convento* at the base of Sentinel Hill have by now been abandoned, though not the Presidio San Agustín across the Santa Cruz River. By the beginning of the Mexican-American War in 1846, all land grants and missions along the Santa Cruz have been abandoned because of attacks by Apaches, except San Xavier, which is protected by soldiers from the presidio at Tucsón and visited at least once a year by a Mexican secular priest, and Tumacácori, which is still populated by a small community of O'odham.

1844

Manuel María Gándara, a Mexican caudillo (military strong-man) from Sonora, engineers the sale of the Tumacácori land grant to an in-law, having falsely claimed that the grant had been abandoned by the O'odham. Nothing is done with the land until 1853 when some German business associates begin to stock a ranch there with cattle, goats, and sheep. This ranching operation has collapsed by 1856, when, after the Gadsden Purchase, Calabazas is occupied by Major Enoch Steen and four companies of United States dragoons. Former settlers begin to return to abandoned ranches and farms. When the military leaves the region at the beginning of the Civil War, Apache attacks on the settlers resume.

6

The Americans Arrive

(1846–1862)

1846

On May 11, the United States declares war on Mexico and General Stephen W. Kearney's Army of the West begins its march south from Kansas down the Santa Fe Trail. At the beginning of the war, a troop of Mormons enlists in the army to escape the persecution they have been experiencing in Illinois and to get help making their way west to Utah. They are formed into the Mormon Battalion in General

Kearney's Army of the West, the only U.S. Army battalion ever to be restricted to a single religion. The Mormon Battalion is given the mission of establishing a second wagon road to California (Anza's had been the first but had not become an established trade route and was closed down by the Yuma Rebellion). The battalion departs Fort Leavenworth, Kansas, comes down the Santa Fe Trail to Santa Fe, New Mexico, then down the Chihuahua Trail toward El Paso, turning west short of El Paso and entering what would become southern Arizona. It arrives in Tucsón in December and raises the U.S. flag there for the first time. Its members continue on west, crossing the Colorado and arriving in San Diego in late January 1847 after a march of 1,900 miles.

1846

As the Mexican-American War had begun to seem imminent, the American-Mexican scalp hunter James Kirker had fled Mexico. He now takes part in U.S. Colonel Doniphan's invasion of Mexico. He will survive the war and lead a party of Forty-Niners to California. In 1852, he will die in Contra Costa County, California, at age 59.

1848

The Treaty of Guadalupe Hidalgo concludes the Mexican-American War. The new nation of Mexico cedes about half of itself to the United States, but the region south of the Gila River that includes Tucsón remains part of Mexico. The treaty recognizes the validity of prior land grants, but the continuing troubles with the Apaches have caused most grants to be abandoned. Grants found to have been abandoned can be auctioned off.

1849

This year, one H. M. T. Powell pencils a sketch of the San Xavier Mission Church that is its first recorded representation. The drawing also represents 12 dome-shaped Indian dwellings in front of the church.

1849

This year the Apache and Yavapai Indians kill 407 people in the new American Southwest and in northern Mexico, the highest total of any year of hostilities. The next-highest totals will be 207 in 1851 and 337 in 1882, two years after the arrival of the railroad in Tucsón and four years before the surrender of Geronimo.

1850

The Compromise of 1850 is passed by the U.S. Congress to decide the question of the status of slavery in the lands acquired from Mexico. In the compromise, California comes into the Union as a free state. In the Territory of New Mexico (which includes present-day Arizona), the question of slavery is left for people to decide in the future. Texas gets debt relief from the United States and gives up its claims to territory in New Mexico and Missouri. The slave states get the Fugitive Slave Law, which requires authorities in free states to return escaped slaves to their owners.

1854

The Gadsden Purchase is ratified by the U.S. Senate, bringing Tucsón and the rest of what is now southern Arizona into the United States. The purchase had been promoted by

James Gadsden of South Carolina, a proponent of slavery, to give the South a railroad route to California. Work on a southern railroad will not begin until after the Civil War.

1854

Aaron Zeckendorf (b. Germany 1835, d. Santa Fe 1872) opens a store in Santa Fe. Soon afterward, he is joined there by his brother Louis (b. Germany 1838, d. New York 1937). They soon extend their operations south to Albuquerque and the Rio Mimbres mining camps in southern New Mexico.

1854

Peter R. Brady and Frederick Ronstadt organize Arizona's first mining company, the Arizona Mining and Trading Co. The company will later develop mines west of Tucson in Ajo, with the copper ore being taken west to San Diego by mule before being shipped to Wales for refining.

1855

The first African-Americans recorded to have come to Tucson in the American period are Mr. and Mrs. Wiley Box, from New Orleans and Oklahoma, respectively. Before the American period, Estévan, the Moor in Marcos de Niza's group, had been the first African in the region. In the 1780s, a Spanish soldier designated "mulatto" (the Spanish designation for the offspring of a European-African union), Sergeant Francisco Xavier Marquez, had served with distinction at the Presidio San Agustín de Tucsón, and an 1801 enumeration of "*ciudadanos*" (that is, "citizens" who were not soldiers or Indians) in Tucsón had included three "mulattos," 7.7 percent of the total number.

1856

The 26 Mexican soldiers remaining in the Presidio San Agustín de Tucsón are replaced by a troop of First Dragoons from the United States. Many Mexican residents choose to remain in Tucson. Solomon Warner (b. New York 1811, d. Tucson 1899), who had gone to California in the Gold Rush, arrives in Tucson 11 days before the Mexican soldiers leave. He is the first Anglo shopkeeper in Tucson after it transfers to the United States. Tucsón has become Tucson, but into the twentieth century, many Anglo residents will continue to pronounce the name as Too SAHN, rather than TOO sahn.

1856

The first Anglo mining operation in the Arizona/New Mexico Territory is in Tubac, run by Charles D. Poston (b. Kentucky 1825, later the Arizona Territory's first representative to Congress, d. Phoenix 1902), with the backing of Ohio investors. Soon afterward, Poston begins other mining operations in the Santa Ritas. He is protected by soldiers stationed at Tubac, until the soldiers leave to enter the Civil War and the region becomes vulnerable to attacks by Apaches and Mexicans. Other significant Anglo mining operations in this region are the Cerro Colorado Mine to the southwest, also known as the Heintzelman Mine, also in operation from 1856 (Poston's brother will later be killed there by Apaches). In 1860, Silvester Mowry (b. Rhode Island 1830) begins to operate a mine to the east in Patagonia that is destroyed by Apaches in 1863.

1857

The Butterfield Overland Mail stage line begins operations between San Francisco and St. Louis. The line was created by Congress after John W. Butterfield and his team won a bidding competition with Wells Fargo. Before this, mail had gone by ship to Panama and by land across the isthmus. Going east from California, the stage line enters New Mexico Territory at Yuma, crosses to Tucson, goes on to Mesilla and Franklin (formerly and later El Paso), Texas, and then up to St. Louis. Stage stations are 12–20 miles apart, with 25 stations in what is now Arizona. The traveling is hard because of heat, lack of water, and Apaches. To support the route, water wells are dug along the Santa Cruz. In 1864, Irish traveler J. Ross Browne writes of this stage line, "An enterprise of greater importance than this had never been undertaken by any private citizen. It was one of the grand achievements of the age to span the continent by a semi-weekly line of stages, under bonds to perform, by the sole power of horse-flesh, a trip of nearly two thousand five hundred miles within the schedule time of twenty-five days. Few believed it could be done; and when the vast deserts through which the route lay, and the hostile tribes of Indians that inhabit them, are taken into account, it is a marvel that it was not only a success but a triumph."

1857

Phillip Drachman (b. 1833 Poland) arrives in Tucson with his cousin Issac Goldberg. They start a business of long-distance freighting to California, open a store in Tucson, and develop farming enterprises along the Colorado River.

1858

Sam Hughes (b. Wales 1829, d. Tucson 1917) arrives in Tucson, coming from California after a diagnosis of tuberculosis. His family had emigrated to the U.S. in 1837 but his parents had died when he was very young and he had gone to work. By the time he arrives in Tucson, he has worked at many different kinds of jobs in many different parts of the United States.

1858

Father Joseph P. Machebeuf, an emissary of Archbishop Lamy of the Catholic Diocese of Santa Fe, visits Tucson and the new San Agustín Church that is under construction. The church he finds inside the presidio walls, also called San Agustín, is half in ruins.

1859

Leopoldo Carrillo (b. Sonora 1836, d. Tucson 1890) arrives in Tucson from Sonora, where he'd had a ranch and a freighting business, and begins his business career in long-distance freighting, with mule-trains bringing goods from the port of Guaymas in Mexico to Tucson. With his wife, Jesusita, he has 10 children from 1863 to 1878 (including Mathilde, Leopoldo, Joaquin, Arturo, Lionel, Bella Amanda). He also later establishes the Republican Party (that is, the party of Abraham Lincoln) in Tucson and serves on the first school board and on the Tucson City Council from 1883 to 1885, but he does not succeed in other campaigns for political office.

1859

In December, a treaty is signed in Veracruz between the U.S. and Mexico, the McLane-Ocampo Treaty, also known as the Treaty of Transit and Commerce, which sells to the U.S. a perpetual right of transit from Nogales to Guaymas, among other rights of transit through Mexico. The treaty would give Arizona a seaport. President Buchanan supports the treaty but the Senate fails to ratify it.

1859

Estevan Ochoa (b. Mexico 1831 into an affluent family, d. Las Cruces 1888) arrives in Tucson. Before coming to Tucson, he had operated stores in Mesilla and Las Cruces and freighted on the Santa Fe/Chihuahua Trail all the way to its starting point (from the American point of view) in Independence, Missouri. The starting point in Mexico is Durango.

1859

Arizona's first newspaper, the Weekly Arizonan, *is printed and published in Tubac. The hand press used will later be acquired by L. C. Hughes of Tucson to print the* Arizona Star.

1850s late

At the southeastern base of Sentinel Peak, William and Alfred Rowlett create a lake by damming springs there, and build a flour mill. The mill will be destroyed by retreating Union forces in 1861 and rebuilt in 1864 by the enterprising Irishman James Lee. A resort called "Silver Lake" is later developed on the site by J. F. Richey and J. O. Bailey, and later by Frederick Maish and Thomas Drisscoll, offering a hotel, bathhouses, pavilions, a one-mile racetrack, and later sailboating, with tram service from Tucson. Floods destroy its earthen dams on several occasions and after the turn of the century, Silver Lake returns to the desert.

1859

William Oury (b. Virginia 1817, arrives Tucson 1853 after serving in the Texas War of Independence and in the U.S. War with Mexico, d. Tucson 1887) and Sylvester Mowry move the *Weekly Arizonan* newspaper from Tubac to Tucson.

1860

According to the U.S. Census, out of a total population of 925 non-Indians in Tucson, 168 are Anglos, of whom 95 percent are male, mostly bachelors. The Mexican residents are more often in families. Though Anglos are a minority, they now control about 87 percent of Tucson's wealth. Anglos in Tucson do not, however, manifest the outright hostility to people of Mexican descent that is found in mining communities like Prescott and will appear later in Phoenix.

1861

In February, at what was supposed to be a peace parley, U.S. Army Lieutenant George Bascom tries to trap and arrest the Chiricahua Apache leader Cochise. Cochise escapes by cutting his way out of the tent with his knife and begins a relentless war against the Americans, with whom he had formerly been more friendly than with the Mexicans.

1861–1862

With the Confederate shelling of Fort Sumter in South Carolina on April 12, 1861, the United States' Civil War begins. Four months later, on August 1, Lieutenant Colonel John R. Baylor, commanding the Confederate Texan troops that had taken Mesilla, New Mexico, issues a proclamation declaring the creation of a provisional Confederate Territory of Arizona, to include all of the former United States Territory of New Mexico south of the 34th parallel north, roughly the southern half of what today is New Mexico and Arizona. In 1861, 68 voters in Tucson elect a Territorial Delegate to the Confederate Congress. Colonel Baylor dispatches to Tucson a detachment of Confederate Texan soldiers commanded by Captain Sherod Hunter that arrives on February 28, 1862. The Confederate Texans occupy Tucson for 10 weeks, giving residents the option of declaring loyalty to the Confederacy or leaving town.

1862

When the Confederates arrive, Estevan Ochoa declines to swear loyalty to their cause and is told to leave. Lightly armed, ill-provisioned, and on horseback, he heads east into Apache country and manages to make his way safely to Union forces on the Rio Grande. When Solomon Warner also refuses to swear allegiance to the Confederacy, his property is seized. He goes south into Sonora, returning after the war with a Mexican woman he had married there. Sam Hughes refuses to swear allegiance and departs for California.

1862

After the U.S. soldiers leave Tubac to fight in the Civil War and during the 10 weeks the Confederate Texans are occupying Tucson, Apaches besiege Tubac, which, thanks to mining in the area, had become the largest town in Arizona. The besieged citizens of Tubac are rescued by an expedition of Confederates from Tucson led by William Oury, but Tubac is afterward abandoned and Tucson becomes the largest town in Arizona. Tubac never regains its former stature. During the Civil War, mining operations in the area are destroyed by Apaches and Mexican bandits returning from the south.

1862

In New Mexico, another detachment of Confederate Texans under General Henry H. Sibley had gone north from Mesilla up the Rio Grande and occupied Santa Fe, with the ultimate aim of continuing north and capturing the gold fields of Colorado. On March 28, one month after the arrival of the Confederate Texans in Tucson, in the Battle of Glorieta Pass, the Confederate Texan forces marching north from Santa Fe suffer an unexpected and catastrophic defeat that results in a complete dispersal of their forces.

1862

From Tucson, patrols of the Confederate Texans had been sallying forth to destroy facilities and supplies along the Butterfield Stage route, hoping to impede the progress of Union troops expected to come from California. On April 15, 1862, west of Tucson at Picacho Pass, a patrol of Confederates encounters a Union patrol that is scouting for a larger body of California Volunteers that has come east from

Los Angeles, troops now called the California Column. A skirmish ensues. Four Union soldiers are killed but the Confederates retreat and on May 14, 1862, abandon Tucson. The skirmish at Picacho Pass (today called Picacho Peak) ends the Confederacy's adventures in Arizona and the American Southwest.

1862

On May 20, 1862, the California Column enters Tucson and creates the military Post of Tucson. Now it is the turn of the Confederate sympathizers to have their holdings confiscated. Sam Hughes returns to Tucson with the California Column. One week after his return, he marries 13-year-old Atanácia Santa Cruz (b. Tucson 1850, d. Tucson 1935). The two will have 15 children, 10 of whom will survive infancy, and Atanácia will come to be called the "mother of Tucson." Atanácia is the younger sister of Petra Santa Cruz, already the wife of Hiram Stevens (see below: 1865).

1862

Silvester Mowry is arrested by General Carlton of the California Column and shipped to San Francisco on charges of disloyalty but never tried. His Patagonia mine is destroyed by Apaches while he is gone. He dies in England in 1871 while on a trip to sell his mines or raise capital to restore them.

1862

The Federal Homestead Act is passed that allows people to patent (i.e., take ownership of) 160 acres, if they build on, reside on, and farm the land for five years. The homesteader need not be a citizen, only to declare an intention to become one, but must not have borne arms against the United States, that is, must not have fought for the Confederacy.

1862

During the Civil War, Congress passes the Pacific Railway Act, authorizing the first transcontinental railroad across the north. Construction begins in 1863, with tracks being laid west from San Francisco and east from Omaha, Nebraska/Council Bluffs, Iowa. The tracks of the first transcontinental railroad will be joined at Promontory, Utah, on May 10, 1869.

1862

Tucson's National (or Government) Cemetery is established at the east end of Alameda and what will become Stone Avenue when some soldiers are buried there. Earlier it had served as Tucson's cemetery. A large walled cemetery for civilians will be in place there from 1870 that will be closed in 1875 when it is realized that the Southern Pacific right-of-way will pass through it. What is now Toole Avenue cuts it in half. Beginning in 1890 the city will develop the site with residences and small businesses.

1862

A survey of Tucson by Major D. Fergusson of the California Volunteers shows the only settled area beyond the presidio to be south of it along Meyer and Main, the area now called Barrio Historico or Barrio Viejo.

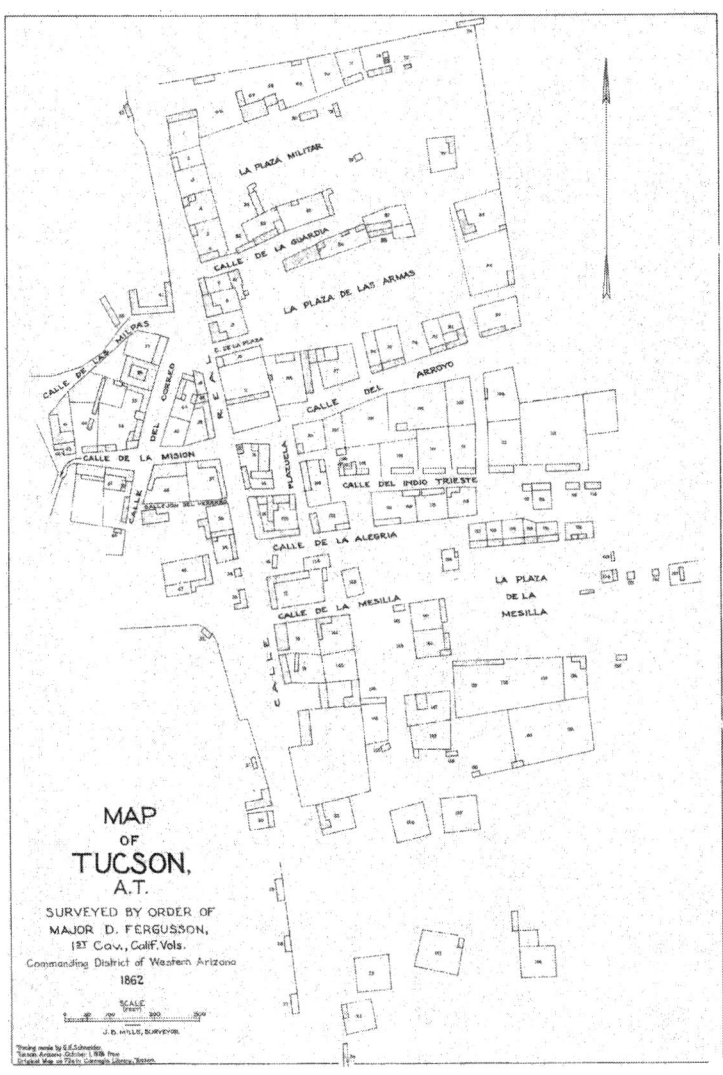

1862 Fergusson map of Tucson (1926 tracing). Immediately after the Union army's California Column drove the occupying Confederates out of Tucson in May 1862, Major D. Fergusson of the Column ordered the city surveyed and mapped. The map, which presents itself as accurately scaled, bases itself not on streets and landmarks but on the outlines of buildings with negative space outside. It shows the Presidio San Augustín (1775-1853) located North of "Calle del Arroyo," with almost all settlement in Tucson to the south of it.

1862

East of Tucson at Apache Pass, a large force of Apaches led by Cochise and another notorious Apache leader, Mangas Coloradas, attacks the California Column on its way east but are driven off. The Column continues east on its mission to expel the Confederate Texans from southern New Mexico Territory. The Column meets no resistance from the Texans and by August 1862, it has reached Franklin, now known as El Paso.

7

Tucson in the Arizona Territory

(1863–1911)

1863

In an act signed by President Lincoln, the Territory of Arizona is created as separate from New Mexico Territory. The first governor appointed for the territory (who serves until 1866) is John Noble Goodwin, a native of Maine. Goodwin chooses the mining town of Prescott in northern Arizona as the first territorial capital (Fort Whipple is nearby) even though it is much smaller than Tucson, probably because Tucson's suspected sympathies with the Confederacy (NB: the Civil War is still on). Goodwin identifies the Apaches as the principal obstacle to civilization and development. Goodwin also chooses Judge William T. Howell to be the principal author of Arizona's first code of laws. He appoints Democrat William Oury (b. Virginia 1817, d. Tucson 1887) as the first mayor of Tucson. Soon after his term ends, Goodwin leaves Arizona never to return, not the only territorial governor to do so. Of Arizona's 16 appointed territorial governors, five will have been born in Pennsylvania, three in Ohio, two in Maine, two in New York, and one each in Kentucky, Georgia, Indiana, and Vermont. Only a little more than half of them will have been in Arizona long enough to qualify as residents. Most would be appointed by Republican presidents. Most elected officials in the state during this period are Democrats.

1863

The foundation for a new St. Augustine Church is laid by Father Donato Rogieri south of Congress (then Calle de la Alegría) at Church Street and Broadway (then Camp Street). The adobe bricks for the church will be manufactured by the Mexican parishioners after Mass. Adjoining the church site on the north is the Plaza de la Mesilla, also known as La Placita, an open area that will be used for ceremonies, festivals (such as the Fiesta de San Agustín), and socializing.

1864

Archbishop Jean-Baptiste Lamy of the Archdiocese of Santa Fe (Archbishop Latour in Willa Cather's *Death Comes for the Archbishop*) visits Tucson.

1864

Tucson's population, with Indians not counted, is 1,200 Mexicans, 150 American soldiers, 100 Anglos. The census shows Arizona's population to be 4,573, also with Indians not counted. The lowest estimate of the peak population of Hohokam in the Tucson Basin alone is 6,000. Tucson's population is still less than a fourth of that total.

1864

The Territory of Arizona has four counties to begin with—Pima, Yavapai, Yuma, and Mohave. The other 11 counties in existence in 2014 are carved out of these along the way, the process beginning with the creation of Maricopa County in 1871. By 2014, the state has 30 districts represented in the state legislature.

1864

The first school in Arizona designated to receive public funds is a school established at San Xavier. It closes after a couple of months because the Indians do not attend.

1864

The first U.S. marshal, Milton B. Duffield (b. 1810 Wheeling, West Virginia), comes to Tucson. In 1865 Duffield resigns because he isn't being paid but remains in Tucson. A pugnacious man, he is shotgunned and killed in 1874 after accosting someone squatting on a mine property he owns on the San Pedro River.

1864

Sam and Atanácia Hughes's first daughter, Lizzie, is born. Lizzie later claims to have been the first Anglo girl born in Tucson even though Hughes is married to a Mexican-American woman, Atanácia Santa Cruz. Lizzie later attends Ward Belmont School in Nashville, Tennessee, and marries J. Knox Corbett (see 1880), dying in 1936. Her grave is in Holy Hope Cemetery in Tucson.

1864

Irish-born writer and world traveler J. Ross Browne arrives in Tucson and is not favorably impressed. In *A Tour through Arizona 1864, or Adventures in the Apache Country* he writes:

> Passing the Point of the Mountain [the stage station northwest of Tucson 18 miles downstream on the Santa Cruz], [the traveler] is refreshed during the remainder of the way by scraggy thickets of mesquit [sic], bunches of sage and grease-wood, beds of sand and thorny cactus; from which he emerges to find himself on the verge of the most wonderful scatteration of human habitations his eye ever beheld—a city of mud-boxes, dingy and dilapidated, cracked and baked into a composite of dust and filth; littered about with broken corrals, sheds, bake-ovens, carcasses of dead animals, and broken pottery; barren of verdure, parched, naked, and grimly desolate in the glare of the southern sun. Adobe walls without

whitewash inside or out, hard earth-floors, baked and dried Mexicans, sore-backed burros, coyote dogs, and terra-cotta children; soldiers, teamsters, and honest miners lounging about the mescal-shops, soaked with the fiery poison; a noisy band of Sonoran buffoons, dressed in theatrical costume, cutting their antics in the public places to the most diabolical din of fiddles and guitars ever heard; a long train of Government wagons preparing to start for Fort Yuma on the Rio Grande [sic] —these are what the traveler sees, and a great many things more, but in vain he looks for a hotel or lodging-house. (131–133)

Traveling on the same stagecoach with Browne is Charles Poston, returning after service in the Union Army and carrying an appointment to serve as Indian agent in the territory. While in Washington, Poston had been one of those exerting himself to get Arizona declared a territory separate from New Mexico.

1864

At Tucson, J. Ross Browne turns south and heads up the valley of the Santa Cruz River toward Mexico. He writes,

The valley of the Santa Cruz is one of the richest and most beautiful grazing and agricultural regions I have ever seen. Occasionally the river sinks, but even at these points the grass is abundant and luxuriant. We travelled league after league, through waving fields of grass from two to four feet high, and this at a season when cattle were dying of starvation all over the middle and southern parts of California.... [T]here is no lack of water most of the way to [the Mexican town of] Santa Cruz. (144)

1864

Estevan Ochoa, who had ridden out of Tucson when the Confederates arrived but has now returned, forms a business partnership with Pinckney Randolph Tully in freighting, mercantile, and military supply. Corral Street, which sits just south of Ochoa Street off Stone Avenue, is named for the corral that was originally the U.S. Army quartermaster's corral and later the Tully, Ochoa & Company's corral. Tully is a Mississippi native who had started west on the Oregon Trail in 1845 with his family. His father had died en route in Missouri, and Tully had gone instead to Santa Fe and then to California, and finally back to Arizona, settling in Tubac and opening a store in Tucson. He finally moves to Tucson, and later serves in various public posts, including twice as mayor. Ochoa later serves as territorial legislator and mayor. Both men later work with territorial governor Safford to promote public education.

1864

John W. "Jack" Swilling (b. South Carolina 1830, d. Yuma 1878) marries Trinidad Mejia Escalante in St. Augustine Church in Tucson. Two years earlier Swilling had fought on the side of the Confederates during their occupation of Tucson, then had managed to join up with the California Column, leading the group that had captured the Apache captain Mangas Coloradas after the Apache attack on the California Column. Three years after his wedding, Swilling

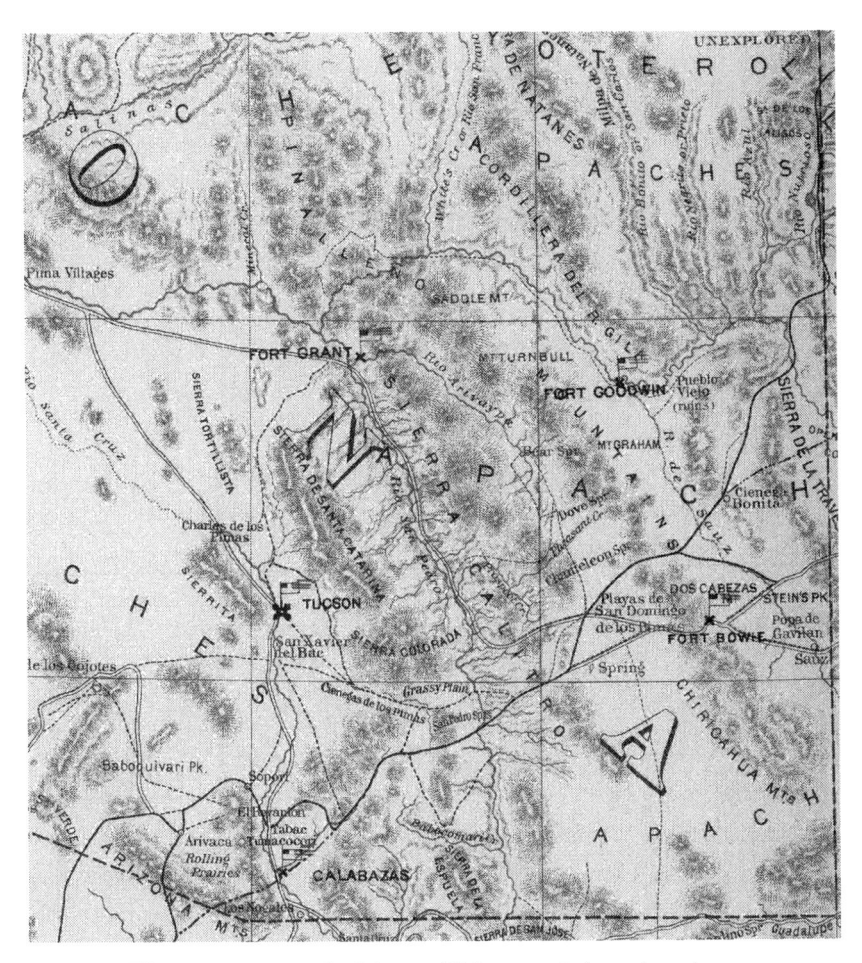

1864 Union army map of Arizona. This map of the region places topographic features in only approximate relation to each other but it would have been suitable for long-distance travel by an army traveling on horseback according to compass directions and landmarks such as mountain ranges, whose names are different from contemporary ones, and the few trails that crossed the terrain.

will have relocated to the Salt River Valley and begun digging the first modern-era canals where Phoenix would later grow. The canals of the Hohokam are thought to have given him the idea. He and Trinidad will have five children and two adopted Apache orphans by the time Swilling dies at age 48.

1860s

The troubles with the Apaches have caused many Mexican land grants to be abandoned. Grants found to have been abandoned can be auctioned off. After the Gadsden Purchase and the Civil War, the legal status of many land grants begins to be litigated, and fraud, by Anglos now, is common.

1865

Hiram S. Stevens (b. Vermont 1832, m. Petra Santa Cruz, d. Tucson 1893) forms a business partnership this year with brother-in-law Sam Hughes (Hughes, Stevens & Company). They get into military supply and freighting, merchandizing, mining, and cattle ranching and begin to acquire buildings in town. Stevens has a serious interest in territorial politics and represents the Arizona Territory in the U.S. Congress in 1875 and 1877. Sam Hughes is elected to various local political offices but serves reluctantly, if at all, possibly because he had never been able to attend school and could not read and write very well.

1866

French Father Jean B. Salpointe arrives in Tucson. Salpointe had been appointed pastor of the St. Augustine Church by Archbishop Lamy of the Archdiocese of Santa

Fe. Lamy, who is himself French and the model for Archbishop Latour in Willa Cather's *Death Comes for the Archbishop*, favors French pastors and bishops over Spanish or Mexican ones. Salpointe will be the first Vicar Apostolic of the diocese and will be succeeded by two other French prelates, Peter Bourgade, who succeeds Salpointe in 1885, and Henry Granjon, who succeeds Bourgade in 1900. Salpointe estimates the current population of Tucson to be 600. In 1864, Marshall Duffield had reported its population to be 1,568, making it the largest town in Arizona by far, with the next largest, La Paz, on the Colorado River, having 352. Work on St. Augustine Church—commonly referred to as a cathedral even then—continues. The main body of the church will be completed under Salpointe in 1868.

1866–1868

Richard C. McCormick (a Lincoln Republican, b. 1832 in New York City, d. 1901 New York City) is the second governor of the Arizona Territory, replacing Goodwin. McCormick is the publisher of the Journal-Miner *in Prescott, started in 1864, and the* Arizona Citizen, *started in 1870. Along with efforts to control the Apaches, he supports development of agriculture and acquiring a seaport for Arizona on the Gulf of California.*

1866

Louis Zeckendorf (b. 1838 Germany, comes to U.S. at 16, d. 1937 New York City) brings merchandise to Tucson from the store he has with his brother Aaron in Santa Fe that is also serving Albuquerque and Rio Mimbres mining camps. The next year, Louis founds in Tucson the Zeckendorf Bros. store on Pearl near Pennington.

1866

After the Civil War, the military presence in the American Southwest had been greatly reduced but conflict with Apaches was unabated, with defense being provided by poorly equipped volunteer groups. This year regular army units begin to replace them, though not in large numbers.

1866 August 29

The Post of Tucson, established by the California Column in 1862, abandoned in July 1864 and reestablished July 1865, is renamed Camp Lowell in honor of Union General Charles Russell Lowell, who died from wounds received during the Battle of Cedar Creek (October 1964) in the Shenandoah Valley of Virginia. The troops and armory are located not far from the presidio, east of what is now Sixth Avenue between what now are 12th and 14th Streets, an area that comes to be called the "Military Plaza."

1867

Lord & Williams store opens in Tucson, co-founded by Charles H. Lord, a medical doctor who had come to Tucson in 1866 as a contract surgeon at the Cerro Colorado Mine south of Tucson, and W. W. Williams. It becomes the United States depository for Arizona Territory and is a leading merchandiser in Tucson until its failure in 1881, though Lord will be accused by Charles Poston of corrupt dealings concerning Indians. Also, an "Indian Ring" of commercial interests in the Southwest is sometimes suspected of fomenting conflict with Indians in order to profit from supplying the military.

1867

A. & L. Zeckendorf store opens in Tucson. Aaron and Louis Zeckendorf, both born in Germany, had been in business in Santa Fe since 1854. Aaron continues in business there until he dies in 1872. Louis continues in business in Tucson with his brother William as Zeckendorf Brothers. Phillip Drachman serves as manager.

1867

Lionel and Barron Jacobs, whose father, Mark, a merchant in San Bernardino, had lent them money for the enterprise, arrive in Tucson having come by wagon from San Diego with a load of canned goods. They rent an empty store next to Lord & Williams from Leopoldo Carrillo and open Mark Jacobs Company.

1867

Phillip Drachman represents Tucson in the 3rd and 4th territorial legislatures in Prescott.

1867

Samuel Drachman, Phillip's brother (d. 1911), comes to Tucson from Charleston, South Carolina, where he had fought for the Confederacy, traveling from New York City to San Francisco by ship over three weeks, making about 240 miles a day compared to 25 miles a day by stagecoach, arriving Tucson September 4. He works at the White House store and Zeckendorfs, and by 1872 is in business for himself.

1867

A report by railroad surveyor William A. Bell describes the Santa Cruz as "a perennial stream" for its first 150 miles, until it disappears beneath the surface near "a spot called Canoa. It then flows underground almost to St. Xavier (twenty miles), and again reappears at a spot called Punta de Agua. Beyond St. Xavier it usually again sinks, rising for a third time as a fine body of water near Tucson, enriching a broad piece of valley for about ten miles around that town, turning the wheel of a fair-sized flour mill, and then sinking forever in the desert to the north-west."

1867

John W. "Jack" Swilling, seeing potential in the remains of Hohokam canals in the Salt River Valley, heads a small group of men who build the first modern-era irrigation canals there, where Phoenix later begins to appear. He develops this enterprise with his old business partner Charles T. Hayden, who will become the father of Arizona senator Carl Hayden (D).

1867

Tucson, still the largest town in the Arizona Territory, is made its capital (until 1877). The Territorial Library is brought to Tucson from Prescott.

1868

Charles O. Brown opens the Congress Hall Saloon on Congress and Meyer, near the meeting place for the territorial legislature. It is Tucson's finest saloon and thrives. On Camp Street nearby he builds his house that in 2014 is the Old Adobe Patio. The next year, Calle de la Alegría's name is changed to Congress Street.

1868

At the eastern boundary of the presidio, Pima County's first courthouse, built of adobes, opens for business.

1868

E. N. Fish & Co. store opens this year on Main and Pennington, just south of A. & L. Zeckendorf on Calle Reál (the main thoroughfare through Tucson, later renamed Main Street) near Congress. Edward Nye Fish is a New Englander who had come to Tucson from the California gold fields in 1865 and become an army post trader at Calabazas in partnership with Simon Silverberg. The Fish-Stevens houses and Sam Hughes's large house are built around this time on Calle Reál. The residences on Main are north of Congress; the businesses are concentrated to the south of it. In his backyard, Sam Hughes will install a windmill water pump, probably the first in Tucson with one. The "windpump" had been invented by New Englander Daniel Halladay in 1854, and then spread throughout the dry West.

1868

Emilio Carrillo (apparently no relation to Leopoldo) homesteads ranch property at the base of the Rincons, calling it La Cebadilla (roughly speaking, "a place where there is good feed for animals"). After Carrillo's death in 1908, Jim

Converse acquires this 640-acre ranch and makes it into a working/dude ranch.

1868

On November 15, Phillip Drachman returns to Tucson from San Francisco with the wife he had traveled to New York to find. He and Rosa (a cousin of Louis Zeckendorf) will have 10 children, including Harry (said to be the first Anglo boy born in the Arizona Territory), Mose, and Emanuel (Manny), all of whom establish themselves in Tucson. The other seven children—Rebecca, Myra, Albert, Minnie, Lillian, Esther, and Phyllis—leave in their adult years. Roy Drachman is the son of Emanuel, grandson of Phillip and Rosa. Most descendants, including Roy, cease practicing as Jews. Phillip dies November 1899, age 66, and is buried with Masonic rites.

1869

Major John Wesley Powell conducts his first wooden boat expedition down the Green and Colorado rivers and through the Grand Canyon, at this time the last unmapped area in the United States, referred to by Powell as he begins the journey as "the great unknown."

1869

Mariano Samaniego (b. Sonora 1844, d. Tucson 1907) arrives in Tucson. He had been in Mesilla since 1852 with his widowed mother in the mercantile and long-distance freighting business. After the Gadsden Purchase, he gets naturalized, graduates from St. Louis University, supports the Confederate cause in New Mexico, and later gets into the long-distance freighting business on the Chihuahua/Santa Fe Trail with Yjinio Aguirre, a childhood friend from Chihuahua. In 1868, he marries Aguirre's sister Dolores and in 1869 goes to Tucson, where Yjinio's brother Pedro Aguirre is in the freighting business, and they become partners in competition with Tully & Ochoa. He has contracts to Camp Grant and to Yuma. In the 1870s he is elected to territorial and county offices. He survives the arrival of the railroad in 1880 because he had also gotten into ranching in Oro Valley and along the Rillito. The Aguirres had major ranch holdings southwest of Tucson, founding the Buenos Aires Ranch, among others. Samaniego also operates an express stagecoach that runs to settlements north and south of Tucson.

1869

Samuel Bostwick opens his barber shop, the first business in Tucson owned by an African-American.

1869

Jacob Mansfeld (b. Pasewalk, Germany, 1832, d. Tucson 1894) arrives in Tucson. He had come to America in 1856, worked in bookstores in San Francisco; Virginia City, Nevada; and White Pine, Nevada, before coming to Tucson. Mansfeld opens the Pioneer News Depot and Bookstore, selling newspapers from New York City, magazines, and books, as well as stationery and other writing materials. In 1871 Mansfeld establishes the first lending library in town, lending books from his store.

1869–1877

Anson P. K. Safford (b. Vermont c. 1830, to California in 1850, arrives Tucson 1869) becomes governor of the Arizona Territory, appointed by President Grant. He will be the longest-serving territorial governor and do much to promote public education, causing John Spring to say he should be called the "Father of our Public Schools." He will also do much to curtail the operations of the Mexican and American highwaymen operating in the territory and will preside over the removal of the Chiricahua and Arivaipa Apaches to reservations in eastern Arizona. As governor, he resides in the then capital, Tucson, in a house on South Main that is destroyed in urban renewal 100 years later.

1870

Alex Levin (b. Bahn Prussia 1934, arrives Tucson 1869, d. Tucson 1891, age 58, after financial reversals) launches the Pioneer Brewery with J. Goldtree, marries a prominent woman from Sonora, Zenora Molina (d. 1891), and becomes Catholic. Levin takes over the Hodges Hotel, buys out J. Goldtree's interest, and over the next decade turns the Pioneer Brewery grounds into a three-acre park (at the corner of today's Granada and Congress), adding a dance hall, a restaurant, an opera house that seats 2,000 people, a shooting gallery, an archery range, an icehouse, a bathhouse, riding stables, and a bowling alley. Levin's Park is very popular and into the 1880s is the location of every important and communal event in Tucson—until the much larger Carrillo Gardens opens in 1885 and Levin's Park declines.

1870

Having traveled by wagon from San Diego across the California and Arizona deserts, seven Sisters of St. Joseph of Carondelet come around Point of Rocks and arrive in Tucson. The townspeople welcome them in a celebration punctuated by gunfire. Before long, they have opened a private school for girls near St. Augustine Cathedral. In 1873, they open a school for Indians at Mission San Xavier (still in existence in 2014, operated now by the Franciscan Sisters of Christian Charity, who teach at the school and reside in the convent at San Xavier). In 1880, they will open St. Mary's Hospital, Arizona's first hospital.

1870

Tucson's population is 3,224.

1870 October 20

The town site of Phoenix is laid out.

1870

John Wasson, a newspaperman from Idaho and Nevada and friend of Governor Safford, comes to Tucson and becomes editor of the McCormick-owned weekly, *Arizona Citizen*. Tucson's newspaper had been the *Weekly Arizonan*, managed by P. W. Dooner, publishing primarily the "acts and resolutions of Congress" with little other "outside information." The *Arizonan* will cease publication this year, however, after an editorial "war of words" with the *Citizen*. The *Citizen* continues agitating for such measures as "the sweeping away of garbage piles, the lighting of the streets by night, the establishment of schools, and the imposition of a tax upon the gin-mills and gambling-saloons" (Bourke 94–95). Newspapermen from elsewhere in the state accuse Wasson of being part of the McCormick-Safford faction, aka the "Tucson Ring."

1870

Throughout the American Southwest, it is the era of the survey. Arizona is made a separate surveying district this year and John Wasson is appointed Arizona Surveyor General by President Grant. He hires S. W. Foreman to survey the Tucson Basin, tricky because of the Apaches. Spanish and Mexican land-grant claims present him with another kind of challenge.

1871

At the insistent instigation of Governor Anson Safford, the territorial legislature sitting in Tucson passes laws creating a Territorial Board of Education and a superintendent of public instruction and authorizing taxes that allow the creation of Tucson School District 1 in Pima County.

1871 March 3

President Grant signs into law a bill authorizing the private Texas & Pacific Railway to run west to California along a southern route. This railroad is never built in Arizona and will be supplanted in Arizona and New Mexico by the Southern Pacific.

1871 April 30

Near a U.S. military fort 60 miles north of Tucson called Camp Grant, over 100 Arivaipa Apache women, children, and old men who had surrendered and are living near the fort are attacked and killed by 140 Mexican, Papago, and Anglo residents of Tucson (likely supplied by Sam Hughes and led by Jose María Elías and William S. Oury, both of whom had lost relatives in Apache attacks), in reprisal for continuing Apache raids. In October 1871, after pressure from the U.S. government, a Pima County grand jury indicts 100 of the assailants for murder. The earliest known photograph of a scene in Tucson pictures the large group of defendants, jurors, and court officials involved in the trial in front of the three-year-old Pima County Courthouse. The six-day trial that takes place two months later focuses on continuing Apache depredations. John Spring later wrote in *Troublous Days in Arizona* (1903), "My own data give the number of murdered men, women and children during the years 1869, 1870 and 1871 at 227." One of the stories told was probably that of Larcena Pennington, who had been captured in the Santa Rita Mountains by a different band of Apaches in 1860. Left for dead, she had survived 16 days in the mountains before making it to safety. In the nine years that followed her capture, her first husband, father, and two of her brothers would be killed by Apaches. J. Ross Browne had written that in 1864 "I saw on the road between San Xavier and Tubac, a distance of forty miles, almost as many graves of the white men murdered by the Apaches within the past few years. Literally the roadside was marked with the burial-places of these unfortunate settlers. There is not now a single living soul to enliven the solitude...everywhere ruin, grim and ghastly with associations

Photo courtesy of Arizona Historical Society, #654 (http://arizonahistoricalsociety.org). The earliest known photograph of any Tucson scene, taken in 1871. It is a photograph of the first Pima County Courthouse, built with adobes on Church Street in 1868. Tucson is in Pima County, which was established in 1864 as one of Arizona Territory's four original counties. Arrayed in front of the courthouse are many of the town's most substantial citizens, including several of the defendants in the trial then being conducted of those who perpetrated the Camp Grant massacre, their defense attorneys, and the judge in the case (middle foreground). The 3"x 4" photograph at the Arizona Historical Society bears the stamp "Edw. J. Muybridge, Photographic View Artist, 12 Montgomery St, San Francisco, Cal."

of sudden death. I have rarely travelled through a country more richly favored, yet more depressing in its associations with the past." It seems unlikely that any evidence was offered that the Apache women and children killed at the camp and the children captured and sold had committed any of these depredations. The jury nevertheless quickly pronounced a general verdict of not guilty upon those who had killed them.

1871

John G. Bourke, captain, Third Cavalry, arrives in Tucson for a posting to Camp Lowell, finding Tucson "as foreign a town as if it were in Hayti instead of within our own boundaries. The language, dress, funeral processions, religious ceremonies, feasts, dances, games, joys, perils, griefs, and tribulations of its population were something not to be looked for in the region east of the Missouri River" (57). At the Shoo Fly Restaurant, "a long, narrow, low-ceiled room of adobe...whose floor was of rammed earth and ceiling of white muslin," run by a Mrs. Wallen, he found "plenty of 'jerked' beef, savory and palatable enough in stews and hashes; eggs, and the sweet toothsome black 'frijoles' of Mexico, tomatoes equal to those of any part of our country, and lettuce always crisp, dainty, and delicious." From Hermosillo, Mrs. Wallen was sometimes able to get "honey-juiced oranges, sweet limes, lemons, edible quinces, and luscious apricots" though the "apple, the plum, and the cherry were unknown...and the strawberry only occasionally seen." When the Apaches interrupted trade from the south, "our sole reliance would be upon the mainstay of boarding-house prosperity—stewed peaches and prunes." Sometimes "the red beet, which in the 'alkali' lands attains a great size, and the black fig of Mexico" would be available. "Chile colorado entered into the composition of every dish, and the great velvety-skinned delicately flavored onions as large as dinner plates ended...the regular list. On some special occasions there would be honey brought in from the Tia Juana Ranch in Lower California... and dried shrimps from the harbor of Guaymas."

1872 April 4

The first public school in Arizona opens in Tucson, for boys only, in an adobe building on the northwest corner of Meyer and McCormick Streets leased from one Mariano Molina. John Spring is hired as its first teacher. Spring (b. Switzerland 1845, m. Manuela Molina of Sonora in 1870, d. Virginia 1924) had come to the United States to fight for the Union during the Civil War and served at military posts in the Southwest before leaving the service. In Pima County, there are said to be 503 children of school age. Average attendance at the school is 98, with ages ranging from six to 21 years, rather a challenge for a single teacher. The primary language of the great majority of the students is Spanish. The school board, led by Estevan Ochoa, begins a campaign for a new building. John Spring later establishes educational standards in both Arizona and Sonora.

1872

Emanual Drachman is born in Tucson to Phillip and Rosa.

1872

Albert Steinfeld is invited by his three uncles, Aaron, Louis, and William Zeckendorf, to come work in the family

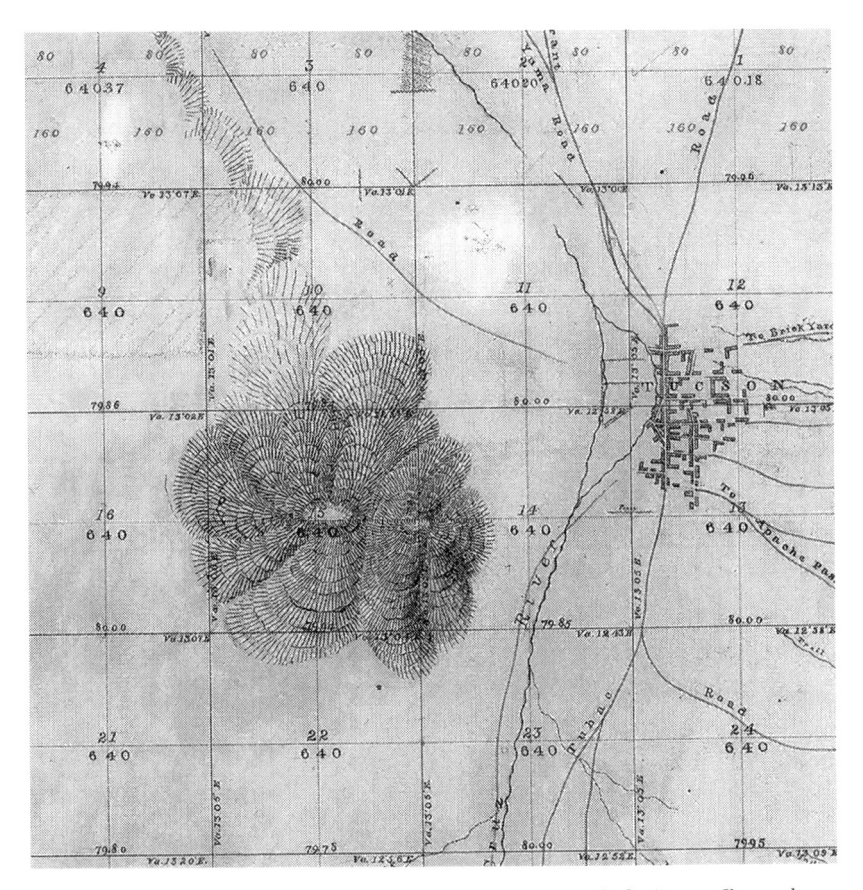

1871 map by S. W. Foreman under the auspices of Surveyor General John Wasson. This map, produced early in the era of the surveying of the West, may be the first of the region that uses the Public Lands Survey System of townships and ranges, still in use today for property descriptions. This map also shows an early and inexact form of indicating elevation and landforms in mountains. Little detail appears outside of the town of Tucson. The Apaches were active and surveying was a risky business.

business in Tucson. From his parents' home in Denver, the 17-year-old travels alone by train to San Francisco, where he boards the weekly boat to San Diego and then takes the tri-weekly stage to Tucson. He is mortified by what he finds Tucson to be, but resolves to try to make a go of it (Aaron dies soon after this and Louis sells out of the Santa Fe business).

1872

The S. W. Foreman survey notes that at San Xavier there are 100 acres under cultivation, 1,900 acres now west of the presidio (compared to 300 acres in 1854). The survey records many streets renamed from the Spanish, some after people killed by Apaches (Pennington, Stone, Cushing, Simpson, Kennedy, Scott, Jackson). What was Camp Street (because it ran east to the northern boundary of Camp Lowell) is now Broadway, Calle de la Alegría is Congress Street, and Calle Reál is Main Street.

1873

The first free public school for girls begins operating in Tucson in a room at Levin's Park. The teacher is Mrs. L. C. Hughes, sister-in-law of Sam Hughes.

1873

Maria Wakefield, a teacher, arrives in Tucson. She is said to be the first unmarried Anglo woman to come to Tucson. Shortly after her arrival, she marries the merchant E. N. Fish. Many Anglo men, including Alex Levin, Sam Hughes, Hiram Stevens, and Governor Anson P. K. Safford, are married to

Mexican women. Many others have common-law marriages with Mexican women.

1873 March 31

The military Post of Tucson, established during the Civil War just east of the city and now known as Camp Lowell, is moved "for sanitary reasons" to a location about seven miles north and east of town just south of where Pantano joins Tanque Verde Wash to form the Rillito. Unknown to the soldiers, a large Hohokam settlement had existed on the site 600 years earlier. Ample water is available here and the new location is closer to a route favored by Apaches coming over Redington Pass on their way to Tucson. In the year of the move, John Brackett "Pie" Allen opens near the camp the Post Trader's Store (and bar), which quickly comes to do a thriving business, especially the bar. He sells out to Frederick Austin the following year. On April 5, 1879, the post's name is changed to Fort Lowell. The fort grows to have approximately 30 adobe buildings, including accommodations, hospital, commissary, stables, trading store, guard house, kitchens, large parade ground, and tree-lined sidewalks. The area back in the city that has been vacated by the troops becomes known as Military Plaza, later Armory Park, and soon begins to be developed by the city, with the number of residences there increasing substantially with the arrival of the railroad in 1880.

1873

William Oury becomes sheriff of Pima County, serving until 1877.

1873

The Jacobs brothers, Lionel and Barron, are charter members of the Tucson Literary Society, which meets Friday evenings in a member's house.

1873

The telegraph arrives in Tucson via Sam Hughes's and James H. Toole's Arizona Telegraph Company.

1874

Cochise, chief of the Chiricahua Apaches, dies. Two years earlier, he had made peace and agreed to reside on a reservation that would take in a large part of southeastern Arizona, the agreement having been mediated by his friend, Indian agent Tom Jeffords. Cochise is believed to be buried in the Chiricahua Mountains but the burial site has not been found. The Chiricahua Reservation is later abolished and merged in 1882 with the San Carlos Reservation to the north along the Gila River, a reservation just south of the White Mountain Apache Reservation that had been established for the Arivaipa Apache and Yavapai tribes. Both of these reservations exist in 2014.

1874

After the Foreman survey, the Tucson townsite—1,280 acres, Main to First Avenue, Speedway to 22nd—is approved for patent under the Homestead Act. The city begins to issue deeds to property within its boundaries. Surveying continues in the agricultural area along the Santa Cruz.

1874

Dentist and photographer Henry Buehman (b. Germany 1851, d. Tucson 1912) arrives in Tucson, pulls some teeth at Fort Lowell, and the next year goes to work for photographer Adolpho Rodrigo. In February 1875, he buys the Rodrigo Photographic Parlor, changes its name to the Buehman Studio, and begins making images, many of which have become iconic, like his 1875 image of the ruins of the *convento* at the San Agustín Mission. His son Albert continues in photography, and so does Albert's son Albert, publishing images in the "Arizona Album" in the *Tucson Daily Citizen* from 1950 to 1964 and occasionally to 1973.

1874

President Grant sets aside 71,000 acres around San Xavier for exclusive use of the Papago (today Tohono O'odham) Indians. After 1880, historical Mexican residents in the area are forced to leave. A much larger reservation will be created later to the west. In 1884, a smaller area near Gila Bend will be reserved for northern Papago groups. After statehood, the Tucson Chamber of Commerce will try to have the Papago Reservation abolished, efforts that will fail in 1916.

1875

Tucson saloon keeper and confirmed bachelor George Hand (b. New York State 1830, d. Tucson 1887) keeps a diary from this year until 1878. Hand had gone from New York to California as a Forty-Niner, joined the Union Army, come to Tucson in 1862 as a member of the California Column, and returned to Tucson to stay in 1867. His place of business is now a saloon located on the corner of Mesilla and Meyer streets (the site now occupied by the Tucson Convention Center). His diary recounts life in a town:

- Where gambling was legal (until 1905 when gambling houses were outlawed in Tucson. Two years later all forms of gambling were outlawed in the Territory of Arizona).

- Where drinking by anyone, anywhere, at any time was legal (until 1883 when public drunkenness was proscribed by a Tucson city ordinance, the first of several limitations on the manufacture, sale, and use of alcohol that came to be instituted in Tucson before 1914, when the State of Arizona instituted Prohibition five years before it arrived nationally via the Eighteenth Amendment to the U.S. Constitution).

- Where firearms were legal, abundant, and in frequent use.

- Where opium use and opium dens were legal (until outlawed in 1880, the first vice to be outlawed, since it was thought to pertain primarily to the Chinese).

- Where bullfighting and cockfighting and rooster pulls were legal (until 1893, when the first two were outlawed, and 1912, shortly after statehood, when the state outlawed killing animals for the entertainment of spectators).

- Where prostitution was legal though restricted by unspoken agreement to a street called Maiden Lane—a kind of extension of Congress that no longer exists—and points south. Public sexual solicitation will be outlawed in 1883, but houses of prostitution are not outlawed in Tucson until 1905.

Hand's diary makes it clear that in Tucson at the time he is writing, all of these activities (except opium use) were common among Tucson's citizens, himself included. An ordinance had been passed, however, against men wearing dresses or women wearing pants, and Hand tells us how a notorious woman he knew named Molly Monroe was arrested for violating it. The manuscript of Hand's diary is now in the holdings of the Arizona Historical Society.

1875

Estevan Ochoa (b. 1831 in Chihuahua) is elected mayor, the only *tucsonense* (American of Mexican descent) ever to be elected mayor (as of 2014), defeating druggist Charles Meyer 187 to 40. Ochoa had been in business since 1859 with P. R. Tully (Tully, Ochoa & Company) in long-distance freighting, mining, cattle ranching, and merchandizing, and later explored the potential of wool and Pima cotton. Ochoa also serves several terms in the territorial legislature.

1875

Estevan Ochoa has constructed two small smelters at Ochoa and Stone to refine the ore from his and Tully's copper mining operations in the Santa Rita Mountains.

1875 October 1

On the northwest corner of Congress and Sixth Avenue, the Congress Street School is dedicated, built on land donated by Estevan Ochoa, now mayor of Tucson. It has three classrooms, one for primary school boys, one for primary school girls, one for boys doing advanced lessons.

1875

The three top merchandizing firms in Tucson are E. N. Fish, Tully & Ochoa, and Lord & Williams. Zeckendorf Bros. is in fourth place. Supplying military posts and mines remains a major part of their businesses, and now Indian reservations, though corruption is not infrequently alleged.

1870s

Carlos Jácome (b. Sonora 1870, m. Dionicia German 1889, 13 children, naturalized 1894, d. Tucson 1932) arrives in Tucson from Mexico, works in Zeckendorf store for 15 years before leaving to found his own mercantile business.

1875

The Court Street (now Tenth Avenue) Cemetery is established north of town, west of Stone and south of Speedway, partly because it is realized that the Southern Pacific Railroad right-of-way will pass through the current Alameda-Stone Cemetery (est. 1862) on the east end of Alameda Street at Stone Avenue. On the west end of Alameda Street, the Presidio Cemetery had been in service from 1776 to the

1860s. After the Court Street Cemetery opens, the Alameda-Stone Cemetery takes only military burials. It goes out of service in 1881. The eastern half of the Court Street Cemetery will contain plots for Catholics, the western half plots for Protestants, Jews, and members of fraternal groups, with a "City" plot on the west edge. Sub-plots exist for volunteer firefighters (the first sub-plot placed there), Masons, Grand Army of the Republic, B'nai B'rith, Knights of Pythias, International Order of Odd Fellows, and other fraternal orders, among them the "Pima Chapter of the Improved Order of Red Men," which will be established in 1897 and acquire a cemetery sub-plot in 1898, the last sub-plot in the cemetery. In 1907, the Court Street Cemetery will begin to be replaced by the Evergreen (non-denominational) and Holy Hope (Catholic) Cemeteries, to the north of Speedway. The Court Street cemetery closes in 1909. In 2014, Evergreen is still in use and owned by the Addison family. In 2006, the Alameda-Stone site will begin to be excavated by Statistical Research, Inc. and in 2010, many of the remains from the National Cemetery at Stone and Alameda will be moved by the diocese of Tucson to All Faiths cemetery on the southeast side. County buildings are to be constructed on the National Cemetery site. In 2011 the Court Street site will begin to be excavated by Desert Archaeology, Inc., now Southwest Archeology. Burials have been found elsewhere in Tucson, with two significant sites on the south side. Many burials from this era are of children.

1875

At the base of Sentinel Hill west of what had been the Mission Gardens, Solomon Warner builds a grain mill that uses water from the dammed springs and Lee's Pond to turn the stones, with runoff irrigating the fields below. Later he adds a stamp mill for crushing ore. Mills and irrigation ditches proliferate in the 1870s.

1875 April 18

An organizational meeting is held on the second floor of the Cosmopolitan Hotel for the first Scottish Rite Masonic Temple. The Scottish Rite disbands in 1886, then restarts in 1903. Nineteenth-century Masons (not all Scottish Rite) include Albert Steinfeld, Morris Goldwater, George Roskruge, and Sam Hughes; later, Phillip, Harry, and Roy Drachman and Levi Manning. The Scottish Rite Creed is "Human progress is our cause, liberty of thought our supreme wish, freedom of conscience our mission, and the guarantee of equal rights to all people everywhere our ultimate goal."

1876

The first Presbyterian Church is organized, with services being held at the courthouse while a church building is constructed, which is completed in 1879.

1876 April

A group of the Chiricahua Apaches who, with Cochise, had agreed in 1872 to reside on the Chiricahua Indian Reservation east of Tucson leave the reservation and kill some citizens near Camp Bowie east of Tucson. Attacks will continue for another decade. Later in the year, the Chiricahua Reservation is abolished and the Indian agent Tom Jeffords (who had negotiated the reservation deal with Cochise) is fired. The Indians remaining on the reservation are moved north to the San Carlos Reservation that had been established, also in 1872, for Arivaipa

Apaches and Yavapai Indians. The Indian agent there, John P. Clum, organizes the Indians into scouting units to be used to track hostile Apaches.

1876

Easterner Walter Vail and English business partner Herbert Hislop buy property east of Tucson along Cienaga Creek Valley from E. N. Fish, who had occupied it in 1871 and bought it later from his brother-in-law, naming it the Empire Ranch. When Hislop departs after a couple of years, Walter's brother Edward joins him. In 1879, the Total Wreck Silver Mine is located on the ranch. In 1884, the brothers expand their holdings in the area by buying the Stock Valley Ranch from Alonzo Sanford (b. New York City 1840), who had founded the ranch and operated it through the 1870s. Apaches are an issue in this area until Geronimo's surrender in 1886. By 1898, the Vails are running 40,000 cattle, mostly Herefords, on a combination of patented land and grazing lots.

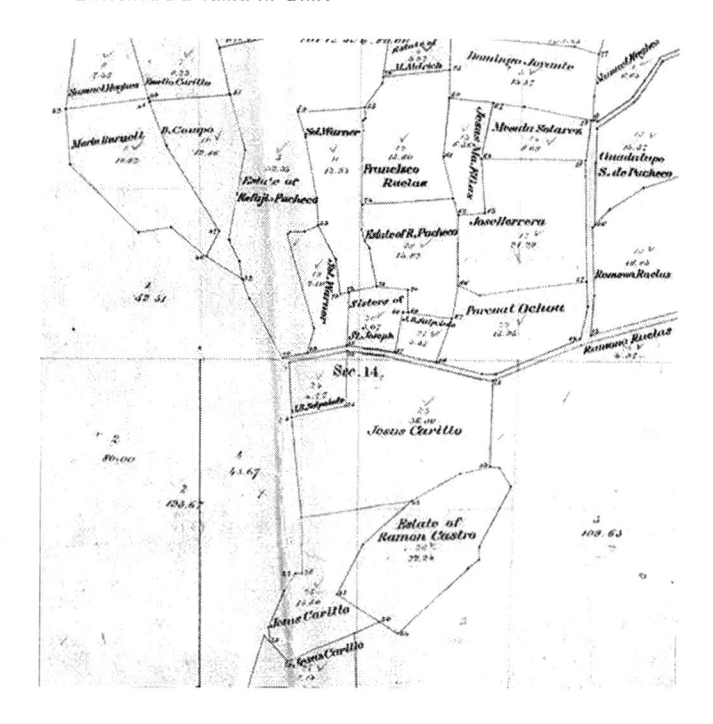

1876 map by F. J. White under the auspices of Surveyor General John Wasson showing the claimants to agricultural plots along the Santa Cruz for purposes of granting title to the land to people who had established a historical claim to it. Most names are Hispanic, but Solomon Warner and Sam Hughes appear among the claimants, as does J. B. Salpointe.

1877

An epidemic of smallpox begins in Tucson. Two hundred people, many of them children, will die of the disease this year, 5 percent of Tucson's population. Measles and tuberculosis, not known in the region until the Europeans arrived, are now a problem, as is malaria because of the standing water in the *cienaga* south of Martinez Hill. The *cienaga* is also home to fish, waterfowl, and even a species of clam.

1877

A report in the *Weekly Arizona Citizen* on March 10 reports fish being caught in Tucson, "some of which were a foot long," by boys fishing "the various mill ponds above the town."

1877

Carlos Tully, son of P. R. Tully, establishes an English- and a Spanish-language newspaper (the *Daily Bulletin* and *Las Dos Republicas*). A few months later the *Bulletin* is acquired by L. C. Hughes and becomes the *Arizona Weekly Star*, with offices at the corner of Congress and Meyer streets. Before the year is out the paper is acquired by A. E. Fay but it is reacquired by Hughes in 1878, who then runs it for many years, turning it over to his wife, Josephine, in 1893 when he becomes governor of the territory. He sells it in 1907. In 1910, the paper is acquired by the Copper Queen Consolidated Mining Company. *Las Dos Republicas* lasts only two years, being supplanted by Carlos Velasco's *El Fronterizo* (see 1878).

1877

The territorial legislature and Governor Safford incorporate the City of Tucson and give it "charter city" status, meaning that it will be governed by its own charter document rather than one developed by the state.

1877–1878

John Philo Hoyt (b. Ohio), formerly secretary of the Territory of Arizona and a lawyer, replaces Safford as territorial governor.

1877

The territorial capital is moved from Tucson back to Prescott. Tucson had requested a court injunction to prevent the move, but it was not granted.

1877

Upon the realization that in the dry West 160 acres isn't enough for a farm or ranch, Congress amends the Homestead Act of 1862 with a Desert Land Act that increases the amount of land that can be homesteaded to 640 acres. The act still requires "improvement" but it lifts the residence requirement, making fraud easier.

1877

The big silver strike is made in Tombstone, 70 miles southeast of Tucson in the San Pedro Valley. Nearby, the town of Charleston is established to concentrate the ore. Tucson merchants start opening stores there in 1879, by which time it has become a wild and wooly place. Another strike has been made in Prescott and yet other strikes are now made across southern Arizona.

1878

Carlos Ygnacio Velasco (b. Hermosillo, arrives Tucson 1862) sells the store he has had since the 1860s, buys the press that in 1869 had printed Tucson's first newspaper, and out of his house on South Stone Avenue begins to publish Tucson's second Spanish-language newspaper, *El Fronterizo,* which he will publish until his death in 1914, with the paper continuing to be published into the 1930s.

1878

Martha Summerhayes, native of Nantucket and now the young wife of an officer in the Quartermaster Corps, comes with him to Fort Lowell for a new posting after four years serving elsewhere in "the Territory," most recently at Fort McDowell (near Phoenix). She writes, "Arriving at Tucson, after a hot and tiresome night in the stage, we went to an old hostelry. Tucson looked attractive. Ancient civilization is always interesting to me."

1878

Of the ten merchandising companies operating in downtown Tucson, most along Main between Pennington and Congress, "six were owned by first generation German Jews, all related to one another by either blood or marriage," according to Bettina Lyons, a descendant of the Steinfeld family. Stores are being operated by E. N. Fish, Louis and William Zeckendorf, Lord & Williams, Jacob Mansfeld (Pioneer Print Shop), Theodore Welisch (White House), Leo Goldschmidt (furniture), the Jacobs brothers, Phillip Drachman, and Issac

Goldberg. There are no banks yet in Arizona Territory. Payment to suppliers is made in store credit or script, payment by customers in Mexican silver dollars, by the military in greenbacks. Tucson has two hotels (the Cosmopolitan and the Occidental), two breweries, ten saloons, four feed-and-livery stables, four boot-and-shoe stores, a photographic gallery, and two jewelers. One of the saloons is the Congress Hall Saloon on Broadway downtown, owned by Charles O. Brown. It had been a popular meeting place for territorial legislators.

1878

Louis and William Zeckendorf terminate their business partnership. Albert Steinfeld is made managing partner of L. Zeckendorf & Co. William departs on travels, returns later to open a competing store, which fails, after which William joins his wife in her hometown of New York City where he lives out the rest of his life.

1878–1881

John C. Fremont (b. Savannah, Georgia) is appointed territorial governor by President Hayes, replacing the popular and hardworking Hoyt, who had been governor for only a year. Hoyt moves on to the Territory of Washington where he enjoys a successful legal and business career. Fremont, a celebrated frontiersman, turns out to be a poor governor.

1879

In its last year of operation, *Las Dos Republicas* publishes a "Directorio de la Ciudad" that lists two churches (Catholic and Presbyterian), three schools (a public school, a Catholic school for boys, and Saint Joseph's Academy for girls), four doctors, eight attorneys, four newspapers, two hotels, three restaurants, seven "cantinas" (though George Hand's diary shows that no less than 36 saloons were in operation), and a number of other businesses, large and small.

1879

The Jacobs brothers, Lionel and Barron, merchants in Tucson since 1867, organize the Pima County Bank, the first official bank in Tucson. Since 1875 they had been making long-term loans and running a currency exchange, exchanging gold (preferred by their customers) for the greenbacks the military paid its debts with. The next year they sell their merchandizing business to Lord & Williams. Over the years, through a series of mergers and consolidations (including with Hiram Stevens and Sam Hughes's Santa Cruz Valley Bank), their bank becomes the Consolidated National Bank. In 1910, Albert Steinfeld becomes its president. In 1935, it is incorporated into the Valley National Bank of Phoenix, and later into Bank One and then Chase Bank.

1879

A first plan is offered for a Tucson water system, devised by former Indian agent Tom Jeffords. Reliance heretofore has been on El Ojito, an artesian well on the east side of the river near the road to the first San Agustín Mission, and a hand-dug well on Main. Each day Adam Sanders and Joseph Phy take a wagon through town selling water at five cents a bucket. For a while now, Papago women have been selling water in town, carrying it in large ceramic *ollas*. The *ollas* sweat and keep the water cool.

1879

The weekly *Star* and *Citizen* newspapers have now become dailies.

1880

A U.S. Census records Tucson's population as 7,007, with Mexicans a majority at 4,469. This number finally exceeds the lowest estimate of Hohokam in the Tucson Basin, 6,000. Population in 1870 had been 3,324. The developed area of the city extends about a mile south from Franklin to 17th Street and a half mile east from Main to Sixth Avenue.

1880

In 1870, Arizona's population had been 10,000. It is now 40,000.

1880

Congress and President Grant had finally authorized a southern railroad route in 1871. Construction of a railroad had begun in Los Angeles and reached Yuma in 1877, with Arizona authorizing the Southern Pacific Railroad to continue east from there. In Tucson, a right-of-way for the railroad was established along Toole Avenue, named for the mayor. This year the Southern Pacific arrives in Tucson, coming to town from the west with Charles Crocker, president of the Central Pacific, and his son Charles F. Crocker, president of the Southern Pacific of Arizona, on board. Celebrations of the arrival of the railroad, "[t]he greatest event in the history of the city" (*Tucson Citizen*), are widespread. One of the first buildings built east of the depot is a liquor warehouse, built by William B. Hooper & Company. The thriving Cactus Saloon is across the street from the depot. A great many changes begin in Tucson, not always to the benefit of the Anglo pioneers and *tucsonenses*. Travel and freighting to and from California now costs much less and takes less time. Merchants in Tucson have to discount goods deeply and some go out of business. Mexican elites begin to decline, unable to compete with the large corporations (Southern Pacific, Phelps Dodge, big land and cattle companies) and their capital and credit. Development begins, which finally and irrevocably initiates the decline of the water table. As the tracks move east, some of the Chinese imported to work on the railroad remain in town, starting farms along the Santa Cruz for table produce they sell door-to-door, then grocery stores, laundries, restaurants, and the Ying On Club Community Center in Barrio Viejo. A hobo jungle called the Isla de Cuba soon appears north of the tracks east of Third Avenue where 9th Street crosses Arroyo Chico. By the 1890s, the jungle has moved south to 16th Street near Park Avenue. For railroad employees, the Pie Allen Neighborhood (named after another Tucson mayor) is established between Euclid/Mountain and Sixth Avenue/Broadway, within earshot of the train whistle.

1880–1883

The Southern Pacific tracks are laid east to the Rio Grande, connecting there in 1881 with the Santa Fe Railroad coming down from Albuquerque and establishing the nation's second transcontinental railroad. From El Paso, the tracks will be laid east where they'll connect at Sierra Blanca with the Texas & Pacific Railway, creating the nation's third transcontinental railroad. In 1883, the Southern Pacific crews building east will meet the Southern Pacific crews building west, completing the fourth transcontinental railroad. Southern Pacific's domain now extends from San Francisco to New Orleans. The journey from New York City to Tucson by train now takes five days, rather than several months by wagon.

1880

With the arrival of the railroad, it is realized that money might finally be made mining not just silver and gold but copper. Facilitated by Albert Steinfeld, dealings begin that result in the founding in 1881 of the Copper Queen Mine in Bisbee. Others involved are Edward Reilly (initiator and speculator from Pennsylvania), Ben Williams (local mining engineer), W. H. Martin and John Ballard (investors from San Francisco), Dr. James Douglas (then inspecting Clifton-Morenci mines for Phelps Dodge). There are only tents, no houses, in Bisbee at this time. Bisbee is named after Judge DeWitt Bisbee, Williams's brother-in-law. Their company consolidates with Phelps Dodge in 1885. Between 1885 and 1908, the Copper Queen Consolidated produces 730 million pounds of copper.

1880

With the arrival of the railroad and construction of the depot about three-fourths of a mile east and uphill from the city, a need for taxi and transit service is recognized and a number of small private operations arise.

1880

Mariano Samaniego begins his political career in Tucson. Between now and 1900, he will serve several terms as town councilman, three times as territorial legislator, several terms as county supervisor, be the first Pima County assessor in 1886, be on the first Board of Regents for the University of Arizona, and be a member and at one time president of the Arizona Society of Pioneers. After 1900, as relations between newly arrived Anglos and Mexicans deteriorate, he works primarily with the newly formed Alianza Hispano-Americana.

1880

At the foot of Tumamoc Hill on Sisters Lane (later Hospital Road and then St. Mary's Road), St. Mary's Hospital is opened by the Sisters of St. Joseph of Carondolet, who had first arrived in Tucson 10 years earlier, having come by wagon from San Diego. Before this, Tucson's "hospital" had been its "pest house," on Alameda Street, much in use during the epidemic of smallpox that began in Tucson in 1877. A maternity ward called the Stork's Nest may also have been in operation by this time on North Court Street. Later, the Stork's Nest building will serve as the main office of the Southwestern Parks and Monuments Association, a nonprofit dedicated to education about and preservation of national monuments in the western United States. In 2014, the Southwestern Parks and Monuments Association has become the Western National Parks Association, with offices in Oro Valley.

1880

Seeking a beneficial climate, Charles Strauss, a student of finance from New York, comes to Tucson and goes to work for Albert Steinfeld as business manager of the Zeckendorf general store, improving the store's accounting and stocking procedures. He is soon elected to Tucson's school board, joins Tucson's new Volunteer Fire Department in 1882, and in 1883 is elected Tucson's mayor, but resigns in 1884 after a political dispute. During his abbreviated term, he does much to transform the appearance of Tucson, shepherding the construction of a city hall, a firehouse, an infirmary, a standalone library, a building and loan association, and graded roads. Strauss and his wife become active in Tucson's social activities: Their home becomes a center for culture, including literary and music programs. In 1886 Strauss is elected territorial superintendent of public instruction and works with Jacob Mansfeld to sell bonds to buy the land and start construction of the University of Arizona.

1880

The Sosa family constructs a house (now a museum) at 151 South Granada. It is perhaps the grandest house in Tucson, built with high ceilings permitted by using materials brought in by the railroad. This house is later bought by Leopoldo Carrillo and lived in by the Carrillo family for the next 90 years. Territorial governor John C. Fremont (1878–1881) leases it at one point for his daughter but never stays there himself. The museum is now known as the Sosa-Carrillo-Fremont house.

1880

Johnston Knox Corbett (b. Sumpter, South Carolina, 1861, d. Tucson 1934) arrives in Tucson. His first job is as a newsboy for the *Arizona Daily Star*, then owned by L. C. Hughes, the uncle of Knox Corbett's future wife, Lizzie Hughes, eldest daughter of Sam Hughes. He then runs a freight delivery line that operates between Tucson and Silver Bell. Later he goes to work at the Tucson post office, is promoted to assistant postmaster, and in 1890 is appointed postmaster, a position he holds under four U.S. presidents—Harrison, McKinley, Roosevelt, and Taft. He also starts Tucson's second lumber company, merging it later with his deceased brother's hardware store. He also engages in ranching near Benson and south of the Rincon Mountains. Along the way, he serves as mayor of Tucson and on the District 1 school board. He dies in Tucson in 1934. His lumber and hardware company thrives in Tucson for many decades. His son, Hiram S. Corbett, for whom Hi Corbett Baseball Field is named, becomes a state senator from Pima County. His grandson, Jim Corbett, becomes court clerk, city councilman, and also a mayor of Tucson.

1881

Population of Tombstone is 7,000, close to Tucson's.

1881

Lord & Williams, the primary merchandizer in town since its founding after the Civil War, had seen several mercantile firms go bankrupt in Tucson over the years. It now goes bankrupt itself, not the only firm to do so after the arrival of the railroad greatly reduces the prices that can be charged for goods.

1881

L. Zeckendorf & Co. opens a store on Main and Pennington that has the new plate-glass show windows on the street. This store will operate until Albert Steinfeld & Co. opens on Stone in 1904.

1881

Northwest of its depot, the Southern Pacific opens the Porter (later the San Xavier) Hotel, which quickly becomes a major hotel in Tucson. It will burn down in 1903.

1881

The Tucson Land and Herdic Coach Company begins scheduled service on a loop south of the city center. "Herdics," named after their East Coast designer, are horse-drawn carriages with a rear entrance in which the passengers sit along the sides facing each other.

1881

Former governor and widower Anson P. K. Safford returns to Tucson and marries Soledad Bonillas, the sister of Ignacio Bonillas, a destitute young man whose education Safford had supported in Tucson who then went on to become the mayor of Magadalena, Sonora. After Safford's term as governor ended in 1877, he had developed mining interests in Arizona and then had gone to the urban Northeast to acquire capital for a development in Florida. His then wife, the former Margarita Grijalva of Magdalena, Sonora, had died in New York in 1880 after giving birth to a daughter. The year after he marries Soledad Bonillas, he closes down his business interests in Arizona and departs for Florida where he founds and develops the city of Tarpon Springs. In 1889, after being heavily recruited by his many remaining supporters back in Arizona after the very disappointing administration of John C. Fremont, he allows his name to be put forward again to be governor of the territory. His detractors manage to derail his candidacy and President Benjamin Harrison does not appoint him. Two years later, in 1891, he dies in Florida.

1881

The towers are completed on the St. Augustine Cathedral, one rounded and one tall and pointed, with the stone coming from a quarry on the north flank of Sentinel Peak.

1881

Tucson's first Masonic lodge is chartered, under the Grand Lodge of California, Tucson Lodge No. 263. This lodge had been preceded in Arizona by lodges in Prescott (1866, Aztlan Lodge), Phoenix (1879, Arizona Lodge), Globe (1880, White Mountain Lodge), and Tombstone (1881, King Solomon Lodge).

1881

Tucson's first English-language City Directory is published this year, compiled and published by G. W. Barber and printed in San Francisco.

- Businesses are included with personal listings. The Index to Advertisers with which the Directory begins lists six dealers in "General Merchandise," three banks, two furniture stores, two hotels, two "houses" of lodging, one dealer in lumber, one hardware store, one grocer, one purveyor of insurance, one "Assayer," one "Soda and Ice Works," one stationer, one stable, one "saloon" (the 29 others apparently felt no need to advertise), one dealer in wholesale liquor, and the Tucson Vinegar Works. Barber notes that the town also boasts E. N. Fish's Eagle Flour Mill, established 14 years earlier, and an Iron Foundry and Machine Shop that had been established when the railroad arrived last year.

- Barber, whose grasp of regional history before the arrival of the Americans is a little shaky—he claims the presidio was established in 1560—writes that "The stranger who arrives and takes his week of observation on the streets is apt to remain in ignorance of the fact that Tucson has a well-defined stratification of good society.... In matters of dress, the formalities of calls, the selection for private balls and parties, in general social intercourse, in the quality of manners and respectability, the best society of no eastern city can excel the better class of society in Tucson."

- Tucson's police force now numbers seven. They are not uniformed but all wear badges, and some "are clothed with authority, and receive fees for making arrests." Barber also notes the existence of "Barrio Libre" in Tucson on Meyer Street south of Congress, so called because of the understanding that the area shall remain free of policing and a police presence. He suggests it is an area enjoyed by Mexicans rather than the "enterprising" Americans who live north of this area but hastens to add that he means only the lower class of Mexicans. The diaries of saloon keeper

George Hand for the period 1875–1878 make it quite clear that Mexicans weren't the only ones who supported the enterprises in Barrio Libre.

- Barber notes the existence of several "societies" in Tucson, five of which are Masonic groups. One society is "Tucson Turn Verein." "Turnverein" is a German word for gymnasium or athletic club and with the immigration of Germans in the second half of the 19th century, such clubs were becoming common in U.S. cities. The final "society" listed is the Brotherhood of Locomotive Engineers (Division 28).

- There are two newspapers in town now, the daily *Citizen*, a paper that Barber says is "Republican in politics" that had been founded in 1870 as a weekly by John Wasson and is owned now by R. C. Brown, and the *Arizona Daily and Weekly Star*, started by L. C. Hughes and Charles Tully in 1877 and now owned by L. C. Hughes, Sam's brother.

- Barber sees a bright future for Tucson, asserting that "In a little time, the introduction of abundant water will make this city cheerful with verdure and blossom as the rose.... In time, by the more economical distribution of water, a large area of land will be brought under cultivation in the Santa Cruz valley, and by means of wells and reservoirs on the mesa lands, much will be added to the agricultural lands in this vicinity."

- Imminent developments Barber notes are a city water system, a gas works and the lighting of Tucson with this gas (kerosene had been used up to now), a "commodious City Hall," street grading, and numbering the houses and putting "the names of streets on the corners thereof."

- One source of revenue it seems the city will not have for improvements from now on is the significant fees they had collected for booth privileges for the annual festival of San Agustín. In 1880, it had been decided that this somewhat rowdy festival should be held henceforth outside the city.

- Barber notes as a sign of progress that the city ordinances have been printed for the first time in a pamphlet, in both Spanish and English.

1881

Average school attendance in the new public school, the Congress School, is said to be 230 (City Directory). A further 130 students attend the St. Joseph's Female Academy, 29 of them being children of Jewish parents, according to Barber. At the St. Augustine's Parochial School for boys, average attendance is about 200. Barber notes the existence of other smaller private schools, among them a "Modern School" conducted by Professor J. M. Silva in Leopoldo Carrillo's garden, where 19 boys and 25 girls attend classes—together. Barber says the total number of students in all Tucson's schools is 804.

1881

Frances Warren (b. Wisconsin 1840, d. Tucson 1928), a widow and the mother of a daughter, arrives in Tucson and begins to teach at the Congress School as a substitute. She will go on to become principal of the school and later of Safford School. In 1895, she will step in for a year as superintendent of the Tucson School District. In 1905, she will run for school trustee, and in so doing may have become the first woman to run for public office in the territory. She loses a close race and retires from teaching in 1907 but continues to serve as a substitute teacher. The Warren Elementary School on Tucson's south side will be dedicated to her in 1975.

1881

The second Pima County Courthouse is begun, at Court and Ott (a street that no longer exists). The first, built by Charles Meyer, a druggist who also served as mayor of Tucson, had been made of adobes. This one is made of brick.

1881

Phillip Drachman has a popular saloon at Congress and Church called the Post Office Exchange. In 1886 he will open a cigar store nearby.

1881

John Spring obtains free fish from the U.S. fish commissioner which are shipped to Tucson on the railroad and stocked in Silver Lake, Warner's Lake, and the pond in Carrillo Gardens. Flooding in 1886, 1888, and 1890 will wash many unfortunate fish downstream but until the turn of the century, carp, suckers and chub are still caught in these waters.

The big building in this photograph is Pima County's second courthouse, built just south of the original courthouse of brick, not adobe. The photograph was taken in 1883 from the Buehman Studio on the second floor of a building on Congress Street, looking northwest and downstream across the valley of the Santa Cruz River. Seen in the foreground are the hall of the International Order of Odd Fellows and the Grand Central Hotel, with signs visible for a dentist, the Chung Kee Laundry, and an unnamed "Carpenter & Builder." This courthouse also housed most federal and county officials, with the jail on its north wing. The building in the distance beyond the courthouse is the two-story adobe Lionel M. Jacobs house on West Alameda, perhaps the finest house in Tucson at the time. None of these buildings survives.

1882

Grand Lodge of Arizona (Masons) established, 48th Grand Lodge in United States.

1882 September

The first water mains open in Tucson, operated by the private Tucson Water Company, owned by Tom Jeffords and associates. There is no wastewater system yet in Tucson. Water for the mains comes from a spring at the Valencia Road headcut (a ditch that intercepts the shallow water table) in the Santa Cruz, traveling most of the way to town in a redwood flume along the Santa Cruz River channel. Downstream from the headcut, an almost immediate drop in the water table is noticed. Warner complains about the effect on his mill at the base of Sentinel Peak (Logan 120). A year later Warner will build on his property a dam that creates a 300-acre lake where the 22nd Street bridge west of the freeway is now and stock it with fish. It becomes a popular recreation spot. This will be the last uncontrolled water resource in the Tucson Basin.

1882

Federico Ronstadt (b. Sonora 1858, d. Tucson 1954) comes to Tucson from Sonora to learn the blacksmithing and wheelwright trades. He then forms the F. Ronstadt Wagon and Carriage Co. to manufacture wagons, buggies, harnesses, and saddles. His business becomes known for the quality of its products. The Ronstadt Hardware Company, its descendant, lasts into the 1980s.

1882–1885

Frederick Augustus Tritle (b. Pennsylvania) is appointed governor of the territory by president Chester Arthur, replacing John C. Fremont. Tritle is an enthusiastic promoter of the territory and will be the first governor to make Arizona his permanent home.

1883

Theodore Welisch & Leopold Wolf's White House store and William Zeckendorf's store both fail this year. Welisch goes to Charleston, Arizona, the refining town for the Tombstone mines, to open a store. In 1890, William Zeckendorf's wife, Julia, leaves Tucson for her hometown of New York City and in 1891 William joins her there in spite of his high social and political standing in the territory.

1883

Selim Franklin (b. California 1859), nephew of the Jacobs brothers, arrives in Tucson and begins to practice law. He will go on to serve in the 13th territorial legislature in Prescott where in 1885 he will make an impassioned speech that secures the university for Tucson. Phoenix is awarded the plum of the insane asylum (funded at four times the amount given for the university) and Tempe is given the Normal School (for the education of teachers).

1883

Teachers at Congress School start teaching boys and girls in the same classrooms, to the consternation of many parents. Playground areas remain separated.

1883

At Church and Camp streets (now Broadway), the first St. Augustine Church is completed with the addition of a stone facade made by master stonemason Jules Le Flein. The church, built of adobe bricks, had been under construction for decades. In 1897, it will be replaced by the cathedral on Stone and later demolished. The facade now appears on the front of the Arizona History Museum in Tucson at 949 East 2nd Street.

1883

Tucson gets its first electric power company, operated by the Tucson Artic [sic] and Electric Light Company. It is housed in a one-story building on North Church Street, across from the present Pima County Courthouse, and is unable to generate enough power even for streetlights.

1883

The Sanborn fire insurance map shows that urbanization now reaches farther south and north of the Presidio Neighborhood than had been shown in earlier maps, also east along Congress, but not yet beyond the Southern Pacific railroad tracks.

1883

Easterner Colin Cameron acquires the San Rafael land grant in upper Santa Cruz Basin, claiming 153,000 acres that extend into Sonora, and begins to run very large herds of cattle there, tens of thousands, which has a large effect on the headwaters of the Santa Cruz River. Before this time, Apache raids had limited growth of cattle operations. The U.S. government eventually recognizes 17,324 acres in the grant. In 1903 Cameron sells to William C. Greene, who had made money mining copper in Cananea, who runs cattle on the land in the U.S. and Sonora and continues Cameron's practice of preventing wood cutting to preserve the watershed. Greene also begins using fencing to manage usage.

1880s

Tucson's primary hotel is the Cosmopolitan Hotel, at Main and Pennington, on the southwest corner of what had been the Presidio San Agustín. (The other hotels are the Palace on Mesilla and Meyer, and the San Xavier at the railroad depot.) It had begun in 1856 as the one-story Phillips House and was built up and refurbished by Hiram Stevens in 1874, with a second story added in 1882 as a meeting room for Masons. In 1889 it will be bought by the Orndorff family and renamed the Orndorff Hotel. The hotel persists into statehood and the building lasts into the 1930s. An effort at preservation is contemplated but in 1934, after a wall falls and crushes a passerby, it is razed. In 2014, the site is occupied by Tucson's City Hall

1883–1884

Tucson and Tombstone City Directories are combined for these two years.

1884

Mining in the region has become extensive, with a number of mines in the Tucson Mountains. Among them will be the Old Yuma Mine on the northeast end, the Gould Mine in Kings Canyon, the Mile Wide Mine on the west side, and the mines at Saginaw Hill on the southwest end. To reach mines southwest of Tucson, Starr Pass (then Boulder Pass) is constructed through the Tucson Mountains in a project financed by the Arizona Telegraph Company owned by Sam Hughes and James H. Toole. Richard Starr was a teamster who supplied mines southwest of Tucson. Gates Pass is constructed by Canadian miner Richard Gates to shorten the trip to his Abbie Waterman Mine in what is now the Waterman Mountains, 33 miles west of Tucson. Mines are also being developed in the Silverbell Mountains by Fritz Contzen, an immigrant from Germany.

1884

In the Military Plaza east of downtown, the Plaza School is completed, in spite of the concern expressed about the children being exposed to the Apaches, "Tucson's inherited foe," who often come in from the east. The school will soon be renamed in honor of Governor Safford. In 2014 it is still there and named Safford Junior High School.

1884

The Society of Arizona Pioneers (now the Arizona Historical Society) is founded by local men, among them Charles Poston, Juan and Jesus María Elías, Estevan Ochoa, Barron Jacobs, Sam Hughes, and John Spring. For its 31 founding members, it is more a social club than a research resource. Anyone who came to Tucson before 1870 is eligible for membership unless you are a woman or an Indian. The first president is William S. Oury; the second is Hiram Stevens. At first Albert Steinfeld is not eligible because he arrived in 1872, but later, after criteria for membership are modified, he becomes president of the society.

1884

The Hebrew Ladies Benevolent Society of Tucson is established. Members, who include Eva Mansfeld, Mrs. Albert Steinfeld, and Mrs. Phillip Drachman, meet trains and offer assistance to Jewish and non-Jewish immigrants.

1884

Levi Howell Manning (b. North Carolina 1864, d. Beverly Hills, California, 1935, buried Evergreen Cemetery) arrives in Tucson at age 20, gets work as a newspaper reporter, then as general manager and cashier for the Tucson Artic [sic] and Electric Light Company, which he later buys into and sells for a significant profit.

1885

Carrillo Gardens opens. Founded by Leopoldo Carrillo (b. Sonora 1836, arrives Tucson 1859, d. Tucson 1890), it is Tucson's first public park, an eight-acre garden on South Main Avenue that is landscaped with 500 peach trees, 2,000 grape vines, 200 quince, 60 pomegranate trees, and nine apricot trees. It will be Tucson's social center through the 1890s. Carrillo's sons, dressed as sailors, will row visitors around "lakes," which were actually ponds over natural springs. The gardens have a racetrack with ponies ridden by monkeys, a shooting gallery, 12 bath houses, a saloon, a restaurant, an ice cream parlor, a dance hall, a zoo, and a circus. Carrillo will operate a mule-drawn wagon "bus" that brings visitors the six blocks from downtown to the gardens. The cost for the ride was a nickel. In his lifetime, Carrillo also built Tucson's first bowling alley and first two-story building made of fired brick and operated a large ranch near Sabino Canyon. He, Sam Hughes, and W. C. Davis leased acres of land along the Santa Cruz River to Chinese vegetable farmers. Carrillo served on Tucson's first school board, was a member of the Society of Arizona Pioneers, and served on the Tucson City Council from 1883 until this year. In 1904, Carrillo Gardens becomes Emanuel Drachman's Elysian Grove.

1885

The University of Arizona is founded as a Morrill Act (1862) land-grant university. Six years later, it opens for classes. To promote the university for Tucson, Jacob Mansfeld had held an initial meeting in his stationer's store. Pima County's representative to the territorial legislature in

Prescott, C. C. Stephens, had wanted to acquire the state capitol for Tucson. But by the time Tucson's representatives were able to get to the legislative session in Prescott, Prescott and Yavapai County had nabbed that. Maricopa County had bagged the insane asylum and Normal School. Tucson lawyer Selim Franklin had then made a deft speech to the legislature on how the "Thieving Thirteenth" legislature might redeem itself by creating a university in Tucson. The bill to do so passes, on the condition that 40 acres be acquired for the purpose. Back in Tucson, and just in time to meet the deadline set by the legislature, Selim Franklin, Charles Strauss (then superintendent of public instruction for the territory), and Jacob Mansfeld convince three businessmen—E. C. Gifford, Ben C. Parker, and William S. Read—to donate the necessary land, which at the time lies in the empty desert some miles east of the town.

1880s and after

Residents and new arrivals are taking advantage of the Homestead Act, usually with no intention of farming the land. Five people homestead the almost entirely vacant section of land east of what is to become the University of Arizona, between what will become the streets of Speedway and Broadway and west of what will become Country Club. These homesteaders are Louis Mueller (who patents 40 acres in the southwest of the section in 1889), Eugene Brunier (who patents 120 acres east of Mueller's land in 1890), William H. Campbell (patents 160 acres in the northwest of the section in 1898, and after whom Campbell Avenue will be named), Charles S. and Alvina Himmel Edmondson (who come to Tucson from New Orleans in 1897 and patent 160 acres in the northeast of the section in 1900), and Hugh Byrne (patents 160 acres in the middle of the section in 1906). The homesteads will later be sold or developed into subdivisions. Alvina Himmel Edmondson, who is divorced from Charles in 1927, will sell part of their homestead to the city in 1934 or 1935 to be made into a park named for her parents, the Himmels.

1885

Vegetable truck gardens along the Santa Cruz now total about 150 acres, started by Chinese families who had come to town as railroad construction workers and then leased land in the floodplain from Sam Hughes, Leopoldo Carrillo, and Solomon Warner. Downstream landowners north of Hospital Road (later St. Mary's Road) complain that they are not getting enough water for their fields. A local court case decides the matter in favor of the upstream users under the doctrine of prior appropriation.

1886

The Reid Opera House is built on the corner of Pennington and Meyer in downtown Tucson. In 1899, Reid will hire Henry Trost to remodel the building and convert it to a hotel, named the Park View Hotel because it overlooks Levin's Park. The two-story building eventually comes to be occupied by offices. In 1958, it is torn down. One of its last occupants is the detective division of the Tucson Police Department.

1885–1889

C. Meyer Zulick (b. Pennsylvania, a lawyer in New Jersey) is appointed governor of the territory by President Grover Cleveland, replacing Frederick Augustus Tritle. He is the first governor who is a Democrat. One of his supporters had described himself as tired of having the territory "governed by second-class Republican adventurers." One of Zulick's challenges will be the smuggling going on between Arizona and Sonora. Another will be the depredations of the Chiricahua Apaches led by Geronimo. During his administration, the territorial capital will be moved from Prescott to Phoenix.

1886 April 27

South of Tucson along the Santa Cruz between Calabazas and Tumacacori, a rancher named Artisan Leslie Peck and his friend Charley Owen are working cattle, neither of them armed, when they are attacked by a band of 20 or 30 Chiricahua Apaches that includes Geronimo, who had escaped from General Crook a month before, and Naiche, the second son of Cochise. Owen is shot and killed and Peck is stripped and left to walk barefoot back to his house two miles up what is now known as Peck Canyon, where he discovers his pregnant wife and 14-month-old son dead at the hands of the Apaches.

1886 September 4

After a five-month rampage of raiding and killing in southwestern Arizona and northern Mexico, much of it around the Rincon and Santa Rita Mountains, Geronimo surrenders to General Nelson A. Miles in Skeleton Canyon in southeastern Arizona. He, Naiche, and others are shipped east to Florida on a train. Contrary to promises made upon their surrender, no Chiricahua who is shipped east, including scouts who had helped catch Geronimo, will ever return to Arizona. Attacks by Apaches in southern Arizona now drop off precipitately but do not stop entirely for several more years. Attacks continue in Mexico, with the last casualties in both sides being suffered in 1932. In Mexico, the Chiricahua do not survive.

1886

Mines in Tombstone strike water, begin to flood, and are shut down. The booming town of Charleston quickly goes out of business.

1886

The second floor of the Tucson City Hall that had been built in 1883 and designated for use as a public library opens this year as the only free public library in the territory, according to the *Arizona Weekly Citizen*. The Society of Arizona Pioneers also has its offices there.

1886

The Owls Club is started as a dining and social club for eligible unmarried (Anglo) men. It meets first in a house on Stone near where the Temple of Music and Art is today, then in a house on the corner of Stone and Camp Street (now Broadway) that is owned by Estevan Ochoa and accounted one of the finest houses in town. The club hires a housekeeper and a cook, Woo Sing, who stays with them for 15 years. Later the club will meet in the Steinfeld and Manning houses until Manning builds a residential facility for the Owls on Main in 1900.

1886

A powerful flood on the Santa Cruz washes out bridges, destroys dwellings on the floodplain, and damages the dams at Silver Lake and Warner's Mill.

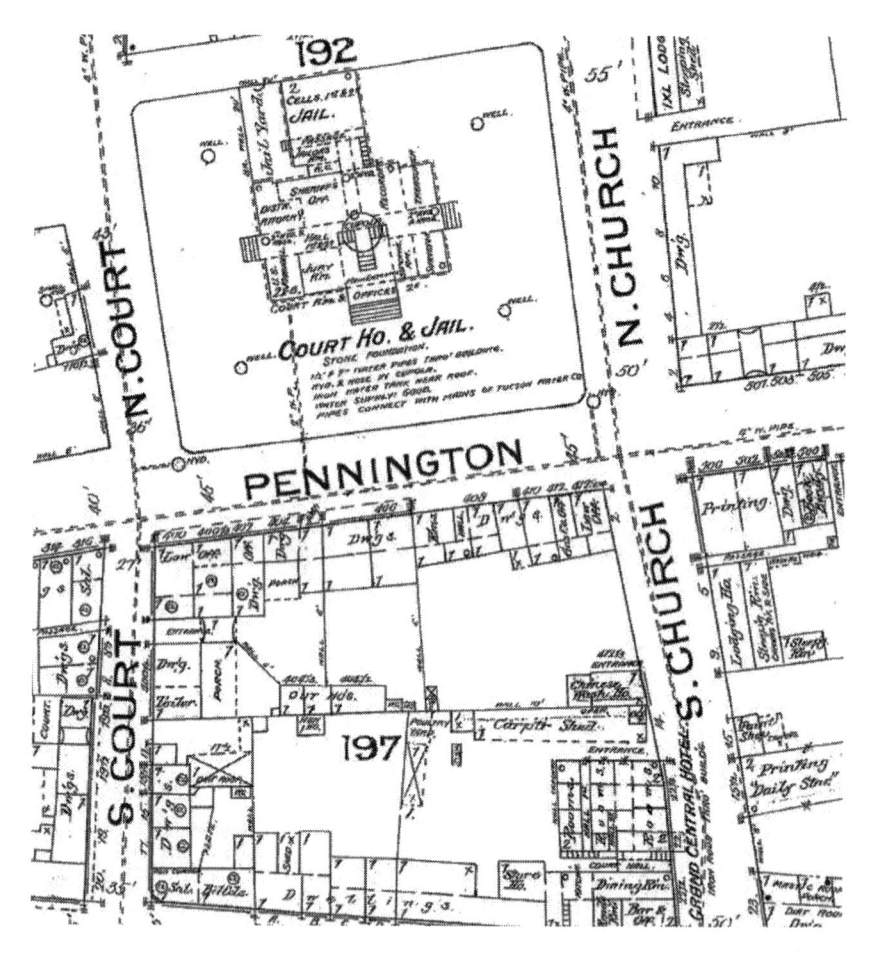

1886 Sanborn fire insurance map. After the Civil War, the D. A. Sanborn National Insurance Diagram Bureau in New York City began to make maps of many U.S. towns and cities to assess fire insurance risks. The maps, which Sanborn made until 2007, are scaled and highly detailed, depicting the functions of buildings sometimes down to individual rooms. Over the years, they have been an important documentary resource for researchers of many kinds.

1887

A giant celebration with parade is put on in Tucson for General Miles, the final captor of Geronimo, during which Miles is presented with a gold sword.

1887

A 7.2-magnitude earthquake with its epicenter just north of Bavispe, Sonora, destroys the town of Charleston in the San Pedro Valley, causes extensive damage at San Xavier, and produces a range of changes in water flows throughout the area. It is followed later in the year by more flooding, especially along the Rillito River.

1887

Charles R. Wores, who had come from San Francisco to Tucson in 1880, had established a thriving ore assaying business. This year he moves the business—The Tucson Sampling Works—into what had been Hooper's liquor warehouse next to the railroad depot. He will operate the business until 1891.

1887

Construction of UA's "Old Main," then known as "the University Building," is begun, to be completed in 1889. The architect is J. M. Creighton. The stone is local but the lumber has to be shipped in from San Diego. The money runs out before the roof is on, but the regents manage to get federal grants under the Hatch and Morrill Acts to complete the job. In 1972, the building, then known as Old Main, will be the first of UA's buildings to be put on the National Register of Historic Places. In 2014, it is completely renovated to become the offices of the new president of the university, Ann Weaver Hart.

1887

The head of the Agricultural Experiment Station at UA, Robert Forbes, notes that olive trees "from Santa Barbara," site of one of the Spanish missions in California, have been planted on the campus just east of Park Avenue, inside the northwest boundary of the campus (these are now among the oldest trees in Tucson). Forbes will go on to plant more olive trees along North Campus Drive and around town. Because he is professionally interested in which Mediterranean plants will do well in Tucson, he will also plant date palms. He discovers that some varieties do well and some don't.

1888

In an effort to produce water to irrigate 15,000 acres he owns north of Hospital Road, Sam Hughes makes an artificial headcut (a ditch that intercepts the water table) in the Santa Cruz near St. Mary's Road. Upstream (south) of the cut, an arroyo forms that becomes greatly enlarged in the floods that follow in July and August 1890 and begins to move upstream.

1888

Estevan Ochoa dies destitute in Las Cruces. His prosperous freighting business had been destroyed by the arrival of the railroad in Tucson in 1880 and a bad accident in which a locomotive had destroyed one of his pack trains.

1889

The territorial legislature moves the capital from Prescott to Phoenix.

1889

Three members of the federal Breckinridge Survey (the author's cousin John R. Norton is one of them), searching for irrigation potentials in the dry West, locate in the Tonto Basin on the Salt River the site for what becomes the Roosevelt Dam, a key element in the Salt River Project that will allow irrigation of the valley downstream and allow agriculture to take off in Phoenix.

1889

The new Tucson Water Company has been diverting the increasingly unreliable surface water into canals. It now installs on a 40-foot well a steam pump that yields an amazing 1,250 gallons a minute. Steam pumps in Tucson are at this time powered by wood and in the next two years they will burn 1,782 cords of wood, not an abundant resource in the desert.

1889

With Frank W. Oury, a mining engineer, Levi Manning opens a general brokerage business dealing in land, mines, cattle, and county and city property.

1889-1890

Lewis Wolfley (b. Philadelphia, a civil engineer, resident of the Arizona Territory for the last six years, and a Republican) is appointed territorial governor by President Harrison to replace C. Meyer Zulick, but there is a conflict with the incumbent, producing for a time two territorial administrations. The popular former governor Safford had also put his hat in the ring.

1890-1892

Republican John N. Irwin (b. Ohio) is appointed territorial governor by President Harrison, replacing Lewis Wolfley. Irwin will be the last non-resident governor.

1890

Tucson's population is about 5,000, a disappointing decline from the population when the railroad arrived. There are 365 children in public schools in Tucson, 60 percent Mexican or of Mexican descent. Plaza School, later Safford, is being attended at this time by the Steinfeld children, who are living in a house on South Main and McCormick and who walk by "Gay Alley" (also known as the "sporting district") on the way to school, thinking nothing of it. Gay Alley, actually Sabino Street, was two north-south blocks between Main and Stone that dead-ended into McCormick Street. No. 12 was a famous house of prostitution whose madam, Mae Palmer, was known as "the Queen of the Tucson Underworld." Barrio Libre begins south of McCormick Street.

1890

Because the Southern Pacific has raised cattle shipping rates to California by 25 percent, the owner of the Empire Ranch, Walter Vail, and his brother 'Ned' decide to drive 900 cattle overland from their ranch east of Tucson to the Warner Ranch, north of San Diego. Leaving at the end of January, they cover the 400 miles in two months and ten days, after which the SP agrees to lower rates for a while.

1890

UA's first paid faculty member is Frank A. Gulley, a graduate of Michigan State Agricultural College. The first actual president of UA, Theodore Comstock, a mining engineer, takes office in 1894 and serves for only a year, being replaced by Howard Billman, who serves for two years.

1890

West University (University District) is platted, the first suburb north of the Southern Pacific tracks. It will be built out into 1930. In 2014, it is the largest Historic District in Arizona.

1890

The farmer-in-charge on the Papago Indian Reservation estimates that 790 acres are now being irrigated at San Xavier. Over the last decade, the number of cattle being run on the land upstream of Tucson has been increasing exponentially.

1890s

The Tucson Pressed Brick Company is opened by architect Quintus Monier, who will use the bricks to construct the new St. Augustine Cathedral Monier has designed that will be built on Stone Avenue. Monier had earlier designed and built Archbishop Lamy's St. Francis Cathedral in Santa Fe. The brickworks are located west of the Santa Cruz and south of Congress Street, close to the site of the original Mission St. Agustín and the *convento*. Over the next seven decades, bricks from this factory will be used to build many structures in Tucson, including buildings inside the West Gate of the University of Arizona. The company is later acquired by Albert Steinfeld. The site of the brickworks will be excavated in the Tucson Origins Project in the early 2000s and the site of the original Mission Church and Convento located, though little of archeological significance has survived.

1891

Fort Lowell closes down, and for the first time since 1775, there is no military installation in Tucson. The adobe buildings—the hospital, the officers' quarters, the barracks, the laundresses' facility—are salvaged by local farmers and the walls begin to erode.

1891

The first farms appear that are entirely dependent on water pumps (steam powered). In the previous few years, arroyoization of the river (also called "entrenchment," something that might have played a role in the decline of the Hohokam) has come to preclude old-style floodplain agriculture. Pump-supported agriculture begins. At this time, the underground water is taken to be "inexhaustible." In 1893, agriculture is extended north of Tucson, into Flowing Wells, for example, an area developed by Levi Manning. The doctrine of "prior appropriation" had been established in 1885 by court cases which said that upstream users on a watercourse, if prior, could take the entire flow if they needed it. Pumping allows downstream users to stop worrying for now.

1891

UA classes begin with 32 students in two colleges, Agriculture and Mines. Most of the students are "preparatory." Besides Frank Gulley, the faculty are Dr. Theodore Comstock, dean of Mines; C. B. Collingwood, an agricultural chemist; J. W. Toumey, botany and entomology; and V. E. Stollbrand, professor of mathematics and irrigation. The cohort is joined later by H. J. Hall, instructor in English. The first head of the Agricultural Experiment Station is Robert Forbes. UA's "library" is in the office of Professor Gulley in Old Main.

1891

A state constitutional convention convenes in Phoenix in September, with 17 Democrats and five Republicans having been selected by the assembly. The Arizona electorate supports the constitution that results as, in Congress, does the Democrat-controlled House, but the Republican-controlled Senate does not, and Congress must act if statehood is to be achieved. In 1889 and 1890, when both houses of Congress were dominated by Republicans, six Republican western states had been admitted.

1892

This year the Electric Light and Power Company is founded, with Albert Steinfeld as its first president. In 1896, it takes over Tucson Gas Company and in 1901 changes its name to Tucson Gas, Electric Light & Power. In 1903, it switches from direct to alternating current and in 1904 moves to a larger generating facility on 6th Street at Main.

1892

Tucson's first telephone exchange, Charles F. Hoff's Sunset Telephone and Telegraph Service, opens with 28 subscribers. By 1899, 225 phones are in operation.

1892

Andrew and Annie Olsen have a dry-goods and curio store at 301–312 Congress. Andrew Olsen now buys 160 acres northeast of UA, land that will later become the Olsen Addition. The street in the subdivision that runs along the west side of the Arizona Inn now bears Olsen's name.

1892–1893

Nathan Oakes Murphy (b. Maine but by now a resident of Prescott and popular long-time businessman in Arizona) is appointed territorial governor, replacing Irwin. When Democrat Grover Cleveland defeats Harrison in 1892, Murphy is quickly replaced but will be appointed again later.

1893

Territorial representative from Globe George W. P. Hunt introduces a bill to create a Territorial Museum. Governor Murphy assigns it to the University of Arizona, where it is placed in a room on the second floor of Old Main.

1893–1896

Democrat L. C. Hughes (Sam's brother, b. Philadelphia to Welsh immigrants, orphaned at a young age, who came to Arizona in 1871) becomes territorial governor, replacing Murphy. Hughes's wife, Josephine Brawley Hughes, who had opened the first school for girls in Arizona in 1872, is a leader in the temperance movement in Tucson. Hughes will travel to Washington to promote statehood for Arizona.

1893

Levi Manning is appointed surveyor general of Arizona by President Cleveland and will be known thereafter as "General" Manning.

1893

Hiram J. Stevens dies of a self-inflicted gunshot wound. Before killing himself, he shoots his wife, Petra (Santa Cruz), but she suffers a minor injury. A large funeral is held in the city for this respected pioneer.

1893

The first city well field is established south of Tucson at the Valencia Road headcut. In 2014, Tucson Water is operating 291 drinking water wells throughout Tucson.

1893 November 20

Spurred by the opening of the university, Tucson's first serious public transit line is the University Hack Line, which sells out to the Orndorff Passenger Works in 1895. Previously, public transportation had been scheduled according to customer demand, using "herdics," small four-wheeled carriages with a rear entrance in which passengers sat along the sides facing each other, and surreys.

1893

Oxford-educated Charles Blenman settles in Tucson and begins to practice law, later becoming a local judge and land developer.

1893

The first class graduates from Tucson's high school. Presiding is Charles Hopkins (Carlos) Tully, the adopted son of P. R. Tully, Tucson's first superintendent of schools (1891–1894).

1894

Carlos Velasco, publisher of *El Fronterizo,* Pedro C. Pellón, Mariano G. Samaniego, Carlos Tully, Carlos Jácome and others found La Alianza Hispano-Americana (the Hispanic American Alliance), a political organization and mutual aid society which soon has chapters throughout the Southwest and in Mexico. Carlos Tully and Pedro Pellón are prime movers. The Alianza will function into the early 1960s.

1895

UA graduates its first class: Charles O. Rouse, Mercedes Ann Shibell, and Mary Flint Walker.

1895–1899

Photographer Henry Buehman becomes mayor. First street grading and first curbs in Tucson.

1896–1897

Benjamin Joseph Franklin (b. Kentucky 1839, fought for the Confederacy, d. Phoenix 1898) is appointed territorial governor, replacing L. C. Hughes.

1896

Tucson Board of Trade established.

1896

UA instructor of English, H. J. Hall, who has been "somewhat informally" designated as custodian of the library, takes the library out of Agriculture professor Gulley's office and puts it in a separate room in Old Main.

1896

Carlos Jácome and Loreto Carrillo open La Bonanza department store.

1896

Tucson's first professional orchestra, the Club Filarmónico Tucsonense, is founded by Frederick Ronstadt (b. Sonora 1858, d. Tucson 1954). In 1926 he helps to found the Tucson Symphony Orchestra, still performing in 2014. Ronstadt and his wife, Sara Levin (daughter of Alex Levin, the owner of Levin's Park) are the parents of Luisa Espinel, who achieves international fame as a serious vocal performer. Luisa Espinel is the aunt of Linda Ronstadt, who becomes a highly popular music vocalist during the second half of the 20th century, one of whose successful albums is *Canciones de Mi Padre*.

1896

Sarah Herring (b. NYC 1861) had moved to Tombstone in 1882, to join her father, Colonel Herring, who was practicing law there at the time. Colonel Herring had successfully defended Wyatt Earp when Earp was charged with murder after the shoot-out at the OK Corral in 1881. Most of the time he represented mining companies. This year, Sarah, who two years earlier had graduated from NYU law school, moved with her father from Tombstone to Tucson to practice law, making her the first woman lawyer in Tucson. Representing a mining company, she wins this year her first case before the Territorial Supreme Court. In 1913, she will be the first woman to argue a case entirely on her own before the United States Supreme Court. She will also win that case.

1896

East of the existing St. Augustine Church on Broadway and Church, Bishop Peter Bourgade lays the cornerstone for the new St. Augustine Cathedral that will be built on Stone Avenue of fired brick rather than sun-dried adobe.

1896

L. Zeckendorf and Company store is thriving. "The principal departments consist of shelf and heavy hardware, agricultural implements, paints and oils, tin and hollow ware, groceries and provisions, dry and fancy goods, clothing, gents' furnishing goods, boots and shoes, furniture, carpets, wall paper and shades," writes Bettina Lyons, selling wholesale and retail over southern and central Arizona and Sonora, Mexico. Louis resides in New York. Albert Steinfeld resides in Tucson and manages the operation.

1897–1898

Republican Myron H. McCord (b. Pennsylvania, now a successful agriculturalist in Phoenix) is appointed territorial governor by President

McKinley, replacing Benjamin Joseph Franklin. He will resign to serve in the Spanish-American War.

1897

The new St. Augustine Cathedral on Stone opens and becomes the seat of the Diocese of Tucson. The original plans call for a gothic structure, but the spires are never completed and it isn't until 1928 that the church acquires its current Mexican baroque form, with a facade inspired by the one on the cathedral in Querétaro, Mexico. The old church is abandoned.

1898

UA enrollment is 115 (32 when classes started in 1891).

1898 November

After a number of earlier efforts to establish a street railway in Tucson had failed, the Tucson Street Railway, with Charles Hoff as manager, begins regular mule-drawn passenger service, from downtown to the Southern Pacific depot on Congress and from the depot to the University of Arizona along a newly graded 3rd Street (now University Boulevard).

1898

North of Speedway (then known as Jefferson Street), Jefferson Park is platted between Campbell and Mountain. Most construction occurs between 1920 and 1927.

1898–1902

Oakes Murphy is appointed to his second term as territorial governor, replacing Myron H. McCord. He sponsors the Northern Arizona Normal School, now Northern Arizona University, which opens in Flagstaff in 1899, and after his term as governor, lobbies in Washington, D.C., against joint statehood for Arizona with New Mexico.

1898

Anna Marie Stattelman (age 26, b. Germany 1871, who had arrived in Tucson by train in 1889 with her parents and a sister) homesteads a large tract of land extending from Park Avenue to Cherry Avenue and from what is now Lester Street to Grant Road (then called North Street). Later this year, she builds a home near North Santa Rita Avenue and East Lester Street. She will name most of the streets in the area after trees, perhaps even including Elm Street, Walnut Street (now Cherry Avenue), Pine Avenue (now Warren), Maple Avenue (now Martin), and Oak Street (now Campbell Avenue). In 1899, she will marry Frank Lester, superintendent of the Mammoth Gold Mines. She builds several Craftsman bungalows in the area, and is one of the first people to rent homes to UA students.

1898

The abandoned St. Augustine Cathedral at Church and Broadway is remodeled by the church and some citizens to make it into a traveler's inn.

1898

The new Tucson Ice and Cold Storage plant is built one block east of Stone south of the railroad tracks, providing a big boost for food items delivered by the railroad.

1898

The city's first fire engine is called "the Chemical." At first, it had to be pulled to fires by the volunteer firemen who would attempt to damp the fire until water could be brought.

1898

A fire destroys the big two-story Radulovich Building at the northeast corner of Congress and Stone, occupied by some of Tucson's principal businesses, including Charles F. Hoff's telephone exchange. Others were W. F. Kitt ladies furnishings, Mrs. Beggs' millinery store, Zeigler's candy and ice cream parlor, Wells, Fargo & Co. express office, and the Western Union telegraph company. The fire shows the inadequacy of current fire protection (the fire department's equipment is pulled by hand until a merchant lends them some horses). Fire is a danger for buildings that have been built with the wood the railroad had brought, though not for the adobe structures.

1899

In what is now known as the Presidio Neighborhood, Frank Treat and Margaret Hughes Treat (second daughter of Sam Hughes and Atanácia Santa Cruz) and family are living

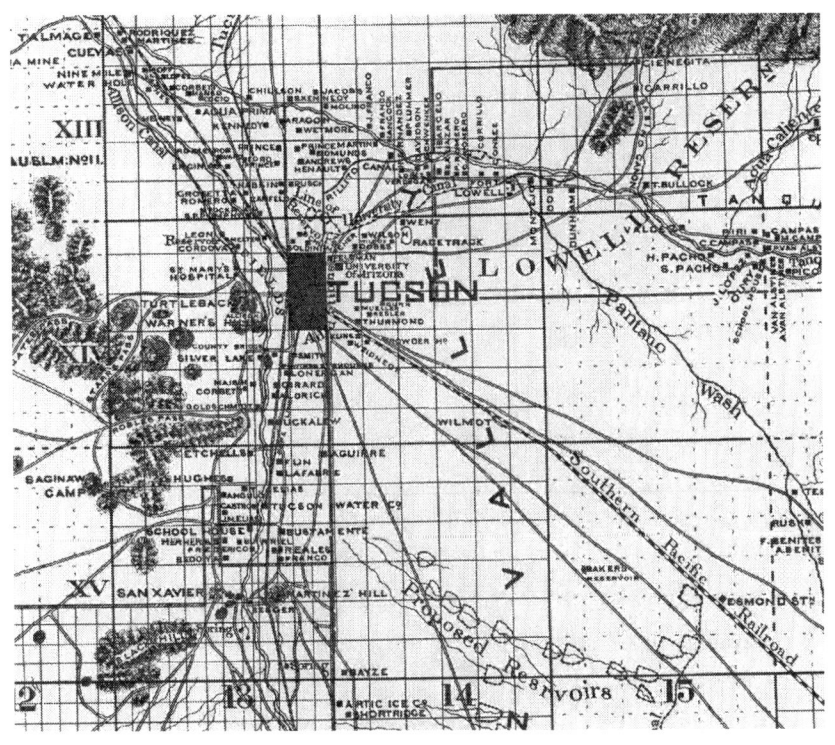

1899 Pima County Board of Supervisors county map. This topographic map, which also employs the Public Lands Survey System with its grid of townships and ranges, focuses on roads and buildings, many of which are ranches or rural homes. The proper names, of which there are many, are offered in the same font as the businesses and institutions. Note depictions of proposed reservoirs and canals, reflecting a growing awareness of water needs.

in the Corner Market Building on the corner of Meyer and Franklin that had been built in 1884 and deeded to them by Sam Hughes. In an interview published in *Voices of El Presidio* (2004) Elizabeth Treat Lazear, their sixth child, reports that when she was growing up in that house, there were all sorts of kids in the neighborhood, black, Indian, Chinese, white. The building later becomes Wing Yen Groceries and Meat (1938–1952).

1899 November

Phillip Drachman dies, age 66, and is buried with Masonic rites.

1899

Andrew Carnegie offers $25,000 for the construction of a public library building in Tucson if the city will provide a site and guarantee a fund of $2,000 a year for its maintenance. The Common Council passes Resolution No. 20 on November 23, 1899, which provides land that was part of the Military Plaza for the site and sets up the Library Fund. The library, designed by architect Henry Charles Trost, opens in 1901. In 2014, it is the city's Children's Museum.

1899

The first auto appears in Tucson, a Locomobile steamer, imported by Dr. Hiram W. Fenner, an Ohioan who had arrived in Tucson in the 1880s, now a member of the Owls Club. In 1905, Dr. Fenner will receive the first driver's license in Tucson and in 1914 or 1915, he will, according to Roy

Drachman, become the first doctor to make his rounds in an automobile. It is not known who was the last to do so.

1890s

The Iron Horse development is built north of the Southern Pacific tracks (Fourth Avenue/Euclid, Broadway/8th Street) to be within sound of the railroad whistle; built up further in the 1920s.

1890s

South of Barrio Libre, Barrio Santa Rosa is established.

1890s

Tuberculosis continues as a scourge in the United States, the cause of one in six deaths during the second half of the 19th century. The idea has caught on across the country that living in a dry, sunny climate can be helpful to "lungers" and the advent of the railroad has made it possible for numbers of them to come to Tucson as health seekers. The city does not have enough housing for all who come and tent cities have begun to spring up.

1900

The City Directory for 1899–1900 is published by Chas. T. Connell.

- The introduction notes that Tucson is "perhaps the oldest place in the United States settled by Europeans or their descendants." (Unfortunately, St. Augustine,

Florida, had been founded by the Spanish in 1566 and Santa Fe in 1610.)

- It goes on to say, "The wealth of Tucson represents the steady accumulation of the merchants, mechanics, and shopmen. No outside capital has ever been loaned here for any kind of improvements. No one brought any money when they came to Tucson; what they have now was made in Tucson." (Fort Lowell and the railroad are not mentioned.)

- The introduction notes that there are churches in Tucson for Catholics, Methodists, Episcopalians, Congregationalists, Presbyterians, and Baptists, with Catholics and Methodists the most numerous.

- Twenty "Fraternal Organizations" are listed, including three for women.

- Small business in Tucson, according to the Directory: four providers of liquor and beer, a number of saloons, two banks, two ice companies, three hardware stores, a shoe store (Harry Drachman), a jeweler, an assayer, a painter and paper hanger, nine lawyers, six physicians, two druggists, two meat markets, two purveyors of guns (one also sells bicycles), several barbers, a livery stable, an ice cream store, among other enterprises. The roundhouse and machine shop for the Southern Pacific Railroad have also been located in Tucson.

- Restaurants include the Maisson [sic] d'Or, the Poodle Dog Cafe, the Oriental Restaurant and Saloon, and Won Tai's Celestial Restaurant. At least until World War I, cooking is done on wood or charcoal fires, with the wagonloads of wood being brought in by Papagos.

- Tucson is still its original two square miles, patented in 1874, with a population now of 7,531 (City Directory claims 10,000), not much increase from 1880, but a good recovery from the 5,000 of 1890.

- Mexicans are still a majority, barely, at 4,122 or 54.7 percent—down from 4,469 in 1880 because of less immigration from Mexico. This is the last decade in which there is a Mexican majority in Tucson.

- African-Americans are numbered at 86.

- Farming, ranching, and to a lesser degree mining are the major economic activities and users of water. There is no agriculture yet in the lower Santa Cruz River Basin but with the introduction of pump irrigation this is soon to change.

- Tucson now has water, sewer, gas, electric light, telephone, and telegraph service (no electric street cars yet).

- The City Directory claims 1,898 students in schools (an increase of 533 since 1890). Private schools listed are the Indian School supported by the Presbyterian Board of Home Missions, St. Joseph's Academy for Girls, and the Orphans Home run by the Sisters of St. Joseph. In Tucson's public schools, both sexes have been in the same classrooms since 1883 and in Tucson's public schools at least, this has become accepted practice

1900

Enrollment at UA is 225, an increase of 193 from 1891 (faculty are 16, up nine; buildings number 14, up 13).

1900

The first African-American neighborhoods are at the base of Sentinel Hill. This year, the Mount Cavalry Baptist Church is established at 210 E. Lester Street, the first African-American church in what will become the state of Arizona. The church will be an anchor for a neighborhood north of Lee and south of Grant between First and Sixth Avenues that is made up largely of African-American families. Later, the church will be joined, on Lee and Fourth Avenue, by the Greater Mount Olive Church of God in Christ, and Mansfield Park and Pool on Fourth Avenue, a block south of Grant. In 2014, the neighborhood will still be known, unofficially, as Sugar Hill. African-American neighborhoods appear in later years on South Park Avenue and near Meyer Street and near other churches, including the Prince Chapel African Methodist Episcopal Church at 602 S. Stone.

1900

With money raised by donations and special performances at the Opera House, Tucson's Fire Department purchases four horses to pull its chemical fire equipment, formerly pulled by hand. Funds can be collected from people whose property is saved, but only if it is saved. Tucson's first salaried fireman, Frank C. Norton, had been hired last year.

The second one, Alex McNeil, is hired this year. McNeil will become chief in 1938 and retire after a 40-year career.

1900

Louise Foucar (b. 1864 in Boston to a family that had emigrated from Germany) had begun graduate study at the University of Arizona in 1898, having come to Tucson from Denver after developing tuberculosis and heart problems. This year she becomes UA's first woman professor, teaching botany. Because of earlier studies, she is also able to teach English, French, Latin, and Spanish. In 1901 she will be made head of the Department of Ancient and Modern Languages. Using money inherited from her parents, she begins buying up raw land around the university, which is still far from downtown but now accessible by the Tucson Street Railway.

1900

The Tucson Women's Club is organized (it remains in existence in 2014). Organizers had not wanted to be a "club" the way men's clubs tended to be (they might have had the Owls Club in mind), but also had not wanted to appear to be only a "good works society." They aspired, they said, to personal, literary, and educational development and to engagement in civic affairs.

1900

Over the last decades, Mexican *ranchos* have been established downstream on the Santa Cruz and in drainages that enter the Santa Cruz from the northwest (Cañada del Oro) and from the east (Rillito Creek, Tanque Verde Creek,

Pantano Wash, Sabino Creek). Over the next two decades, most will be lost to Anglos, one way and another, except for a Mexican settlement that emerges this year in the region of Old Fort Lowell called "El Fuerte." By 1908, the population in this area is large enough to support a school and a two-room schoolhouse is built on land donated by a local dairy farmer with construction materials donated by J. Knox Corbett. In 1929, this Fort Lowell School will be replaced by a larger one on East Pima. A little more than a decade after the school is replaced, the San Pedro Chapel, which had been the center of El Fuerte's community life, will be supplanted by St. Cyril's Catholic Church on Pima and Swan. In the late 1930s and 1940s, with the water table falling, farming declines. By 1948, more Anglos have moved into the area and El Fuerte has faded away though its graveyard remains on Fort Lowell Road and Laurel Avenue.

1900

Also at this time, west of El Fuerte where Dodge meets the Rillito, on a 60-acre parcel purchased from Alexander Johnson Davidson, Mormon families form the settlement of Binghampton (named after the 19th-century settler Nephi Bingham) on both sides of the Rillito, where they engage in dairy farming, among other enterprises, and develop ditch irrigation in the area. In 1899, a Latter-Day Saints cemetery had been established in the area (still in use on North Alvernon Way in 2014). More Mormon families come in 1908, some settling around El Fuerte. Yet more come as those who had settled in northern Mexico in order to be able to continue to practice polygamy are forced by the Mexican Revolution to leave the country. In 1910, the Tucson branch of the Church of Latter-Day Saints, called Binghampton, will be organized in Tucson.

1900

At its site west of the Santa Cruz, St. Mary's Hospital opens a large circular sanatorium for tuberculosis patients, designed by Dr. Hiram Fenner. At Fort Lowell, three of the officers' quarters and their kitchens are purchased by Mrs. Dolly Cates and her two nieces for use as a sanatorium. Shortly afterward, Dr. and Mrs. Swan begin operating a sanatorium called Swan Ranch out of the old Post Trader's Store (and bar) that "Pie" Allen had opened next to the new fort in 1873. In the 19th century, tuberculosis had been the leading cause of death: one in four in the first half, one in six in the second half.

1900

For the first time since its founding in 1874, the City of Tucson performs an annexation, bringing in an area around the original city that increases its area from 2 to 3.75 square miles. The City Directory of 1881 had noted the existence of several possible "additions" around the original city limits: Buell's Addition (160 acres adjoining the city on the east), Allen's Addition (a smaller area next to Buell's), Real Estate Associates (adjoining the city to the northwest), Osborn's Addition (3 blocks southwest of South Main), Bruckner's Addition (30 blocks adjoining Osborn's to the south), and George L. Lynde (also south of the city). The Bruckner Addition to the south will be the city's first.

1900

City of Tucson buys the privately owned Tucson Water Company.

1900

To promote agriculture, the California Development Company begins constructing irrigation canals to divert Colorado River water into California's Salton Sink, a dry lake bed on the San Andreas Fault. In only two years, one of these, the Imperial Canal, becomes filled with the river's silt. In 1905, heavy rainfall and snowmelt cause the system to fail and for a period of two years the entire flow of the Colorado River is sporadically diverted into the sink, creating the Salton Sea. Efforts made to return the river to its channel fail. The current superintendent of the Southern Pacific Railroad in Tucson, Epes Randolph, is called in. Randolph, born in Virginia, had become prominent back East in railroad construction and management, and had come to Tucson in 1894 because of a deteriorating lung condition. In one of the most remarkable civil engineering feats of the era, Randolph and workers from the Southern Pacific manage to stop the river's flow before the diversion becomes irreversible. Continuing intermittent flooding of the Imperial Valley leads to proposals for a dam on the Colorado. The construction of the first of these, Hoover Dam, begins in 1929 and is completed in 1935, creating Lake Mead. In 2014, the Salton Sea is drying up. Lake Mead is also shrinking.

1900

Oren Anderson (b. Norway) begins constructing the first of many custom brick and stone homes he will build in Tucson, several along Granada, marking the transition from adobe to fired brick structures in the city. By 1930, Anderson will have built many of these homes in the downtown and midtown area.

1900

Henry Granjon becomes bishop of Tucson, replacing Peter Bourgarde. He takes a great interest in preserving and restoring the San Xavier Mission, which has been essentially vacant and has had no work done on it since 1821. Without the work Granjon does there over the next 12 years, the church probably would not have survived in any form, let alone as it has into 2014.

1900

At Franklin and Main, near the Rosalia Verdugo House on the northeast corner that had been built in 1877 of adobes in the Sonoran style, large brick houses are built for Judge Francis Hereford and Albert Steinfeld at 340 and 300 North Main, and at 378 North Main the Owls Club Building, all designed by architect Henry Trost. Steinfeld's is the first house in Tucson with a bathtub. Public baths along the Santa Cruz now begin to decline. The Owls Club, constructed by Levi Manning as a residential facility for eligible unmarried (Anglo) men, had been started in 1886. In 1902, after the Owls Club commissions another facility farther north on Main, Owls Club resident Leo Goldschmidt will persuade Albert Steinfeld to buy the original building from Manning. In the 1930s, the Manning Building will be acquired by the Moose Club. In 1912, Leo Goldschmidt will buy the other remaining member's interests in the new Owls Club Building and live there until his death in 1944. The building will later become a real estate developer's office and in 2014 be acquired by the Center for Biological Diversity, known locally for its efforts to protect the pygmy owl and other desert owls.

1900

First sewers are built in Tucson. Earlier, residents had only backyard outhouses and later some septic systems. The new sewers deliver untreated sewage to the Santa Cruz, and sometimes to agricultural fields (Webb et al. 160).

1901

North of Speedway, between Euclid and Sixth Avenue, Feldman's subdivision is platted. Alther Feldman, an immigrant from eastern Europe, had arrived in Tucson in 1878 after a 70-day journey from San Francisco, having already bought a house (later the Kappa Alpha fraternity house on North 1st Street) and 160 acres in what became Feldman's Addition north of Speedway. Most houses in the addition will be built from 1920 to 1927.

1901

The Arizona Territory passes a miscegenation statute that makes illegal marriages between whites and "Negroes, Mulattoes, Indians, Mongolians" and their descendants. The statute is not repealed until 1962. The U.S. Supreme Court does not outlaw such statutes until 1967.

1902–1905

Alexander Oswald Brody is appointed territorial governor, replacing Oakes Murphy.

1902

The Federal Reclamation Act is passed to fund irrigation projects in 20 western states, strongly promoted by John Wesley Powell, who since his expeditions down the Colorado River had been trying to educate people in the East about how dry it was beyond the 100th meridian.

1902

Ten subdivisions have been platted by this time, including Feldman, Sunnyside (after the city subdivides Military Plaza), University Home, and University Extension.

1902

The downtown area west of Stone between Maiden Lane (no longer there) and Congress, known as "the Wedge" and known also for illicit activity including prostitution, begins to be taken down by workers under the supervision of home builder O. M. Anderson. Removal will be completed in 1904.

1902

The Tucson Board of Trade becomes the Tucson Chamber of Commerce.

1902–1904

Tucson Street Railway routes are added from downtown south into Armory Park and Barrio Libre and east past the University of Arizona to "Railway Park" on the northwest corner and the Tucson Country Club on the northeast corner of what is now Campbell and Speedway.

1900s

Starting in the late 1800s, Yaqui Indians fleeing oppression in their homeland in northern Mexico take up residence at several locations in southern Arizona, including, in Tucson, an area southwest of Grant and Oracle that becomes known as Old Pascua; in Barrio Libre; and around 39th Street. They get what work they can in the region, such as in the cotton fields in Marana, and return when they can to the struggle in Mexico.

1903

McKinley Park—what later becomes Barrio Anita—is platted by Thomas Hughes Sr., brother of Sam Hughes, north of 6th Street and south of Speedway, west of Stone and north along the railroad, with Annie Street running through it, named after Hughes's unmarried sister Annie who lived with him and cared for his children. Hughes names Oury Street in honor of William and Granville Oury. Most building is completed by 1920. In 2001 the park next to this neighborhood that in 1931 had been named Oury Park is renamed the David G. Herrera and Ramon Quiroz Park.

1903

Henry Ford starts Ford Motor Company.

1903

Joining the McCormick, Feldman, and Jefferson Additions along Jefferson (later Speedway), Olsen's Addition is platted between Campbell and Tucson Boulevard, south of Elm to Jefferson, with half-block-sized lots and wide streets. Parcels of one block or more are sold over the next 10 years.

1903

North and east of Olsen's Addition, Judge Blenman patents land he had homesteaded earlier, one square mile between Speedway/Grant and Tucson Boulevard/Country Club.

1903

On land bought and leased by the Tucson Chamber of Commerce on Tumamoc Hill, the Carnegie Institution of Washington establishes the Desert Laboratory to study how desert plants survive in the heat on so little water. Important botanists from around the world will come to do research here, including Francis Lloyd of Columbia University, who will bring with him a journal called *The Plant World*, acquired by the Ecological Society of America and renamed *Ecology* in 1920. Publications in the journal will help Tucson acquire a reputation as a place of interest to naturalists. In 1906, with the construction of a five-mile barbed wire fence around the land, grazing and quarrying on the land is stopped, and the Tumamoc Ecological Reservation becomes what its website claims is the world's first ecological restoration project.

1903

Tucson Water asks citizens to limit water usage for lawns and gardens during peak usage times. It had first requested this, tentatively, in 1893.

1903

After the railroad started using dining cars, the Southern Pacific's San Xavier Hotel had declined, finally becoming a boardinghouse. It burns down now but with no loss of life.

1904

The Santa Rita Hotel opens in the Military Plaza area, designed by Henry Charles Trost, with Levi Howell Manning and Epes Randolph as principal investors.

1904

Last year, Louise Foucar had resigned her position at UA, where she was the first woman professor, to devote herself to her real estate business and had hired Thomas Marshall, a former student, to help with maintenance of her rental properties. This year she and Thomas Marshall marry.

1903

The second major building at UA, Herring Hall, UA's first gym, designed by UA faculty member David Holmes, is completed. After Henry Trost, Holmes is the first of what will be a line of local architects who over the next several decades will build many distinguished homes and buildings in Tucson. This building is named after William Herring, local lawyer and chancellor of the Board of Regents. Over the years, the building will be home to many different entities at UA. In 2014, it is UA's plant archive. The third building at UA, also designed by Holmes and completed the next year, is first the library, then the College of Law, the Arizona State Museum, and the Department of Psychology. Today it is named the Douglass Building, after the UA faculty member who was a man of many parts, an astronomer who was hired first as a physics professor and later invented the science of dendrochronology (tree-ring dating).

1904

Elysian Grove, formerly Carrillo Gardens, opens, now owned by Emanuel Drachman. It quickly becomes Tucson's principal venue for recreation, dancing, and entertainment. Tucson Street Railway extends a line to the Grove.

1904

Professor George P. Smith, who had come to Tucson with a PhD from Columbia University in 1900 and became a water expert, builds for himself the first residence north of Speedway, now the Smith House at 1195 East Speedway.

Two years later, the second house north of Speedway, the Cannon-Douglass House, will be built next to it. Professor Cannon was a botanist who had come to Tucson in 1902 and became the first resident director of the Desert Laboratory on Tumamoc Hill. Professor Douglass will buy the house from Cannon in 1913. The Smith House, which in 2014 is next to the College of Law, is the UA College of Architecture's Center for Preservation Studies. Both houses are now on the National Register of Historic Places.

1904

The Dunbar/John Spring subdivision is platted between Speedway and 6th Street, Stone and Main Avenues, on the site of the old Court Street Cemetery (1875-1909). It becomes an ethnically mixed area, Anglo, Black, Chinese, Mexican, and Yaqui.

1904

The South Park and Native American Additions are platted, the latter by George Pusch, along with Southern Heights and, in 1905, Papagoville south of 22nd Street and west of Sixth Avenue.

1904

A new electric power plant is completed on 6th Street between Court and Main. Tucson Gas, Electric Light & Power Company will now be able to produce enough power for streetlights and electric street cars.

1904

Mariano Samaniego becomes a charter member of the Arizona Cattle Growers Association. He runs his cattle north of Tucson on the Rillito Ranch and the Cañada del Oro Ranch near Oracle.

1904

After a complex and contentious dispute with Louis Zeckendorf arising out of their ownership of stock in the Silverbell Copper Mine 45 miles northwest of Tucson, Albert Steinfeld buys out the partnership interest of Louis Zeckendorf and is now in sole control of the store. He changes the business's name to Albert Steinfeld & Company, and builds a big new store on the corner of Stone and Pennington that has a grand opening in 1906. Betinna Lyons writes, "The *Citizen* [of March 16, 1906] marveled that only two other department stores in the West—one in Denver and the other in San Francisco—rivaled Tucson's new emporium. 'When Steinfeld arrived in Tucson, thirty-four years ago, the Zeckendorf business amounted to only $40,000 per year,' it reminded its readers. 'It had just two clerks to wait on customers and keep the books. Now the annual business of A. Steinfeld & Co. aggregated $1,500,000 and required a force of 150 people.'" Steinfeld and his descendants will operate the business into the 1980s, when it closes down and the building is demolished.

1905

UA's library moves out of a room in Old Main to a separate building, the third major building at UA, which also houses the Territorial Museum, the President's Office, and classrooms (in 2014, the Douglass Building).

1905

The Cheney House is built at 252 North Main by the Holmes & Holmes firm for Annie Cheney, the widow of mining chemist George Washington Cheney. In 1981, a fire burns part of it, but it is refurbished in 2001 by Gerald and Emma Talen and in 2014 is private apartments.

1905

The *Arizona Daily Star* worries about the danger of "fast automobiling" on the streets of Tucson. Horses and buggies are still much in use.

1905

UA enrollment is 200. Old Main is damaged by a fire this year.

1905

The Tucson Rapid Transit Company (TRT) buys the existing mule-drawn streetcar system in Tucson. By 1906, electricity has replaced mules.

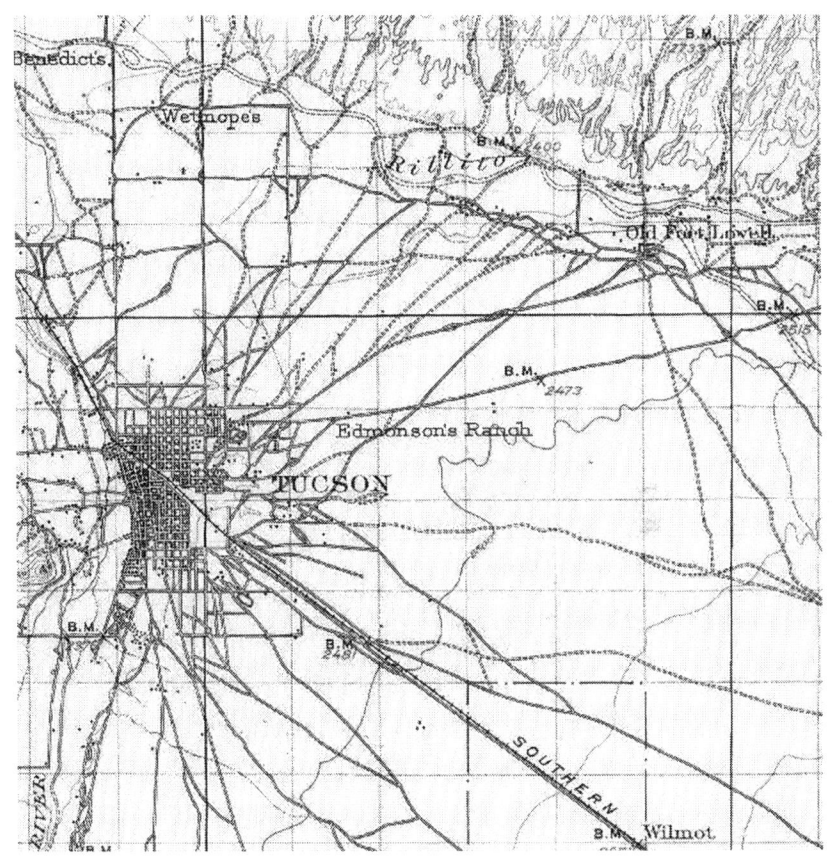

1905 Tucson USGS quadrangle map. This map is the earliest example of a U.S. Geological Survey topographic map of Tucson. Topographic contours are represented as they still are today on USGS maps. Appearing on this map are Fort Lowell and the loop containing Old Main on the University of Arizona campus, beyond which little development is shown to have taken place.

1905

Bisbee has become the largest town in Arizona, and the largest between Santa Fe and San Francisco; Douglas, Bisbee's smelter town, is incorporated this year, with the Calumet and Arizona (1902) and Copper Queen smelters (1904) in operation there.

1905–1909

Joseph Henry Kibbey is appointed territorial governor, replacing Alexander Oswald Brody. The federal government supports Arizona and New Mexico coming in as one state: Kibbey and most of Arizona's citizens oppose this.

1905

Levi Manning and Leo Goldschmidt subdivide the land they had bought between Main and the Santa Cruz River, then known as "the Flats," later as the "Goldschmidt Addition" and then as "Snob Hollow" on Granada Street. The houses will be two-story houses in set-back American (not curb-side Sonoran) style. Goldschmidt (b. Hamburg 1852, d. Tucson 1944), brother-in-law of Jacob Mansfeld, had worked in Zeckendorf's store after coming to Tucson, then started a furniture store that did well, then in 1888 had bought into the Eagle Flour Mill (with four stories, Tucson's tallest building) that had been founded in 1898 by E. N. Fish and partners two blocks northwest of the train depot. Goldschmidt ended up owning it, and remained president of the company until 1922 when he sold out to a Phoenix firm and retired. In 1919, with Mose Drachman and Judge W. H. Sawtelle, he will build the Hotel Congress and the Rialto Building, both now on the National Register of Historic Places.

1905–1907

Levi Howell Manning is elected mayor. As he had promised in his campaign, he outlaws gambling and requires the police to start wearing uniforms. In 1907, he builds a 37,000-square-foot mansion in Snob Hollow at the foot of Paseo Redondo, designed in a combination of architectural styles by Henry Charles Trost; it has stables and what may be the first private swimming pool in Tucson. The house is sold to the Elks Club in 1949, then is operated as a wedding and meeting venue, and is purchased in 2013 by the El Rio Community Health Center for its administrative offices.

1906

On the lower Salt River, the Granite Reef diversion dam begins to operate, the first dam of the Salt River Project.

1906–1907

J. Knox Corbett constructs a house on Main, designed by UA faculty member David Holmes, who had by now designed Herring Hall, UA's second building, and what is now Douglass Hall, its third. He also designed the Southern Pacific depot and Heidel Hotel (MacArthur Building) on Toole, the original Tucson high school that became Roskruge Junior High School, the Chicago Store, the Rockwell and Kingan Houses on Franklin Street, and South Hall on the UA campus, his last building in Tucson. In 1912, Holmes moves to San Diego. The Corbett House completes the building out of North Main. Granada (the Goldschmidt Addition) now begins to be built out.

1906

Hyman Capin (b. Lithuania 1874, d. Tucson 1935), a tailor in the business of making military uniforms, comes briefly to Tucson, going then to El Paso and finally Nogales. In the 1920s, the Capin family starts opening department stores in Nogales and becomes an important merchandizer on the border, later opening a few stores in Tucson. In 2014, no Capin stores are in operation in either location.

1906 June 1

Electric street cars begin to operate under the auspices of Tucson Rapid Transit. On June 1, the symbolic last horse car and two electric cars proceed down Congress and north along Stone to the car barn at 5th Street, where the mule car turns off into the barn. TRT is now owned by Mayor Manning. On June 8, Alther M. Feldman dies from injuries suffered when he jumps off a moving streetcar, becoming the first electric streetcar fatality. The streetcar arrives at UA's Main Gate on the half hour and students are allowed 10 minutes to get to class. Classes at UA therefore start at 20 minutes to the hour and do so until after World War II. Electric streetcar service continues to 1930.

1906

Tucson High School, Tucson's first high school, opens at 1010 E. 10th Street (in 2014 this is the administrative offices for Tucson Unified School District 1).

1906

Levi Manning begins his first venture into cattle farming with his purchase of what would become known as Scotch Farms, a 500-acre ranch between Tucson and Mission San Xavier.

1906

Calvert and Kathryn Wilson of California sell to James W. Wheeler, a land developer from Seattle who had contracted tuberculosis, 120 of the 160 acres north of Elm they had bought from the federal government in 1891, and the 160 acres south of Elm that will become Olsen's Addition. Wheeler digs an 83-foot well on the property and, in 1910, installs two windmills and a 5,000-gallon tank, and digs an 80-foot circular concrete pool, probably the second private swimming pool in Tucson (the one at Levi Manning's new house is probably the first). In 2006 Wheeler's pool is filled in by the then-owners of the property because the empty pool was being used at night by skateboarders.

1907

Albert Steinfeld builds a warehouse this year by the railroad tracks. His Pierce-Arrow automobile is the 66th registered in the City of Tucson. In 1909, his "colored" chauffeur will be given the city's first speeding ticket for driving more than 20 miles per hour, three times the speed limit, which is seven mph. In 1913, it is raised to 10 mph.

1907

The Old Pueblo Club is incorporated, a "gentlemen's club for social purposes" and "to work for a greater and better Tucson." The building completed at 101 South Stone in 1908 will offer rooms for bachelors but does not exclude married men, as did the Owls Club. Among the 69 charter members are seven current and former members of the Owls Club.

1907

The grand Eliza Ward Rockwell House is built at Franklin and Granada in the area that comes to be known as "Snob Hollow." In 2014, the house is still well-preserved, now occupied by law offices, in what is now the El Presidio Historic District.

1907

A larger passenger depot is built by the Southern Pacific Railroad downtown on Toole Avenue. Designed by the Southern Pacific's architect, Daniel J. Patterson, it features Spanish and Mission Revival details. In 2014, the somewhat altered building houses the Tucson Transportation Museum, Maynard's Restaurant, and small businesses.

1907 October

A financial panic follows a number of others that had started occurring in the 1870s. Many bankruptcies result. Discussions begin that lead to legislation in 1913 authorizing the Federal Reserve System.

1907 October 25

The cornerstone is laid in the northeast corner, according to Masonic ritual, for the new Tucson High School Building (later Roskruge Junior High School), on the north side of 6th Street. The school has 191 students in 1908. The superintendent of schools is John Ruthrauff Jr. (b. Illinois 1886, arrives Tucson 1904, BA in metallurgy from UA in 1909, d. 1926). Ruthrauff will be the city engineer from 1912 to 1917 and, after service in World War I, will be the county engineer, guiding all work in paving and lighting Tucson's streets, the construction of the Fourth Avenue underpass (Tucson's first underpass), the construction of City Hall, and the construction of Congress Street Bridge over the Santa Cruz. He dies in 1926 at age 39.

1908

New prison built by the inmates themselves opens in Florence, to replace the Territorial Prison in Yuma (also inmate constructed) that had been created by the territorial legislature in 1875.

1908

General Motors is founded by William "Billy" Durant, Buick its first brand.

1908

Arturo Carrillo (b. Tucson 1870, d. Tucson 1937), son of Leopoldo and a furniture maker who recently had fled from Cananea in the run-up to the revolution, opens the Tucson

Undertaking Company. Arturo is the father of Leopoldo Robles Carrillo (d. 1984) and the grandfather of Leopoldo "Leo" Arturo Carrillo, who marries Carole Coulter in 1962, and takes over in 1964 what is now the Tucson Mortuary. L. A. Carrillo is the brother of Irene, Eloise, and Walter Carrillo. L. A. Carrillo's son Leo Coulter Carrillo takes over the mortuary in 2004.

1908

Tucson's firehouse at Broadway and Sixth Avenue acquires a steam engine.

1909–1912

Richard Elihu Sloan (b. Ohio, a lawyer and a Republican) replaces Joseph Henry Kibbey as territorial governor. Sloan will focus on achieving statehood and will be the last territorial governor.

1909

College of Agriculture faculty member John James Thornber, who has been interested in bringing desert plants from Africa to Arizona, imports the salt-tolerant tamarisk (salt-cedar) tree to Arizona. The tree spreads widely in the Southwest. Unfortunately, it consumes large amounts of groundwater and has become a scourge on watercourses in the Southwest, another "invasive species." Efforts are being made to eradicate it but many are still to be found in Tucson, on the El Rio and Randolph Golf Courses, for example.

1909

The College of Agriculture buys 20 acres at Campbell Avenue and River Road to be the Campbell Avenue Farm, a teaching facility for the college. In 1984, it is renamed the Campus Agricultural Center.

1909

Charles Loebs (b. Germany 1861), who first came to Tucson as a worker on the railroad and later came to own a saloon in town, holds the grand opening of his Pastime Park facility on North Oracle designed to offer various indoor and outdoor amusements for Tucsonans. In 1917, Loebs is murdered in his saloon by robbers. Pastime Park then becomes a sanatorium for veterans of World War I with lung injuries and for people suffering from tuberculosis.

1910

In a Republican Congress, the House passes an Enabling Act saying that the election of 1908 would be the last one under territorial law in Arizona. The Senate passes the bill in June and President Taft, a Republican, signs it that month. Statehood has been achieved, pending approval of the state's constitution, of course. A week after Taft signs the act, territorial governor Sloan calls for an election in September of delegates to a constitutional convention. Forty-one of the 52 delegates elected by Arizona's voters are Democrats. A major question will be whether to authorize "direct democracy"—the initiative, referendum, and recall—considered a "progressive" plank. The convention convenes on October 10, and elects George W. P. Hunt of Globe as its president. It completes its work after 60 days, on December 9. A provi-

sion making racial segregation constitutional had been considered and rejected. It recognizes women as "citizens" and grants them the right to vote and hold office, seven years before the Twenty-Second Amendment to the U.S. Constitution does. It also provides that "The university and all other state educational institutions shall be open to students of both sexes, and the instruction furnished shall be as nearly free as possible," and establishes "eight hours" as constituting "a lawful day's work in all employment by, or on behalf of, the state or any political subdivision of the State." It provides for the initiative, referendum, and recall. Territorial governor Sloan says, "Arizona stands just as much chance of annexation as a province of the Russian empire as it does of admission to statehood under the constitution." Arizona's voters approve it by a margin of more than three to one.

1910

The U.S. Census says Tucson's population is 13,193, the first time over 10,000. Tucson's black population is 222. The population of Pima County is 22,818.

1910

Total enrollments with change from previous decade: UA 195, a decrease of 30 but the total increases the next year by 106; number of faculty 30, an increase of 14; buildings 17, up by three.

1910

Tucson has six schools, including a high school and Mansfield Junior High School, along with the elementary schools. It also has the Indian School (agricultural, industrial, and domestic arts for boys and girls) that had been run in

Tucson by the Presbyterian Mission since 1888, and 15 other schools spread throughout Pima County. In 1907, Reverend Haddington Brown and the Presbyterian Mission had moved the Indian School farther south to a new location on South 12th Avenue and an unnamed road that came to be known as "Indian School," which, since 1950, has been known as Ajo Way.

1910

Tucson's City Directory for this year is compiled and published by F. E. A. Kimball of Tucson, Arizona.

- Advertisements now appear in the Directory, including one for "Albert Steinfeld & Co., Arizona's Greatest Department Store."

- Among the cultural amenities now listed is Drachman's Opera House. An "employment agency" has appeared.

- The Heidel Hotel, across from the Southern Pacific depot, advertises a "long-distance phone in every room."

- Three "stage lines" offer transportation to settlements nearby.

- A new company advertised is the "Tucson Farm Pump Engine Co., Capt. J. H. Yundt, General Manager." Professor Arthur E. Yundt has opened a "Violin, Mandolin, Banjo & Guitar Studio" and also the "Tucson Bicycle Motor Club."

- Ten churches are listed, with a new one for Lutherans and another for Christian Scientists.

- Eleven Masonic and 26 "Other" fraternal organizations are listed, along with 30 "Unions," although included in that last group along with several labor unions is the Mexican Consulate, the Old Pueblo Club (Albert Steinfeld, president), the Agricultural Experimental Station at UA, the St. Joseph's Orphans Home, the Rifle Club, and the Arizona Pioneer Historical Society.

- One classified listing is for the Consolidated Telephone, Telegraph and Electric Company.

1910

Speculators from the eastern U.S. and England form Tucson Farms Company and begin to acquire land from the San Xavier Reservation to Canoa Ranch. The company develops a system of 19 wells cutting across the Santa Cruz River south of Sentinel Peak, with plans to deliver water in concrete conduits for new farms. The project is not a success. By the 1920s, the crosscut has been acquired by the Flowing Wells Irrigation District north of Tucson and Midvale Farms has taken over the land in the south between San Xavier and the city (Logan 168).

1910

Stone Avenue Temple is established at 564 South Stone in Barrio Libre. It is the territory's first house of Jewish worship, with Samuel Drachman as its first president. In 2014, it is the home of the Southwest Jewish Museum.

1910 February 19

The first airplane flight in Tucson takes place, at Elysian Grove. Emanual Drachman and George F. Kitt had persuaded several other local businessmen to pledge $2,000 as a guaranteed fee for the exhibition by the aviation pioneer Charles Hamilton in his biplane, brought in by rail from an airshow in Phoenix nine days earlier.

1910

The Clearwater Swimming Pool opens on the east side of Grande Avenue, south of Clearwater Drive, on land owned by the Austad family (Mr. Austad was a welding and steel contractor), in use to the 1930s. The oval-shaped pool is about 70 feet long and 40 feet wide and has a springboard and a tower. The pool is surrounded by cottonwood trees, picnic areas, changing stalls, a concession stand, and a dance floor where dance marathons take place—until the floor burns up in a fire. Because the pool's water isn't filtered, it is frequently drained, with the water used to irrigate the Austads' watermelon fields.

1911

Roosevelt Dam on the Salt River is dedicated. The dam is the key to the Salt River Project in Phoenix.

1911

J. F. McKale becomes the football coach at Tucson High School, coming to Tucson from Wisconsin. Tucson High's mascot becomes the Badger and its colors red and white.

1911

President Taft vetoes the joint resolution of Congress that provides for statehood for Arizona, citing the "pernicious" provision for the recall of judges. On December 12, the Arizona legislature amends the state's constitution to remove the provision.

1911

Robert G. Fowler lands his Wright biplane on the UA campus during his attempt to win the Hearst prize by being the first to fly across the United States in under 90 days. Departing San Francisco in September 1911, he arrives in Jacksonville, Florida, in February 1912.

Tucson in the State of Arizona

(1912–2014)

1912

In Brooklyn, New York, Harold Charles Warnock, the author's father, is born to Harry G. Warnock, a Scotch-Irish orphan, and Magdeline Leunig, the daughter of German immigrants.

1912

The City Directory claims 100 miles of streets that are "macadamized through the principal business district." The first one was Congress from Toole west to the new El Paso and Southwestern Railroad depot. Grant is not yet a listed street, nor are any streets listed south of 24th Street.

- Tucson's area is 10 square miles, according to the City Directory, and its population is 13,125 (22,500 "with additions"), which makes it the most populous city in Arizona, followed by Phoenix (at 11,134), Bisbee, Globe, and Douglas. For comparison purposes, the Directory lists the populations of many cities in other states. In New Mexico, the only city listed is Albuquerque, at 11,020. Three cities have more than a million people, New York, Chicago, and Philadelphia. Of the 45 cities listed as having more than 100,000, three are in California, one in Colorado (Denver), and none in Utah or Nevada.

- The police department consists of a chief, two sergeants, and six patrolmen.

- Forty-two attorneys and 20 physicians and surgeons are listed.

- Tucson High School has seven teachers, a principal, and a staff member designated as "Commercial branches and Librarian." The junior high school—seventh and eighth grades—has six teachers.

- Among the 13 churches listed is an African Methodist Church on 17th Street, all the other churches being downtown.

- The vast majority of the many grocery stores have Chinese names, with many located on South Meyer. Many will remain in business in Tucson until the advent of franchised "convenience stores" in the 1960s and 1970s.

1900s early

At the base of the Rincon Mountains on Tucson's far east side, four large ranches are now in operation: the X-9 owned by Jefferson Rukin Jelks; the Tanque Verde, later and still in 2014 the Tanque Verde Guest Ranch; the Rincon Ranch, which belongs to Melville Haskell and later becomes part of the Rocking K master-planned development by Diamond Ventures; and La Posta Quemada (aka Mountain Springs and the Shaw Ranch).

1912

Statehood for Arizona when President Taft signs the statehood bill on February 14.

1912

Carl Hayden, who was born in 1877 at Hayden's Ferry, now known as Tempe, is elected to the U.S. House and later to the U.S. Senate. He will serve 57 years under 10 presidents (William Howard Taft to Lyndon Johnson) and die in 1971. He is the person without whom, it is said, the Central Arizona Project (see 1968) would never have become a reality.

1912

On November 5, Arizona's voters restore to the state's constitution the provision for recall of judges.

1912

At statehood about 30 percent of Arizona's population has been born outside the United States with 31 percent born in Arizona; 11 percent were born in Arkansas, a much larger percentage than from any other U.S. state.

1912

Arizona's first legislature passes a law requiring segregation in schools, and a voting rights statute that requires voters to pass a literacy test. The territorial legislature had mandated segregation in 1909. Before that time, miscegenation laws had been in place that prohibited blacks as well as Indians and Asians from marrying whites. The state's first miscegenation statute had been passed in 1865, but races had not been segregated, in Tucson's schools at least. The state's segregation laws will not be repealed until 1951. The state's miscegenation laws are not repealed until 1962.

1912

The first governor of the state is Democrat George W. P. Hunt (b. Missouri 1859, d. Phoenix 1934). Between now and 1933, Hunt will go on to serve six terms, with brief interruptions by the election of two other governors. Hunt will commute several death sentences early on and be one of two Arizona governors ever to commute a death sentence.

1912

Tucson's first mayor after statehood is Dr. I. E. Huffman.

1912

Arizona's first legislature enacts a provision forming the Arizona Schools for the Deaf and Blind in Tucson. The first classes are held in a converted former professor's residence at East 2nd Street and Park Avenue near UA.

1912

After an absence of 76 years, the Franciscans return to San Xavier and are put in charge of the religious supervision of the Papagos. The new Franciscan period begins at San Xavier with the appointment of Father Ferdinand Ortiz as priest in 1913. They remain in charge of the mission in 2014.

1912

Tucson's second railroad, the El Paso and Southwestern, owned by Phelps Dodge, enters Tucson from the south, with the terminal on Congress west of Granada. A large celebration is mounted. The new railroad had been promoted by a citizens group led by Hugo J. Donau, manager at Steinfeld's, brother-in-law of Albert. A beautiful terminal in Classical Revival style opens in 1913. In 1924, the railroad is bought by the Southern Pacific and all passenger traffic moves to the Toole Avenue terminal.

1912

John E. White (b. Illinois 1875) arrives in Tucson after having been employed by the Union Pacific Railroad in Cheyenne, Wyoming, for nine years. In Tucson, he serves 13 years as an auditor and assistant treasurer of the Arizona Eastern and Southern Pacific Railroad, is a member of the District 1 school board from 1917 to 1925, and is the 25th mayor of Tucson for two terms from 1924 through 1928. While mayor, he helps to push through an $800,000 bond issue to develop Randolph Park, construct Hi Corbett Field, and finance a water development program and several new city parks. While he is on the school board, District 1 taxpayers approve the bond issue that allows the present Tucson High School to be built.

1913

In Paducah, Kentucky, Mary Louise Phelps, the author's mother, is born to Early Clay and Bertha Humphrey Phelps.

1913

West of the Santa Cruz River and north of Congress, Menlo Park is platted by Henry Schwalen, a recovered tuberculosis patient from Wisconsin who had stayed earlier at the sanatorium at St. Mary's Hospital, and Manuel King, from California. "Negroes" and "Mexicans" are excluded. The development is named after a California town that Schwalen had heard about but never seen.

1913

The school board opens the "Colored School" at 215 East 6th Street, established as a result of the state law that mandates segregation of African-Americans.

1913

More than half of Tucson's population (and of several other southwestern cities) have come to town as health seekers.

1913

Automobiles are now being used to travel longer distances and the Arizona Good Roads Association, with headquarters in Prescott, publishes the *Arizona Good Roads Association Illustrated Road Maps and Tour Book* showing the good, and sometimes not-so-good, roads that connect the larger towns with other destinations and points of interest. None of these roads is paved. The "Explanatory" page for the collection claims that Arizona has the "best natural roads in the Union" as well as "accessible deposits of the best natural road materials known." It also announces that "a system of State Highways is now under construction" and that "it will be but a short time until the whole State will be gridironed with travelable roads, giving easy and comfortable access to the scenic, agricultural and industrial sections of this rich commonwealth." The entry for Tucson, Arizona's largest town by 2,000 people, according to the guide, touts its charms and advantages, as do the entries for the other towns thought to be significant enough for an individual entry.

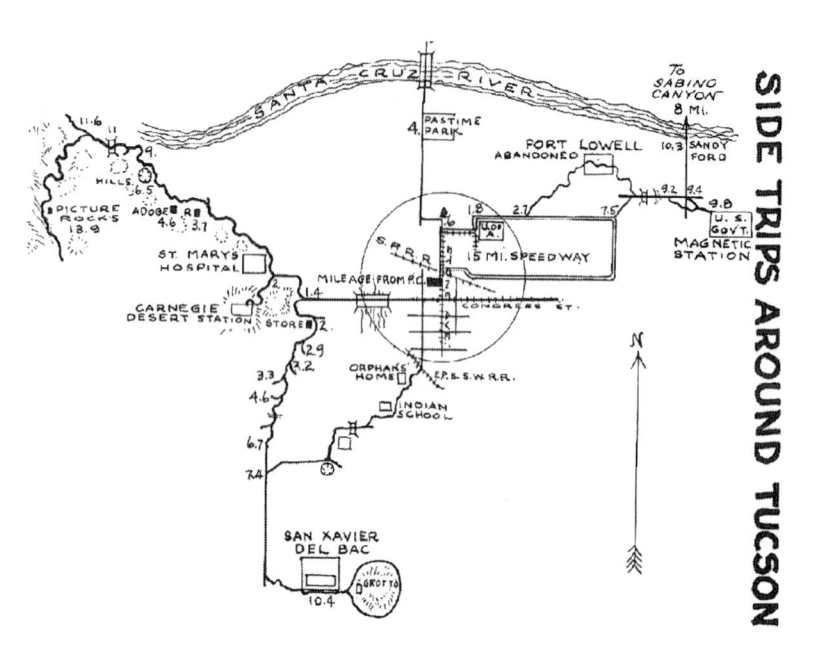

1913 Arizona Good Roads guide overview of Tucson area attractions. This "Good Roads" map, which is not to scale and mistakes the Rillito for the Santa Cruz, shows some recognizable attractions around Tucson. Note the "Speedway" loop and the "sandy ford" cars would have to hazard on the way to Sabino Canyon.

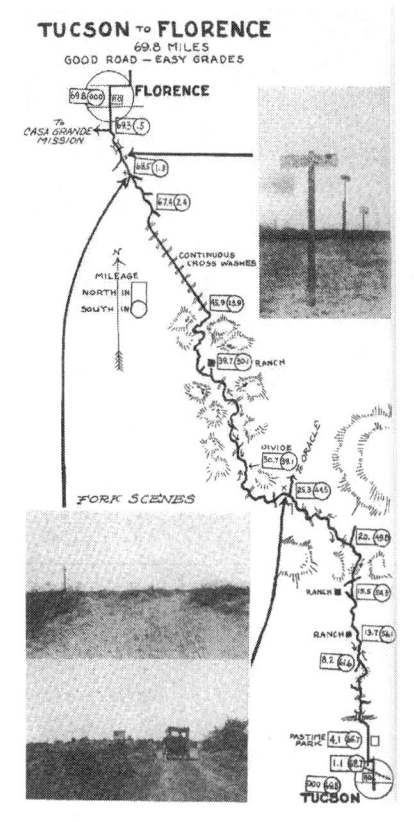

1913 Tucson to Florence driving map from Arizona: Good Roads Association Illustrated Road Maps and Tour Book, originally compiled and published in 1913 by Arizona Good Roads Association, Prescott, AZ. This early tourist guide, published in the early days of the automobile, shows routes between towns and sights along the way. Most "roads" are still dirt trails. Driving between one town and another called for a knowledge of local landmarks, road hazards, and possible wrong turns. Casa Grande is referred to as a "mission."

1914 March

Tucson's first golf course had been a nine-hole course on the northwest corner of Speedway and Campbell. The first 18-hole course is the Tucson Golf and Country Club that is established now at Broadway and Country Club. Albert Steinfeld's brother-in-law Hugo Donau is the prime mover. The "greens," 40 to 60 feet in diameter, are oiled sand, with carpet-wrapped "sweepers" provided for a sweep of the putting line. This course lasts into the 1940s, when the area is converted into a residential subdivision.

1914

Levi Manning buys the entire Canoa land grant, which at this time spans west from the base of the Santa Rita Mountains across Avra Valley (c. 40,000 acres), and goes on to develop it into what will be considered one of the finest cattle ranches in the American Southwest, running mostly Hereford cattle, and breeding Arabian horses. After 1921, his son Howell (b. 1899, d. 1966) will manage the ranch.

1914

President Wilson signs the Smith-Lever Act that establishes and funds Cooperative Extension Services for land-grant universities in the United States like UA. States must match the federal funding. The aim is to establish at least one office in every county in the state to give the people of the state access to the scientific and technical expertise of university faculty and researchers, primarily in agriculture. Agriculture remains the primary focus today, though expertise has been offered also in areas such as engineering and mining, and is still offered in the areas of home economics and government.

1914

South of Old Main, ground is broken at UA for a major new Agriculture building.

1914

The International Order of Odd Fellows Building, designed by Henry Jaastad, is completed on the southeast corner of Broadway and Sixth Avenue, near the old Armory building, now lost. The Odd Fellows are an order of Masons more oriented to artisanal work. They occupy the building for about 50 years, being succeeded by tenants who are often artists and artisans. In 2014, the building is the site of the Etherton Gallery, Janos Wilder's Downtown Kitchen restaurant, and the sculpture studio of Barbara Grygutis.

1914

A Young Men's Christian Association is established on Congress and Court with money donated by El Paso and Southwestern Railroad. The first YMCA had been established in London in 1844 to promote a healthy "body, mind, and spirit." In the 1940s, the author will learn to swim at this "Y."

1914

Arizona passes Prohibition for the state, joining a number of other states that have done so.

1914

J. F. McKale is hired away from Tucson High School to be athletic director and coach of all sports at UA. In the 1914 season, his football team defeats Pomona College 7–6 in the last game of the season and wins the Southwest Football Championship, Arizona's first athletic title, a victory that inspires one of the players to begin a campaign to put an "A" on Sentinel Peak. In the next two years, McKale's basketball teams go undefeated at 9–0 and 5–0.

1914

Rufus Bernhard von KleinSmid (b. Illinois, a professor of psychology and philosophy at Northwestern) becomes the seventh president of the University of Arizona and begins to convert what has been called Tucson's university into the University of Arizona. He terminates the preparatory school (feeling that high schools are now adequate to the task), adds to the original College of Agriculture the College of Letters, Arts, and Sciences and the College of Mining and Engineering, and institutes a building program. In 1921, he will leave to do the same kind of thing for the University of Southern California.

1914

With the start of World War I, the economy of Tucson improves, especially with the entry of the United States in 1917 (fiber, minerals, other agricultural products).

1914

Kress opens on Congress, possibly Tucson's first chain store.

1915

The second mayor of Tucson after statehood is the postmaster, J. Knox Corbett, who serves until 1917.

1915

Tucson's population is 20,000, up from 7,531 in 1900.

1915

UA president von KleinSmid recruits pioneer archaeologist Byron Cummings to build up the Arizona State Museum and head a new Department of Archaeology. In 1917, the nonprofit Arizona Archaeological and Historical Society is founded to support this work.

1915

The Holy Family Church is consecrated in 1915 by Henry Granjon, bishop of Tucson. It had been constructed at North Main and University for Yaqui Indians after a donation from Sister Katherine Drexel, daughter of eastern financier Francis A. Drexel. Sister Drexel had taken a mission with Indians and Negroes in Arizona in 1902, which she will pursue until 1935 when she retires after suffering a heart attack. She dies in 1955 and is later sainted by the Catholic Church.

1915

Diesel engines begin to be used to generate electric power and for water well pumps. The introduction of pumps powered by the internal combustion engine allows farmers, ranchers, and others to locate wells wherever they expect to find groundwater within 80 feet of the surface.

1915

South of Tucson along the Santa Cruz, Continental Farms is established on the northern 9,700 acres of the Canoa land grant that had been purchased from Levi Manning in order to grow plants for rubber thought to be needed for World War I. After the war, the land goes over to cotton farming. In 1948, the land will be acquired by Keith Walden's Farmers Investment Company, which will run cattle on it, then grow pecans.

1915

A flood on the Santa Cruz destroys the Congress Street Bridge.

1915

Teatro Carmen, "the most elegant theater in town," according to Thomas Sheridan in *Los Tucsonenses*, is opened at 380 South Meyer by prominent *tucsonense* Carmen Soto de Vasquez, whose ancestors had settled in southern Arizona when it was still part of Spanish Sonora. The theater offers performances by renowned artists, in Spanish, of everything from 17th-century dramas to 20th-century musical comedies until 1922. It remains open until 1926 as a venue for dancing and boxing. In 1937, after housing a number of other businesses, it becomes the site of Pilgrim Rest, Elks Lodge #601, a black Elks Club, which it remains until 1986. It is then used for a couple of years by the Borderlands Theater, which had begun life in the early 1970s as the activist Teatro Libertad.

In 1996, the building is acquired by the Rollings family and in 2014 it remains vacant.

1915

Emanuel Drachman's Elysian Grove, originally Carrillo Gardens, closes, a victim of declining income and Prohibition in Arizona. For more than a decade, the Elysian Grove had offered "a baseball park; a beer garden; Tucson's first swimming pool; a sizable pavilion used as a skating rink, a dance hall, and a movie theater; and an outdoor 'airdrome,' which boasted a theater with a stage, an orchestra pit, and a projection room, which doubled as the lighting booth for stage productions." Today the area has been filled in and is known as Barrio el Hoyo, in Barrio Viejo. Carrillo Elementary School now occupies the site. Drachman's house was just north of the Grove on South Main, a site that is now under a parking lot for the Community Center. Drachman soon becomes manager of Tucson's Opera House on Congress, a principal venue for traveling performance troupes.

1915

Prostitution is outlawed in Arizona. Gay Alley closes down. Arizona had instituted Prohibition in 1914, but soon afterward a thriving trade had arisen in bootleg whiskey and whiskey smuggled into Arizona from Mexico, with gambling continuing in private clubs and in roadhouses that appear outside of town.

1915

In a project inspired by a UA civil engineering student who was a member of the football team, the freshman class begins to construct a large "A" on Sentinel Peak out of stones and whitewash, completing the job in 1916. Sentinel Peak becomes known thereafter to many Tucson residents as "'A' Mountain."

1915

The Marist Brothers School for Boys is completed on St. Augustine Cathedral grounds, the last important building to be built in Tucson of sun-dried adobe. It operates as a school into the late 1960s, is vacated in 2002, and is entered with two companion buildings in the National Register of Historic Places in 2011. In 2014, it is still standing but in serious disrepair with its fate uncertain.

1915

During three days of the Pima County Fair, teenager Katherine Stinson, known as the "Schoolgirl Aviatrice," gives aerobatic exhibitions in her Partridge Tractor biplane. She also delivers—that is, drops—a pouch of mail at the downtown post office. Tucson is the first city in Arizona to have an aerial mail demonstration and the first to have sanctioned aerial mail service.

1915

Harness racing and auto racing are conducted at the Southern Arizona Fairgrounds, even though the state had prohibited all forms of gambling in 1907.

1915 December 8

The cornerstone of the Scottish Rite Temple on Scott is laid. The temple, designed by Trost & Trost, is completed in 1916. The first Venerable Master of this Lodge of Perfection, in 1903, had been George Roskruge, with Peter E. Howell the Venerable Master in 1911–1912. Both men later had Tucson schools named after them.

1915

The total number of vehicles registered in Arizona is 7,318, an increase of more than 2,200 over the previous year. Of this number 6,851 are gasoline motor cars, 22 are electric cars, 435 are trucks, and 405 motorcycles. In the motor registration Ford cars lead with a total of 2,785. Studebakers are next with a total of 702, Overlands are third with a total of 627, and Buicks are fourth at 540. Maxwells total 304 and Hupmobiles 259. There are 117 Chalmers and 122 Hudsons. Cadillacs number 237. Maricopa county has the most motor vehicles, 2,571; Cochise is second with 1,216, and Pima is third with 754.

1916

The U.S. National Park Service is created.

1916

The last significant house in the Presidio District is built, the Howell Manning (son of Levi) House on Paseo Redondo, Henry Jaastad, architect.

1916

Also in the Presidio District, on Granada, Hinchcliffe Court opens, a horseshoe of 10 cottages in the California Bungalow style, built by local businessman Charles Hinchcliffe on land purchased from Colonel and Mrs. William Herring. The Court, next to the Owls Club Building in Tucson's "best" residential district, is intended as a winter resort/tourist court for well-heeled visitors and seems to have been Arizona's first of both. In 2014 the cottages are attractive rentals.

1916

The Fourth Avenue underpass, the first tunnel under the railroad tracks, is constructed by the Southern Pacific Railroad and city engineer John Ruthrauff. The area on the far side of the tracks becomes the location of warehouses, industrial firms, and a red-light district called Isla de Cuba. Later, small businesses emerge—a butcher shop, a Chinese grocery, a boardinghouse, a hardware store, the Coronado Hotel, and in 1937 a bar called the Shanty that in 2014 advertises itself as the "oldest continually licensed bar in Arizona." A block from the tunnel, a new post office building designed by Roy Place will be built on Fourth Avenue that is now the site of a Goodwill Industries store.

1916

Motor bus transit service is being provided by two small independent operators, supplementing the electric streetcars.

1917

Thomas Edward Campbell, a Republican, replaces George Hunt, a Democrat, as governor of Arizona. By the end of the year, George Hunt is back in office. Campbell replaces Hunt again in 1919, and Hunt replaces Campbell again in 1923.

1917

Olva Clayton Parker becomes mayor of Tucson, until 1926.

1917

The "Colored School" is relocated from East 6th Street to 300 West 2nd Street and renamed Dunbar Elementary and Junior High. The architect for the new school is Henry Jaastad. Graduates of the school cannot go on to high school until 1920 when Tucson High permits them to attend. At Tucson High, they are placed in segregated homerooms, and integrated extracurricular activities are limited to sports and band. There is no restriction on African-Americans attending the university but, until 1932, those who do are not allowed to live in the dormitories or eat in the dining hall.

1917

In Arizona's mines, labor and management had enjoyed stable relations until the turn of the century when there was a wave of strikes, including one in 1903 in Globe, 100 miles north of Tucson. In these actions, white miners had tended to see Mexican miners not as comrades but as strike breakers. Miners go out again this year in Globe, Miami, and Jerome, Arizona.

1917

Tucson's second City Hall is built by John Ruthrauff. It will not be replaced until 1972, during major urban renewal in the downtown area.

1917

Monte Mansfield (1884–1959), the son of Jewish German immigrant Jacob Mansfeld (Monte has added the "i" to his name), opens the first Ford dealership in Arizona.

1917

The Bisbee Deportation takes place. Protesting miners are kidnapped at gunpoint by local authorities, loaded onto train cars, shipped out east, and put off in rural southern New Mexico. The CEO of the Calumet and Arizona Mine in Bisbee at this time is John Greenway.

1918

The Tucson chapter of the National Association for the Advancement of Colored People (NAACP) is formed, having been preceded in Tucson by the "Wide-awake Colored Club" that had been formed in 1884.

1918

Elysian Grove is gone but the lake south of Congress remains until 1953.

1918

The last battle with Indians in Arizona takes place, in Bear Valley, near the Mexican border southwest of Tucson, when U.S. troops skirmish with Yaquis (who have been technically violating U.S. neutrality in entering Mexico with arms to resist government oppression in their homeland in Mexico). One Yaqui Indian is killed.

1918

The school board purchases its first gasoline-powered vehicle, a Buick truck, for $905. Also, last year, the school board had voted to allow dances at the high school.

1918

The Mines and Engineering Building is built on the UA campus.

1918

The author's father, Harold "Hal" Warnock, arrives with his family in Douglas, Arizona. Hal's father, Harry, had contracted tuberculosis, forcing them to leave New York City and come to the West. Hal grows up on the border with Mexico in the new smelter town of Douglas.

1919

At a 13-acre recreation site on the northeast corner of Oracle and Pastime Street called Pastime Park, several thousand Tucsonans gather to begin work on a facility to treat veterans suffering from tuberculosis or lung damage from World War I.

1919

On the southwest corner of South 6th Avenue and 22nd Street, the Santa Cruz Catholic Church opens, Tucson's third Catholic church after San Agustín and Holy Family. Construction began in 1916. Designed by Bishop Granjon and built by Manuel G. Flores, its 90-foot tower, resembling a minaret, reflects Moorish influence on Spanish architecture. Adobe bricks from the Tohono O'odham are used in the 22-inch thick walls.

1919

On 6th Street, an elementary school is added to the current Tucson High building that had been designed by David Holmes in 1908. The elementary school, designed by architect Henry Jaastad (b. Norway 1872, arrives U.S. 1886, arrives Tucson 1910, d. Tucson 1965), is named after prominent citizen and Mason George Roskruge. Jaastad will eventually design 50 schools and 35 churches in Arizona as well as over 100 homes in and around Tucson and serve as mayor of Tucson from 1933 to 1947.

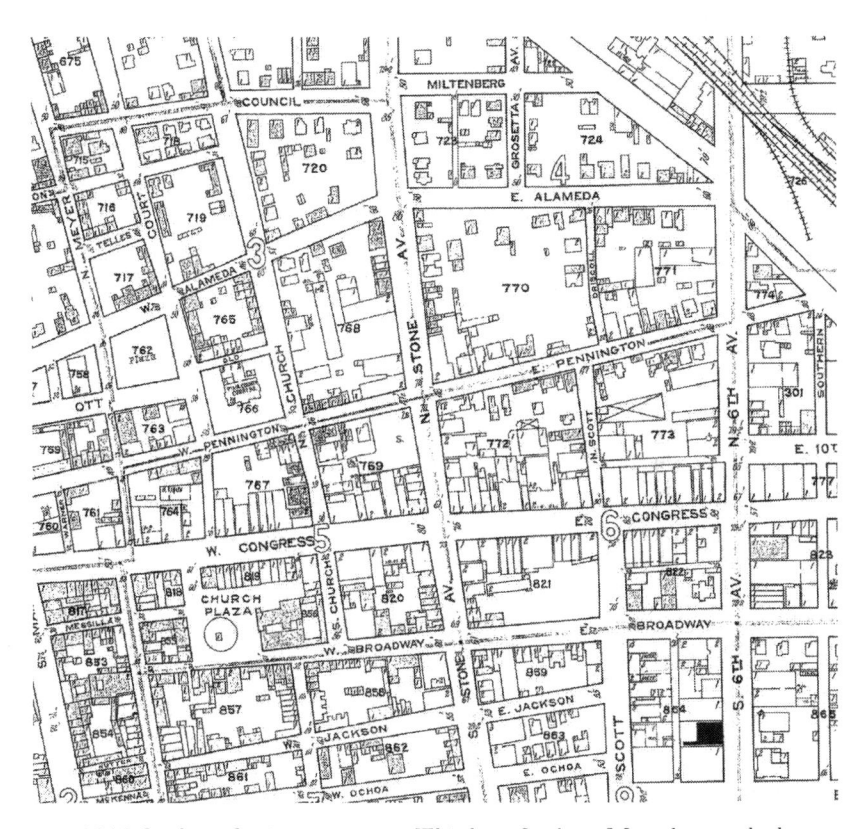

1919 Sanborn fire insurance map. This later Sanborn Map shows only the larger outlines of buildings. Areas of the city are numbered, however, and for each numbered area maps like the 1886 Sanborn map on p. 124 that have much more detail are provided elsewhere.

1919

At South Sixth Avenue and Irvington, the Tucson Chamber of Commerce Aviation Committee establishes the nation's first municipally owned airfield, currently the site of the Tucson Rodeo Grounds. The airfield was named Tucson Municipal Flying Field in 1927. Tucson's first airstrip had been between Oracle and Stone, at the current site of Amphitheater High School. In the early days of aviation, Tucson was on the well-used "Borderland Airway" used for the first two transcontinental flights. It allowed pilots to skirt the mountains.

1919

Hotel Congress is built at Congress Street and Toole Avenue, just past the Fourth Avenue tunnel exit into downtown.

1919

Between Campbell/Mountain and 6th Street/Broadway, Rincon Heights is platted, built out into the 1940s. Forty-one additions have been platted in Tucson since 1903, including, to the south and west, South Park, Native American, Papagoville, Mission View, and Menlo Park. To the north and east, Olsen's, Mountain View, Rillito Park, Paseo Redondo, and Speedway additions.

1919

After the expulsion of the Jesuits from the New World in 1767, the story of Father Kino (d. 1711 Magdalena, Sonora), along with his burial site, had disappeared from view. In 1907, a Protestant professor of history at the University of California, Herbert Bolton, discovered Kino's lost autobiography, Favores Celestiales, *which is published in 2014. Interest in Kino begins to awaken.*

1919–1922

Best-selling novelist Harold Bell Wright (b. Rome, New York, 1872, grew up in Ohio), who had come to Arizona in 1915 seriously ill with tuberculosis, builds a large Pueblo Revival-style home in the desert east of Tucson (now a housing development on the southeast corner of Speedway and Wilmot).

1919

The father of the mother of the author, Early Clay Phelps, is now in Phoenix with the Jordan, Grace and Phelps land firm, which plats Arcadia and acquires the F. Q. Story neighborhood (developed after the mid-1920s by other owners). By 1925, the author's mother, Mary Louise Phelps (b. 1912), and her three sisters will have come from Kentucky to join their father, who is prospering in the land development business in Phoenix.

1920

Tucson, having grown from 3.75 square miles in 1905 to 5.75 square miles, has tripled in population from 1900 (7,531 to 20,337, with Pima County now at 34,680).

- Mexican-surnamed people have only doubled (4,122 to 7,489), and are now just over one-third of the total, with two-thirds of them blue-collar workers.
- Tucson's black population is 346, up from 222 in 1910.

1920

The census confirms that Phoenix (population 29,000) has passed up Tucson as Arizona's largest city, having benefited from canals funded by the Reclamation Act and agriculture in the Salt River Valley.

1920

Tucson's high school has 19 teachers while the grammar schools have 89 teachers in nine schools: Roskruge, Safford, Holladay, Mansfeld, Drachman, Davis, University Heights, Menlo Park, and Dunbar. Total enrollment at the high school is 538 students and there are 3,582 students in the elementary schools. The school budget is $249,782.20.

1920

The UA has 1,171 students, up 976 from 1910 (faculty 95, up 65; buildings 21, up four).

1920

The City Directory for this year is published by the Western Directory Company, 123 East Congress.

- Advertisements for automobile dealers have appeared, for Buick, Ford, and Nash automobiles—also, not surprisingly, advertisements for auto wrecking and salvage companies, and businesses that deal with batteries, tires, and "ignition."
- "Auto Stage Lines" and "Taxicabs" are now advertised.
- 34 lawyers are listed and law firms have appeared.
- A new "steam laundry" has appeared.
- One store now sells "Sporting Goods."
- "Shorthand reporters" now offer their services and there are shops that sell and repair "typewriters."
- A new club listed is the Old Pueblo Club.
- Commercial enterprises now appear in the Directory in bold type.

1920

5.7 miles of roads are now paved, on Congress and Stone and in the Presidio Neighborhood. The roads are likely macadamized rather than paved with asphalt or concrete.

1920

The Rialto Theatre opens as a performance venue in Tucson. In 1922, Emanuel Drachman, former owner of Elysian Grove, takes over management. With 932 seats, the Rialto is larger than Tucson's Opera House and becomes the favored venue for traveling performers.

1920

South Menlo Park (west of Santa Cruz, south of Congress) is platted by Knox Realty and the Pachecos. Mexicans are not excluded in this part of Menlo Park. There are no sidewalks, paved streets, or street lighting in either the North or the South Menlo Park subdivisions until the urban renewal of the 1970s.

1920

South of Congress, Barrio El Membrillo is platted in Barrio Viejo. Most of this barrio will later be lost to the Convention Center and the freeway.

1920

The Santa Cruz arroyo has reached Martinez Hill at San Xavier, 18 miles from its origin in the headcut made by Sam Hughes in 1889 at St. Mary's Road. Pumped groundwater is now the only option for agriculture along this reach. The former Spring Branch of the Santa Cruz has become the main stem.

1920

The Southern Pacific main line has acted as a barrier to expansion north and east from downtown. The first underpass had been constructed in 1916 on Fourth Avenue but Campbell is still the eastern limit of the city. To the west, the Santa Cruz River is a barrier. The flood in 1915 that destroyed the Congress Street Bridge sets back development there.

1920

Out east beyond Campbell on Broadway, Country Club Heights is platted a half mile north and south of Broadway between Alvernon and Columbus (then called Thoreau), with streets laid out in the usual grid pattern. The development does not attract buyers until Stanley Williamson buys it in the late 1920s and begins superimposing winding streets, adding deed restrictions that include a $6,000 minimum cost for each house built. The area is developed into 1959.

1920

On Broadway west of Campbell, Miles School opens, built in Mission Revival style; architects are Lyman and Place.

1920

University Heights (Miles Neighborhood) is platted on East Broadway by Walter E. Murphey, the father of John Murphey (b. Tucson 1898, d. Tucson 1977). There is still no tunnel east from downtown on Broadway under the Southern Pacific tracks, but in ads for Murphey's development it is promised as coming soon. John Murphey graduates from UA this year and declines a Rhodes Scholarship, continuing instead in the construction business he had started in 1918.

1920s

East of Campbell between Speedway and Grant, Blenman-Elm begins to be developed, into the 1950s.

1920s

The first turbine well pumps are introduced in Tucson. Before this, windpumps had been able to get water from no more than about 32 feet below the surface, 80 feet for fossil-fuel powered pumps. Turbine pumps have no depth limit.

1920–1930

More than 40 sanatoria are now in operation in Tucson, including the Desert Sanatorium (opened at Grant and Craycroft in 1927 under the directorship of Dr. Bernard L. Wyatt, with buildings designed by Henry Jaastad); the Pastime Park Veteran's Facility (Oracle and Pastime); St. Mary's (St. Mary's Road and Silverbell); Comstock's Hospital, aka Adams Street Mission (1036 East Adams Street), run by Baptist Reverend Oliver Comstock; St. Lukes in the Desert (1917, Episcopal); and Tentville for destitute patients, also known as "Bugville" (on Park Avenue just north of the UA campus). The Cates sanatorium at Fort Lowell will close in 1928; the land and buildings are sold to the Adkins family, who will start a steel tank manufacturing business there.

1921

Northwest of Tucson, a 40-acre tract along the Southern Pacific tracks is established in hopes that the Yaquis living in different locations in the Tucson area (Marana, Cortaro, Jaynes, Tierra Floja, Barrio Anita, Barrio Libre, Mesquital) will locate there, which would make it easier to prevent violations of U.S. neutrality through their gunrunning to Mexico. The area becomes known as "Pascua Village." At first many Yaquis decline to move but it later becomes a significant settlement.

1921

The Sunnyside School District is established in a large area on the south side of Tucson. Sunnyside High School will be established there only in 1955, Desert View High School in 1987.

1921

The Naturalization Act of 1790 had limited immigration into the U.S. to whites. The Emergency Quota Act of this year limits immigration of those whites to 3 percent of the number of that country's population already in the U.S. The effect is to limit immigration mostly to northern Europeans. Another act in 1924 requires visas for the first time and reduces quotas to 2 percent of the number in the U.S. in 1890, limiting further the immigration of southern Europeans (Jews, Italians, Slavs), Asians, Indians, and Arabs. In 1929, a maximum of 150,000 is set with the percentage derived from the 1920 census. This law governs until 1952 and isn't much changed until 1965.

1922

At the "East Gate" of UA, the University Manor subdivision is developed along 3rd Street by Southwest Improvement. Southwest Improvement's president, Monte Mansfield, puts deed restrictions on the houses in University Manor, the first time this has been done in a Tucson subdivision, prohibiting the construction of any business, apartment house, hotel, bar, or oil rig in the subdivision; requiring a minimum expenditure of $5,000 on each residence; requiring setbacks; and excluding "African or Asian" residents. Deed restriction, which was the only way to control development before zoning is legalized in 1927, continues in wide use though with the racial restrictions. Monte Mansfield's is one of the first houses in the subdivision. The area will later be expanded to become the Sam Hughes subdivision that now covers the square mile from Campbell to east of Tucson Boulevard, and from Speedway to south of 6th Street. Development continues to 1950 in this area with most building being done between 1923 and 1932 and most houses in the "Spanish Eclectic" style.

The 1920s

The "neo-native" movement begins in Santa Fe, fueled by wealthy eastern visitors, who begin to make Santa Fe into a center of southwestern "authenticity," with Pueblo Revival architecture, southwestern art, etc.

1922

Leighton Kramer, a businessman from Philadelphia and a tuberculosis sufferer who has been visiting Tucson since 1918 after cavalry service on the Mexican border during World War I, buys the land and structures owned by James and Alta Wheeler, and other property up to what is now Grant Road between Campbell and Tucson Boulevard. At the site of the Wheelers' house on the north side of what is now Elm Street, he begins constructing a large house he will call Rancho Santa Catalina.

1922

Superintendent of Schools C. E. Rose institutes "ungraded classrooms," the first official accommodation in the schools for children with disabilities.

1922

Classes begin at the handsome new campus of the Arizona School for the Deaf and Blind on West Speedway, built in part on land donated by the City of Tucson. In 2014, the school is operating at the same location as a public corporation.

1922

To promote tourism, the Sunshine Climate Club is formed by local boosters. One of their fliers touts "Man-building in the Sunshine-Climate" and says "Here is the place, Mothers, for your pale inactive children." Boosters make much use of

Harold Bell Wright's essay "Why I Did Not Die" in *American Magazine* about his recovery from tuberculosis after he came to Tucson.

1922

The Colorado River Compact, an initiative of Secretary of Commerce Herbert Hoover, is signed by representatives of six of seven western states along the river's course, with upper- and lower-basin states each getting 7.5 million acre-feet of water per year. This puts California and Arizona in competition for lower-basin water. California immediately proposes Boulder Dam and the All American Canal for its Imperial Valley agriculture. Arizona objects to terms, and doesn't sign the compact until 1944. (By the 1960s it is clear that the compact over-allocates the river's water.)

1922

Between 1892 and 1922, the city had instituted seven water-related bond issues. Dependence on pumped groundwater is now obvious. Booster stations are required to move water up from the Santa Cruz River to properties eastward. The search begins for additional sources. (Perhaps build a dam in Sabino Canyon? Perhaps get access to the water to the east of the Tucson Basin in the Pantano Valley?)

1922

Louise Foucar Marshall develops a block of businesses in an area later known as Main Gate Square, across from the university's main entrance at Park and 3rd Street (now University Boulevard). It is Tucson's first suburban shopping center.

1922

The City of Tucson annexes the southern half of Olsen's Addition (Speedway to Drachman). East-west streets in the addition acquire their current names, north-south names remain what they were.

1922

The Ku Klux Klan makes an appearance in Tucson, with fliers claiming to promote "moral improvement." The KKK will apparently lose its purchase in Tucson by 1924. A KKK outbreak at this time in Phoenix is worse, with some cross burnings and violence.

1923

The first checkpoints are established by the Immigration Service on the border with Mexico. Until this time there had been no physical barriers to migration back and forth, although the Immigration Service (which was based in El Paso, Texas) had employed occasional mounted patrols. The principal concern had been the influx of Chinese trying to evade the Chinese Exclusion Act of 1882 (not repealed until 1943). With Prohibition in place since 1920 and the passage of the Emergency Quota Act of 1921, a need for greater border enforcement had been perceived. The Border Patrol will be established in 1924 and assigned the task of securing the border between inspection stations.

1923

The city extends city limits to include the remaining (north) part of Olsen's Addition. The city limits are now at Elm.

1923

North of what is now Prince Road and east of Tucson Boulevard, helped by his son Randall and best friend Frank Thibault, George Phar Legler begins construction of a venue called the Valley of the Moon on land he bought when he moved to Tucson in 1917. In 1932 he begins offering free Fairy Tours there to children and adults. In 2011, Valley of the Moon, now owned by the George Phar Legler Society and still run by volunteers who offer free tours on the first Saturday of the month, is placed in the National Register of Historic Places.

1923

The Steward Observatory opens on the UA campus, designed by Lyman and Roy Place. It has a telescope in a dome designed by Godfrey Sykes that has a 36-inch reflecting mirror, very large for the time. Before this, UA had been using a telescope with an 8-inch mirror that had been lent to A. E. Douglass and UA by Harvard University. Douglass, hired by UA in 1906, had promoted the Steward Observatory project for years. It had been made possible finally by a gift from Mrs. Lavinia Steward of Oracle, who died before it was completed. With archaeology and astronomy well established at UA, the university has in place two anchors it will rely on in efforts to emerge as a research university.

1923

Southwest of Tucson, the Missiondale subdivision and Drexel Road are recorded in Pima County, Drexel Road probably being named after Sister Katherine Drexel (see above: 1915). The Drexel Heights subdivision is now in this area south of the Tucson Mountains.

1923

Thamar Richey (b. 1858, d. 1937), who had taught Mohave children in Needles, California, asks the TUSD superintendent C. E. Rose for permission to build a school for the Yaqui children at Pascua Village. She teaches the Yaquis first in a shack constructed by the Indians of cardboard and tin and later in a small adobe building constructed by the district, remaining with the people of the village for the rest of her life.

1924

The big new Tucson High School Main Building (Lyman and Roy Place, architects) is completed south of 6th Street and southeast of the Roskruge Building. Roskruge becomes a junior high and elementary school, later a junior high only. Tucson High School is at this time still Tucson's only high school. Amphitheater School District had been founded in 1893 to the north in Pima County. Its high school will be the city's second when the area is later annexed.

1924

The University of Arizona awards its first PhD degree, to J. V. Gorm Loftfield, whose dissertation is entitled "Quantitative Studies on the Vegetation of the Grazing Ranges of Northern Arizona." In 2014, the UA will offer master's degrees in more than 170 fields and PhDs in 85, and will be awarding about 400 PhD degrees a year.

1924

North of Elm, Leighton Kramer completes his Rancho Santa Catalina, an 8,000-square-foot two-story home with 22 rooms and five baths and a roof of green Ludowici tiles. It is "easily the largest and most pretentious of Tucson's private residences," according to a reporter from the *Citizen* writing in 1925. Kramer also establishes the Arizona Polo Association of Tucson. In 1925, with other local boosters, he will found Tucson's Fiesta de los Vaqueros and Rodeo Parade, both still going in 2014.

1924

UA's polo team, after defeating strong teams at the Western Polo Championship in San Antonio, is the first UA team to compete in a national championship. In Fort Hamilton, New York, it loses its two matches with Princeton. UA's polo team had been organized in 1922 by Lieutenant Colonel Ralph M. Parker of the UA's Department of Military Service and Tactics. The first polo field at UA is southeast of Old Main between Vine and Cherry (the site of the current UA football stadium), with stables constructed at Cherry and 3rd Street. Polo is also played on Leighton Kramer's Catalina Field. With the strong support of Ina Gittings, director of physical education for women, Parker had also established women's equestrian classes.

1924

Captain Lowell H. Smith lands his Douglas World Cruiser, "the Chicago," at the Tucson Municipal Flying Field while completing his record-setting around the world flight, staying for only a few hours. Captain Smith reappears in Tucson's history 18 years later as the commander of Davis-Monthan Field. He dies in Tucson after a fall from a horse.

1924

The silent film *The Mine with the Iron Door* is filmed in Tucson and Oracle. It is based on a Harold Bell Wright novel of 1923 that is set in Tucson.

1924

Frank O'Rielly opens a Chevrolet car dealership in Tucson. His is the ninth dealership on North Sixth Avenue, Tucson's "Motor Car Row."

1924

Congress passes the Indian Citizenship Act, granting citizenship for the first time to Native Americans born in the US. Before this, Native Americans could be naturalized but would have to leave their tribe. Many non-naturalized Indians had fought in World War I.

1925

This is the first year of the Fiesta de los Vaqueros at the Kramer Ranch grounds (Catalina Field) and downtown. The Blackfoot painter Lone Wolf (d. 1965) draws the art for the first flier and rides in full Blackfoot regalia in this and later rodeo parades. A painting of his also is given the place of honor over the fireplace in Rancho Santa Catalina. In *Progressive Arizona* for 1925, Kramer writes that "La Fiesta de los

Vaqueros [is] a name destined to be as famous in the annals of the Sunshine City as the Mardi Gras of New Orleans, the Beauty Pageant of Atlantic City, or the Flower Show at Pasadena."

1925

The silent film *Ridin' Wild* is filmed in Tucson at Toole railroad depot and at "Santa Catalina Field" north of Kramer's Rancho Santa Catalina house. It tells the story of a young man who comes west on the train thinking he has contracted "the Con" (consumption, tuberculosis, the "White Plague") and disembarks in Tucson with no resources and no introductions. He nearly falls in with some bad guys, but doesn't. Having attracted the attention of a winsome lass, he trades the cloth cap he was wearing when he came to Tucson for a Stetson and quickly learns how to ride and rope, which doesn't seem to be that hard, or wasn't for him, anyway. The couple sees a poster advertising a rodeo that is a "contest," not a "wild West show"—the poster we see in the film is the actual poster for the first Fiesta de los Vaqueros—and the lass encourages him to enter, with the suggestion that if he wins something at the rodeo, he will also win her. We see the events taking place on a field that has the Catalina Mountains in the background. The hero wins, well, everything, including the girl. It even turns out that he doesn't have the Con after all.

1925

Arizona Highways *magazine begins publication, with a focus on scenic outdoor photography and travel in Arizona. "Auto camps" are appearing in the state, including the All Auto Camp on North*

Oracle Road at Jacinto in Tucson. In 2014, the Arizona Department of Transportation is still publishing Arizona Highways.

1925

The main streets on the UA campus are paved this year and the campus is connected to the city's water mains.

1925

Tucson Rapid Transit purchases the franchise from White Star Bus Line and enters the bus business, serving the north and east at 10 cents a ride. TRT establishes Tucson's first bus depot at Congress and Scott. Roy Laos is operating a second private bus line, started in 1924, that serves the south and west of Tucson.

1925

A local newspaper, the *Independent*, publishes UA salaries, claiming that the president makes $10,500 (about $150,000 in 2014), with seven faculty salaries averaging about $3,500 (a low of $1,900 to a high of $7,000 for a noted professor in Mines and Engineering) and three deans' salaries averaging $5,600.

1925

Randolph Park opens on a 480-acre parcel of land on East Broadway, deeded to the city this year by Willis Barnum on a long-term purchase agreement after Barnum and his wife had bought the land for a city park. Randolph Municipal Golf Course opens. It is named after railroad executive and prominent citizen Epes Randolph (b. Virginia 1856, d. Tucson 1921), who had become prominent back East in railroad construction and management. He came to Tucson in 1894 because of a lung condition and became superintendent of the Southern Pacific Railroad. At the time of his death in 1921 in his apartment in the Santa Rita Hotel, he was president or director of several regional railroads as well as chancellor of the Board of Regents of the UA and president of the Old Pueblo Club. Tucson's second Masonic lodge, named for him, had been founded in 1922.

1925

Roy Drachman (b. Tucson 1906, d. Tucson 2002) drops out of the UA because of the declining health of his father, Emanuel (d. 1933), and begins to manage the Rialto Theatre downtown.

1925

Near 5th Street and Craycroft Avenue, west of the Harold Bell Wright residence, Frank Craycroft builds an "imposing country home" of "Spanish architecture." Craycroft had come to Tucson in 1904 from Louisville, Kentucky, and in the mid-1920s was allegedly Arizona's only certified heating engineer. In 2014, the home is an office building.

1925

Davis-Monthan Municipal Airfield is established on 1,280 acres bought from the state as a refueling and service stop for U.S. Army airplanes. It is named after two Tucson natives and military aviators who had died earlier in air accidents.

1926

John E. White becomes mayor of Tucson, until 1929.

1926

The Indian House development begins with the purchase of 70 acres of land south of 5th street between Craycroft and Wilmot by eastern industrialist Charles Morgan Wood and his wife, artist Nan Wood, who employ a Santa Fe architect who favors Pueblo Revival architecture. In 1949, it is subdivided under a later owner, May Carr, and developed until 1950.

1926

Bear Down Gymnasium is completed at UA, the "finest facility in the Southwest" (Chanin 15), architect Roy Place. It gets its name from the words said to have been spoken to J. F. McKale by UA athlete and student body president John Byrd "Button" Salmon as a message to his football team while in the hospital after an automobile accident north of Tucson the day after the first game of the 1926 season, an accident from which Salmon later died. In 1990, the building was put on the National Register of Historic Places.

1926

Federal highway investment leads to the construction of US 80, coming from the east through Douglas, Bisbee, and Benson, and US 89, which comes up from Nogales and the border with Mexico, along the course of the Santa Cruz River. The highways join south of Tucson, and US 80 runs

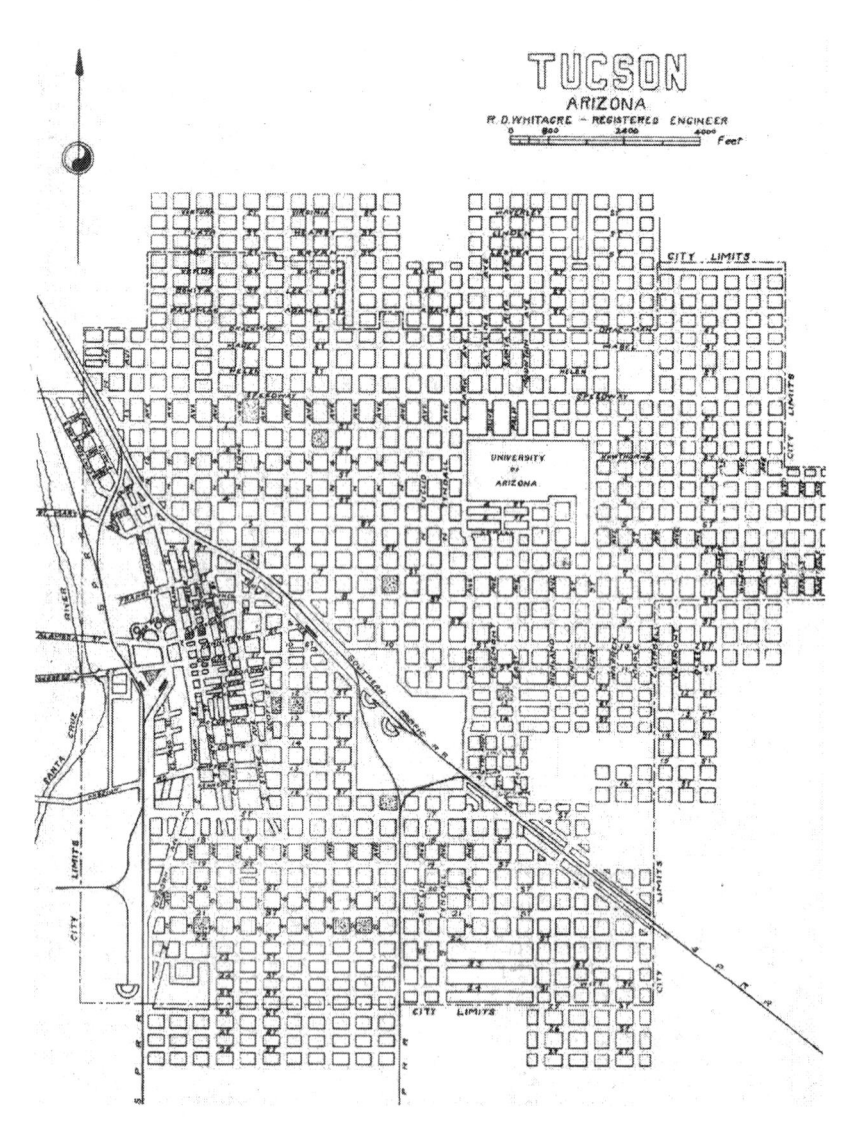

1926 City of Tucson street map. This official city map, though scaled, still focuses on blocks rather than on the lines of roads. As cars become more common, city and county maps come to focus primarily on roads rather than buildings or blocks.

north through town toward Oracle, Florence, and Phoenix. Just north of Grant Road, US 84 begins, a road that turns west off Oracle Road toward Casa Grande, where one route continues west toward Gila Bend, Yuma, and San Diego and another goes north to Phoenix and Los Angeles. The road that turns west off Oracle Road is soon crowded with colorful motels and roadside businesses and becomes known as the Miracle Mile. It is the area's first divided highway.

1927

Ford's Model A car is introduced, replacing the Model T that had first been manufactured in 1908. The Model A will be manufactured until 1931.

1927

The first traffic light is installed in Tucson, at Congress and Sixth Avenue. For the last year, an officer had been placed at this intersection to direct traffic.

1927

Sam Hughes Elementary School is completed in the University Manor development east of Campbell, Roy Place architect (b. San Diego 1887, arrives Tucson 1916, d. Tucson 1950), in the Mission Revival style. Place designs many of the Tucson School District and UA buildings that go up in 1920s and 1930s.

1927

John Murphey, owner of a construction company he started in 1918, has by now built some 200 homes in Tucson. This year the Swiss architect Josias Joesler comes to Tucson and begins to design houses for Murphey in Murphey's Old World Addition (north of Speedway between Mabel and Elm, Campbell and Martin, razed in the 1970s to clear land for UA's medical school). Since 1920 Murphey has been living in a house he built in the 2000 block of Speedway that he and his family will occupy until 1961 (later the Ronald McDonald House).

1927

Just west of the Armory Park area, the elegant Temple of Music and Art performance venue is completed. Harold Bell Wright is a substantial contributor and many other citizens support the project.

1927

UA's major new library building is dedicated, located just inside the western boundary of the campus, with former UA president von KleinSmid speaking at the ceremony. It replaces the first library that since 1905 had been in what is now the Douglass Building. In 1925, the College of Law had moved into that first library building where it will remain for the next 30 years. In 1977, the new library will become the Arizona State Museum building. Designed by Lyman and Roy Place, it will be listed in the National Register of Historic Places in 1979.

1927

UA's "Old Main" acquires that name this year, having been called "University Hall" since 1901, during which time it had provided rooms for faculty and male students, a dining area, and the library.

1927

The Tucson School District purchases a "special" bus from O'Rielly Motors, the Chevrolet dealer, to collect the students who have long distances to travel to school. The bus, which could carry 30 students and sold for $3,675, "was a tall, ungainly vehicle concocted from a GM body and other parts," according to recollections of old-timers.

1927

The municipal airport moves from its site on South Sixth Avenue (in 2014, the Rodeo Grounds) to the current site of Davis-Monthan. Charles Lindbergh flies into town on September 23 for the dedication of Davis-Monthan Field, the largest municipal airport in the U.S. The first military presence at the field begins soon after its dedication when Sergeant Dewey Simpson relocates his refueling/service operations to the new municipal airport, bringing with him a logbook in which he has recorded the comings and goings of the earlier field's many customers. Included within its pages are names such as Foulois, Lindbergh, Earhart, and James H. Doolittle, later to be awarded a Medal of Honor for the raid he will lead on Tokyo during World War II that used bombers that would have to try to land in China after launching from aircraft carriers. Doolittle was the first official military customer at the field. For the dedication, florist Hal Burns constructs the "Spirit of Tucson," a replica of Lindbergh's "Spirit of St. Louis," that is made out of cactus pads.

1927

Reverend Beal and the First Baptist Church at Sixth Avenue and 5th Street sponsor lectures this fall promoting creationism and attacking evolutionary theory. The *Arizona Daily Star* writes editorials defending the scientific point of view. Letters to the editor take both sides.

1927

At Broadway and Craycroft, out east far from town, the Williams Addition is platted. Its developer will have serious troubles.

1928

Carlos Jácome opens Jácome's Department Store.

1928

Standard Airlines (later to be absorbed by American Airlines), which owned the first building on Davis-Monthan Field, begins a regular schedule of flights to and from Tucson.

1928

The Veteran's Hospital opens south of downtown, built on 116 acres donated by Albert Steinfeld, in the Spanish Colonial Revival/Mission Revival style, and designed by architect Roy Place. The hospital replaces the Pastime Park facility on North Oracle and is one of the second generation of "national homes" for veterans being built across the country. In 2012 an application is filed to list the structure in the National Register of Historic Places.

1928

East of Country Club and south of Broadway, Colonia Solana is founded by John Murphey (110 homes on 158 acres developed over the next 40 years, landscape architect Stephen Child, four Joesler homes). On the north side of the development just south of Broadway, a 50,000-gallon water tower is built to serve the development. In 1932, it will be encased in a handsome Spanish Colonial building designed by architect Roy Place. In 1944, the tower is bought by the city and retired from service. Over the years it narrowly escapes destruction but in 1980 is placed on the National Register of Historic Places.

1928

East of Country Club and north of Broadway, El Encanto is also founded by John Murphey, also with curved streets inspired by the "city beautiful" (and anti-automobile) movement. M. L. Starkweather is supervising architect. Pueblo Revival style is not permitted in the development. Streets in this development and in Colonia Solana depart from the grid pattern that had been standard in earlier developments.

1928

The city annexes the area east of Alvernon and west of Wilmot between Speedway on the north and Irvington Road on the south, including the current site of Davis-Monthan Air Force Base. No schools have been built yet in this area.

1928

Frank Boice and partners buy the Vail Empire Ranch southeast of Tucson to continue to be a cattle operation. Boice acquires sole control in 1951.

1928

Downstream on the Santa Cruz at the end of Roger Road, Tucson's first sewage treatment plant is constructed to remove solids from the waste stream.

1928 November

The federal government issues a patent to the city for Sentinel Peak to be used as a park. A local couple, James and Christine Dodson, had filed timber and stone claims on the peak and the city had appealed to the Department of the Interior, which decided in its favor in 1927. A road to the top of Sentinel Peak will be completed in the early 1930s (Menlo Park Historical District application).

1928 November 22

On Broadway near the new developments of Colonia Solana and El Encanto, on the site of what had earlier been a tuberculosis sanatorium, the El Conquistador Hotel opens (Henry Jaastad, architect) after a big civic promotion involving Leighton Kramer, Levi Manning, and other rodeo and Sunshine Climate Club people, meant to help answer the recognized need for hotel rooms in Tucson.

1928

At the vacated site of the Presbyterian Church at 138 Scott Street in downtown Tucson, Isabella Greenway is now operating the Arizona Hut where disabled veterans make furniture and other domestic products for sale. The furniture is sold to the best department stores of the day, Marshall Field's in Chicago, Abercrombie and Fitch in New York, and others. Greenway builds a house for herself this year at the north end of Olsen's Addition.

1929

John Calhoun Phillips, a Republican, replaces George Hunt, a Democrat, until 1931, when Hunt resumes the Arizona governorship.

1929

W. A. Julian becomes mayor of Tucson, until 1931. Rincon Road becomes Second Avenue.

1929

Half of public school students are Mexican-American but only 5 percent of teachers are. The total enrollment is 6,119 children: 2,929 "Mexican," 2,898 "American," 100 "Negroes," 192 "others."

1929

In the Catalina Foothills, John Murphey builds what will be the elite Hacienda del Sol School for Girls, fifth grade through high school. At the beginning of World War II, the school closes. Afterward it reopens as a guest ranch. In 2014, it is a high-end resort and restaurant with historic photographs very much in evidence.

1929

UA president Homer Shantz directs removal of UA's large cactus garden from the west to the east side of Old Main. The garden, with over 600 species of cacti and succulents, had been planted west of Old Main by UA's first professor of botany and entomology, J. W. Toumey. Boojums, native to Baja California, will be brought to Tucson and installed in the relocated garden in 1932. In 1952 the garden will be vandalized and three big saguaros destroyed. In 2014, what remains is the much smaller Joseph Wood Krutch Garden in the Mall which contains two boojums and a collection of other Sonoran desert plants.

1929 June 22

On this day, it becomes possible for the first time to date prehistoric ruins with precision. While working at Lowell Observatory in Flagstaff before coming to UA, Professor A. E. Douglass had begun to develop the science of dendrochronology, or tree-ring dating, as a way of dating sun-spot cycles. Eventually he assembled a tree-ring chronology that went back to AD 1260. On this date, UA archaeologist Emil Haury and Lyndon Hargrave of the Museum of Northern Arizona have found a piece of charcoal in Show Low, Arizona, that bridges the gap between that date and the record given by older samples. This would be the only way to date archaeological sites until the development of radiocarbon dating.

1929

Charles A. Belin, related to the DuPont family of Delaware, had moved to Tucson after World War I, seeking a cure for his tuberculosis. The Belins' first home was built about 1927 at what is now 5045 E. Grant and sold not long afterwards to Hubert and Helen (Congdon) d'Autremont who had come to Tucson from Duluth because of one of their children's respiratory problems. Belin's second Tucson home, a Spanish Colonial Revival-style mansion, is built around this time on a half-section parcel south of the Harold Bell Wright residence and east of Wilmot Road. Decades later the Belin House will be sold to the Sisters of St. Joseph of Carondolet to become the new home of St. Joseph's Academy for Girls. It later became Villa Campana, a nursing home. Also this year, eastern industrialist Bill Woodin Sr. comes to Tucson. On the east side of Wilmot north of Speedway, he builds

"Desert House" which later becomes Pioneer East and the Monaco before being razed. El Dorado Hospital is now on this site.

1929

The Pioneer Hotel opens (owned by Albert Steinfeld; Roy Place, architect). Albert Steinfeld's son Harold moves into the penthouse. Other hotels in Tucson are now being upgraded: the Santa Rita, Congress, Palomar, and, on Fourth Avenue north of the underpass, the Coronado. To the south and east, the 85-room, four-story Presidio Hotel opens this year on East Broadway between South 4th and 5th Avenues. It will survive the Depression but be demolished by October 1989. Its lot remains vacant in 2014.

1929

The Consolidated National Bank Building, the first skyscraper in Tucson (10 floors), is completed downtown on land purchased from Levi Manning in 1901. An earlier Consolidated Bank building on the site designed by Henry Charles Trost had been demolished. The new building is designed by Percy A. Eisen (b. 1885, d. 1946) and Albert R. Walker (b. 1881, d. 1958). In 1935, it becomes the Valley National Bank Building. In 2014 it is the Chase Bank building.

1929

Lieutenant Colonel John Arthur Magee homesteads 640 acres on Tucson's northwest side.

1929

A new Pima County Courthouse is completed (architect Roy Place) on the east end of the site of the old Presidio San Agustín. The building still exists and is now in the National Register of Historic Places.

1929

The Tucson office of M. M. Sundt Construction Company opens, run by John Sundt, a son of the founder. Its first building is the First United Methodist Church, west of the UA campus. The company will go on to build many structures in and around Tucson, among them the Stone Avenue underpass; Randolph Park; the Pond mansion; aviation facilities at Davis-Monthan, Tucson Municipal and Ryan airfields; the Tucson Community Center; Loews Ventana Canyon Hotel; and many buildings for the Tucson School District, the University of Arizona, and Pima Community College. (Beginning in 1942, the firm will build, in the Jemez Mountains of New Mexico, the facilities for the Scientific Division of the Manhattan Project, and in 1957 will begin to build underground missile silos for U.S. ICBMs and launching pads for the Apollo rockets.)

1929

The author's parents, Hal Warnock and Mary Louise "Bunny" Phelps, begin to attend UA and in their first semester meet in an insurance class in the basement of Old Main. Bunny begins the semester living in one of the first houses built in El Encanto. The crash of the stock market

The third Pima County Courthouse, built on the site of the previous one, which had been demolished a year earlier, opened in 1929. It was designed by the architect Roy Place in the Spanish Colonial Revival style, with (controversial) pink walls and a striking mosaic dome. Place also designs many of the buildings at the University of Arizona from this era, almost all still in use at the University. The courthouse, which served as a courthouse for 46 years, still exists and is now on the National Register of Historic Places. This photograph, taken in 1934, is of the east side of the courthouse. Presidio Park, on the site of land that had been enclosed within the Presidio San Agustín, now lies to the west of the building.

this year will wipe out her father, and in fall 1930, she will be living with a relative in El Paso, without enough money to return to UA. Friends coming through El Paso with a space in their car will give her a ride back to Tucson and she will get a job as treasurer of her sorority, Kappa Kappa Gamma, which will enable her to continue at UA. Eventually she will receive an MA in psychology from UA. Hal's economic circumstances, already straitened, are less affected by the crash. He will play baseball for J. F. McKale (being chosen later by McKale for his all-time team) and basketball for Fred Enke and will attend UA's law school on the 3-3 plan.

1929

West of downtown, Tucson Mountain Park is established by Pima County (about 20,000 acres), with the Pima County Park Commission established to oversee it.

1929

At UA, a new football field is constructed on the site of what had been the polo field. The first football field, located west of Highland behind the Agriculture building, is dedicated to women's sports. Roy Place designs the west stands of the new field, still to be seen under the vast superstructure later built above it. A new polo field is constructed north of Speedway between Cherry and Warren (on land later to be occupied by University Medical Center). South of the new polo field is UA's poultry farm. At the northeast corner of the polo field, new stables for the ROTC's 92 cavalry horses are constructed in 1936. The old stables, constructed in 1920, had been just north of the old field.

1929

On Speedway west of the Southern Pacific tracks and the Santa Cruz River, El Rio Golf Club is founded by Hi Corbett, George Stonecypher, Don Fogg, and Doug Leech, a Canadian who wintered in Tucson—Tucson's first golf course with grass. The course is popular with golfers. A residential development is associated with it but sells only a few homesites.

1929

Using the new technology that allows sound to be recorded with film, out-of-town journalists Charles and Lucile Herbert begin making documentary films for Fox Movietone that are set in Arizona. Locally, they feature the San Xavier Mission Church and the saguaro cactus at the Desert Laboratory on Tumamoc Hill. Other subjects are the Grand Canyon and, to the south, a cattle drive. The Herberts, who have been globe-trotting journalists, will move to Tucson in 1939–40, establish Western Ways films, and for another fifteen years produce nonfictional and fictional footage that represents the cultures and landscapes of the Arizona-Sonora borderlands.

1929

By the end of the 1920s, Tucson is the nation's center of dude ranching, which flourishes through the 1930s (16 ranches near Tucson, seven around Phoenix) and continues into the 1960s. One of these is a ranch to the north on Ina Road that is the precursor of Westward Look. Another, in northeast Tucson in the Catalina Foothills at the mouth of

Ventana Canyon, is the Flying V (owned by Lynn and Patsy Gillham from the early 1900s, a guest ranch after 1927, and in 2014 a golf course development). Along Sabino Creek is the Double U Guest Ranch (earlier the site of the Gonzales-De-Baud Ranch), and another east along Tanque Verde Creek is the Tanque Verde Ranch (originally the La Cebadilla Ranch of Emilio Carrillo, owned now by the Converse family).

1929

Since 1920, 71 new subdivisions have been platted in Tucson.

1930

According to the City Directory, compiled by Houston L. Walsh of Tucson:

- The automobile makes now being offered for sale at 14 dealerships include, among others, Studebaker, Pontiac, Hupmobile, Auburn, Pierce Arrow, Hudson, Essex, Marquette, Chrysler, Cadillac, and La Salle.
- Seventeen "Auto Camps" are advertised on North Oracle Road and on South 6th Street.
- Most grocers are listed under the names of individuals, many Chinese. A Piggly Wiggly makes an appearance. Piggly Wiggly, the first ever self-service grocery store, had been founded in 1916 in Memphis by Clarence Saunders.
- The three bottling works in town: Nehi, Purity, and Tucson Bottling.

- The five department stores in town now are Steinfeld's, Baker Dollar Store, Jácome's, J. C. Penny, and the White House.

- There are 47 listings for lawyers and 52 for physicians.

- Isabella Greenway's Arizona Hut is offering for sale "Pocket Books, Bill Folds, Hand Bags, Book Covers, Furniture, Wooden Toys, Copper, Novelties, Cactus Canes, Candy Boxes" that are made by disabled veterans.

- A great many insurance companies have appeared under the headings "Accident," "Automobile," "Bonding," "Burglary," "Casualty," "Employers Liability," "Fire," "Life," "Marine," "Plate Glass," "Tornado," and "Tourist."

- Eighteen labor unions are listed. Among the "clubs" listed is "Kuo Min Tang," the Chinese Nationalist Party. The Ying On Club, a community center for Chinese, has existed in the Barrio Viejo since the 19th century.

- Tucson is said to have four golf courses, two polo fields, and eight city parks.

- Fourteen restaurants are listed.

- Prohibition had begun in the United States in 1920 when the Eighteenth Amendment to the U.S. Constitution came into effect: no listings appear for taverns or sales of liquor and beer.

1930

The City of Tucson now covers 7.15 square miles, up from 5.75 in 1920, with a population of 32,506, up from 20,337 in 1920 (the 1930 City Directory claims 46,500, with 3,000 outside city limits).

- Tucson's black population is 1,003, up from 346 in 1920.

- Mexican-Americans go from 7,489 in 1920 to 11,000 in 1930, now 30 percent of Tucson's population: Mexicans 75 percent blue collar, Anglos 96.5 percent white collar. There is a drop in the number of businesses owned by Mexican-Americans, from 132 in 1920 to 108, despite the increase in population.

- South of downtown, Barrio Libre (aka El Convento, Calle Meyer, the Strip) has been primarily a Mexican neighborhood since the first days of the territory. Two smaller barrios lie west of it: El Hoyo and Membrillo. On the other side of the Santa Cruz, east of Mission Lane and south of Congress, are Barrio sin Nombre (east of Grande) and Kroeger Lane.

- Running along the Southern Pacific tracks northwest of downtown, Barrio Anita is somewhat more mixed. East of Barrio Anita extending to Stone is the Dunbar/Spring Neighborhood, mixed but with a higher concentration of African-Americans and few Anglos.

- West of the Santa Cruz River and north of Congress is Menlo Park, at first legally restricted to "caucasians" but becoming mixed. South of Congress is

Menlo Park South, which had been platted later without racial restrictions.

- New ethnically concentrated neighborhoods—other than the ones to the east and north of downtown in which Anglos predominate—have begun to emerge:
  - To the south, Millville (between Park/Cherry and Fremont/22nd and the Southern Pacific tracks), with African-Americans concentrated west of Fremont in a region called South Park.
  - Two other tracts are:
    - National City, south of downtown from the intersection of South Sixth Avenue and Indian School/Ajo Way, started in the 1930s with Anglos in mind, still mostly Anglo in 1940, then mostly Mexican-American.
    - Riverside Park/Barrio Hollywood, west of the Santa Cruz to Speedway in the north, mostly Mexican-American from its start in the 1920s. This barrio is south and east of the area north of West Speedway that in the 1930s will become El Rio Country Club.
  - East of Main and north of Speedway, Anglos predominate, with one small concentration of African-Americans east of Stone between Grant and Speedway (known to African-Americans as "Sugar Hill").

1930

Seventeen schools are listed in the City Directory (seven more than in 1920) with a peak enrollment in the high school of 1,481 (an increase of 943) and an enrollment of 7,001 in the elementary schools (an increase of 3,419).

1930

UA's enrollment is 2,164 (an increase of 993 from 1920) with 182 faculty (up 87) and 24 buildings (up 3).

1930

UA's polo team again competes for the national championship, beating Army 11-4 but losing this time to Yale, 11-3.

1930

William R. Mathews assumes control of the *Arizona Daily Star*, which he will run for the next 35 years. In 1940, a joint operating agreement with the *Tucson Daily Citizen* creates Tucson Newspapers, Inc.

1930

Rose Sosnowsky Silver (b. Vienna) becomes the first woman and graduate of the UA law school to practice law in Tucson when she partners with John L. Buskirk. In 1934, John Dillinger will hire her to represent him in a civil matter after his arrest that year. She will end up with his blue Packard and its numerous concealed weapons, of which she will be unaware for two years. In 1970, she will be appointed Pima County Attorney by the Board of Supervisors, the first woman to hold that position. The mother of five children, she will live until 1994.

1930

Louise Foucar Marshall, the first woman professor at UA, now a well-established property owner and businessperson in Tucson, establishes the Marshall Charitable Foundation with the aim of creating a permanent scholarship fund for students attending the UA.

1930

On the north side of Sentinel Hill, a quarry for volcanic stone (*malpais* in Spanish, sometimes called "malpai" or "malapai" by Anglos), in operation since the 18th century, is shut down. The rock was used in many structures at UA, including the walls at the west end of the campus, and in homes in Menlo Park. On the north flank of the hill, the quarry is still clearly visible.

1930

On a half section east of Tucson on Wilmot, just north of the Harold Bell Wright place, south of Bill Woodin's "Desert House," construction begins on Florence Pond's mansion ("Stone Ashley"), 17 rooms on 318 acres, 20 landscaped, the rest desert. Florence Pond was descended from the man who developed Pond cosmetic creams.

1930

Since 1920, 85 additions have been platted including, to the east and north of downtown, Barnes Old World, El Encanto Estates, Colonia Solana, University Heights, Jefferson Park, several "Speedway" additions, several "Catalina" additions, Blenman, several "Country Club" Additions, Himmel, Pastime Acres, Richland Heights, Vista del Monte, Amphitheater Acres, and Wetmore; and, to the south and west, South Menlo Park, Elysian Grove, Pasqua, Missiondale, Government Heights, and Randolph.

1930

In 1928, at a federal land auction, John Murphey had bought 7,000 acres north of River Road between Oracle and Sabino Canyon Roads. This year he plats the "Catalina Foothills Estates" subdivision on the land, at one square mile the largest restricted subdivision yet attempted in Tucson. There has been no building yet between Leighton Kramer's Rancho Santa Catalina on Elm Street and the Catalina Foothills, though some streets have been lined out. Catalina Foothills Estates No. 2 will not be subdivided until 1947. Murphey dies in 1977 but by the end of the 1980s, homes are being built in Catalina Foothills Estates No. 10. High-end development continues in the Foothills today. The area is no longer strictly residential. Though annexation of the area has been discussed, it is still not included in the city limits.

1930

East of El Conquistador Hotel on Broadway, the El Montevideo Neighborhood is platted. Not much will happen there for a decade, but after World War II, it will fill in rapidly.

1930

At Congress and Stone, the Fox Theatre is completed (adding to the Plaza, Rialto, State, and Lyric theaters downtown, the last a Spanish-language theater).

1930

The 6th Avenue underpass is constructed by the Southern Pacific.

1930 October 15

The first cross-country airmail-and-passenger flight, performed by American Airways, passes through Tucson eastbound. It had departed that morning from Burbank, landing in Quartzite, Phoenix, Tucson, and Douglas in Arizona, before departing the next day for Dallas and Atlanta. Western Air Express had regular passenger flights along this route by this time. Navigation was still by landmarks, roads, and railroad tracks. By 1934, most airlines were able to fly by instrument, though not always reliably.

1930 December 18

At Olsen and Elm, across from Leighton Kramer's 200-acre Rancho Santa Catalina, the Arizona Inn (first phase, architect Merritt Starkweather, landscape architect James Oliphant) is opened by Isabella Greenway on 14 acres, adjoining the home she had built at the site two years earlier. The inn is to be open half the year, from November to May.

1930

Groundwater pumping begins to predominate in the San Rafael Valley, at the headwaters of the Santa Cruz.

1930

The Gila Pueblo Archaeological Foundation had been established in 1928 by New York financier Harold S. Gladwin. Emil Haury now becomes its assistant director. This year ushers in the "seven years that reshaped Southwest prehistory," which will produce, among other things, the first good account of the Hohokam culture. This period will also see the establishment of the Museum of Northern Arizona in Flagstaff, the Amerind Foundation in Dragoon, and the Heard Museum in Phoenix.

1930

In the U.S., the death rate from tuberculosis reaches an all-time low of 50 in 100,000. In 1943, with the discovery of streptomycin, the rate will drop to 10 in 100,000. Tucson loses thereby its attractiveness to wealthy and not-so-wealthy sufferers from the disease, though it retains its reputation as a healthy outdoor area.

1930s early

Scattered subdivisions are now in place east on Speedway out to Alvernon and beyond. On Broadway and on Grant, not much is happening yet.

1930s

Anti-Chinese sentiment rises during the Depression. The Chinese Exclusion Act, passed by Congress in 1882, the first law to prevent a specific ethnic group from immigrating to the United States, is still in force and will not be repealed until 1943. At the end of World War II, Tucson will have 2,000 to 3,000 Chinese residents.

1930s

South of Orange Grove Road, Leonie Boutall, a health seeker from Tennessee, builds a luxury guest ranch called Rancho Nezhone that attracts a number of celebrities. She sells out in 1948.

1930s

In the lower Santa Cruz Basin, downriver from where the Rillito enters the Santa Cruz, over 98,000 acres of new farmland are now in operation, growing cotton, wheat, barley, alfalfa, and pecans, all irrigated by pumped groundwater, while south of the Rillito to the Mexican border (middle and upper Santa Cruz Basins), 22,000 acres are being irrigated. In the early 1900s, the Tucson Farms Company had attempted to farm the lower Santa Cruz Basin, then desolate, by constructing dams, levees, catchbasins, canals, and a large reservoir to catch seasonal runoff. The rate of evaporation in the reservoir had proved a serious problem. Floods in 1914 and 1915 had destroyed a diversion dam and altered the course of the river, moving it to the west. With the advent of groundwater pumping, however, agriculture began to develop in this region. During World War II, it takes off. In 1952, pumping approaches 10 million acre-feet a year. The water table has begun to fall. In places, the land subsides.

1931

George K. Smith becomes mayor of Tucson, until 1933.

1931

Tucson Rapid Transit's electric streetcars have now been replaced by gasoline-powered buses. In 1951, these begin to be replaced by diesel-powered buses.

1931

Jacob Levy's sons Leon and Aaron convince their father to buy a dry goods store in Tucson and go into business as Levy's of Tucson. Jacob (wife Mamie) and his brother Ben had operated Levy Brothers in Douglas from 1903 and done business with Pancho Villa.

1931

Louise Foucar Marshall, who in 1901 had become the first woman UA faculty member, shoots her husband, Thomas, five times, suspecting that he and their ex-housekeeper are having an affair and are poisoning her. He survives, but three weeks later, dies of an infection and she is charged with first-degree murder. In a trial that is moved to Nogales, defended by local lawyers James Boyle and George Darnell, she offers the defense of temporary insanity. After a long trial, the jury deliberates for half an hour and acquits her. She returns to developing her properties in Tucson and building the Marshall Foundation. When she dies in 1956 at the age of 92, the holdings of the Marshall Foundation are worth more than $900,000. Currently, the foundation has offices on University Boulevard, is receiving income from 76 commercial and retail tenants, and donates $1 million to scholarships and other charitable and educational causes in Tucson.

1931

Cele Peterson (b. Florida 1909, moved to Bisbee 1912, later to Tucson, d. 2010) opens a store at Stone and Pennington, selling upscale women's clothes. As downtown declines, she will outlast many other retailers and remain in the business (and deeply involved in supporting the community) for more than 75 years, dying in 2010 at 101 years old.

1931

The Southern Pacific opens the handsome new tubercular sanatorium it had constructed for its workers next to the old El Paso and Southwestern Railroad terminal downtown, with 100 beds and a separate "Negro ward." In 1946, it will become a general hospital for employees, be opened to the Tucson community in 1964, and named for U.S. Senator Carl Hayden in 1967.

1932

The rodeo of the Fiesta de los Vaqueros moves from Kramer Field to the abandoned municipal airport grounds on South Sixth Avenue. Fiesta founder Leighton Kramer had died of tuberculosis in 1930 but through the 1930s, the fiesta continues to increase in size and significance. The fiesta is still mounted in February, the schools still close for two days, and the Tucson Rodeo is one of the top 25 professional rodeo events in North America.

1932

The state of Arizona eliminates funding for kindergarten.

1932

Carlos Jácome dies. His department store is taken over by his six sons.

1932

In the 1920s, Maurice Reid, a health seeker who had arrived in Tucson in 1923, had planted Tucson's first citrus orchard north of Tucson and east of Oracle Road near where the Rillito and the Cañada del Oro join the Santa Cruz. He planted his trees above the streambed where he had realized the trees would not have to survive frost. He now records the Ranchos Palos Verdes subdivision in the area and is responsible for naming Orange Grove Road. By 1935, he is shipping produce all over the country. In 1947, he sells the citrus operation to Desert Treasures but continues in real estate in Tucson. His son Gene Reid becomes the first director of Tucson Parks, with Randolph Park being renamed for him.

1932

A real-estate investor from Kansas City, Barney Goodman, purchases and remodels the Santa Rita Hotel. It becomes a cattleman's hotel, hosting livestock auctions. The town's social spots are the Pioneer Hotel and the Blue Moon.

1932

Around Tumacácori, Talbot T. "Tol" Pendleton, an easterner and Princeton graduate who had made money in Texas oil, forms the large (over 90,000 acres) Baca Float Ranch from properties bought from three stressed investors who had been trying without success for a number of years and in various ways to make the land pay. For the next three decades, Pendleton will do some cattle ranching there, but this ranch, unlike Levi Manning's Canoa Ranch just north of it, will be primarily a cowboying resort for wealthy corporate executives and movie stars like Stewart Granger and John Wayne, with the well-lubricated social activities ranging up and down the Santa Cruz Valley from the Cavern bar and restaurant in Nogales, Sonora, to the Arizona Inn and Mountain Oyster Club in the Santa Rita Hotel Tucson. From time to time, Pendleton will sell off property to make ends meet. Some homesteaders, many of them Mexican-American, remain in the area but their numbers are dwindling.

1933–1937

Benjamin Baker Moeur, a Democrat, becomes governor of Arizona, replacing George Hunt, also a Democrat, after Hunt's sixth and last term in the office.

1933

Henry O. Jaastad becomes mayor of Tucson, until 1947.

1933

The State Bar of Arizona is created by the legislature as a mandatory membership organization. At this time 654 attorneys and 22 judges are working in the state and only 175 belong to the voluntary Arizona Bar Association. UA's College of Law had been established in 1925. The author's father entered law school there in 1931. In 1948, 1,000 lawyers will be licensed in Arizona, in 1983 more than 7,000, and in 2014 17,600.

1933

Natural gas arrives in Tucson from Texas, to great fanfare.

1933

As development approaches from the west, Harold Bell Wright leaves Tucson and his large house at Wilmot and Speedway for California (d. 1944 near Escondido).

1933

Construction begins on a highway to the top of the Catalina Mountains along its south face. To supply labor, a prison camp is constructed near the bottom of the mountain that during World War II will be used as a Japanese internment camp, with internees also working on the highway. In 1973, the camp will become the first home of what becomes Intermountain Centers for Human Development, a behavioral health facility for adjudicated Native American youth.

1933

Saguaro National Monument (Saguaro National Park after 1994) is created by President Herbert Hoover, with one district west of Tucson in the Tucson Mountains and another district east of Tucson in the foothills of the Rincon Mountains. UA president Homer Shantz, a well-known botanist, had persuaded the UA to acquire the land close to the Rincons to support botanical study.

1933

North of River Road and south of Orange Grove on Camino de la Tierra, Green Fields boarding school is founded by Howard and Rubie Atchley. In 2014, the school is still in operation, claiming to be "Arizona's oldest independent school" with a goal of blending "East Coast academic traditions with Western outdoor ranch life."

1933

Roy Drachman begins to manage the Fox Theatre downtown. Among many other promotions, the venue will go on to feature the Mickey Mouse Club on Saturday mornings.

1933

The Twenty-First Amendment to the U.S. Constitution is ratified, repealing Prohibition. An increase in the number of automobile accidents is observed.

1934

Tucson is feeling the full effects of the Depression. Steinfeld's misses a payroll.

1934

Walter Bopp (b. Switzerland c. 1902, d. Tucson 1980), the salad chef at the Pioneer Hotel, and his wife, Mae, open Bopp Health Food Store on South Sixth Avenue near Broadway, the first of its kind in Tucson. The shop sells items such as teas, grains, herbs, oils, and supplements.

1934

The Civilian Conservation Corps builds the infrastructure for Colossal Cave Mountain Park southeast of Tucson. Colossal Cave had been discovered in 1879 by Solomon Lick, the owner of a nearby hotel, but earlier had been used by Indians from the Hohokam onward. Lick mined the cave for guano, abandoning it at the beginning of the 1900s. In the valley below the cave's entrance lies La Posta Quemada Ranch, formerly the Mountain Springs Ranch, which got its name from a stagecoach station there that burned in the 1870s.

1934

UA president Homer Shantz manages to get Works Progress Administration money and state legislative support for a building program at UA. He also supports reorganization of the university into schools, colleges, and departments that look much more like those currently in place.

1934–1935

Under the auspices of the Gila Pueblo Foundation, Emil Haury directs an excavation of the major Hohokam site of Snaketown on the Gila River 30 miles southeast of Phoenix. His report will be published in 1937. Haury will return to the site in 1964 for major additional work under the auspices of the National Science Foundation. In 1972 the site will be declared a National Monument, though in 2014 it is not open to the public. In the 1920s and 1930s, New Mexico and Arizona are sites of intense archaeological research and development. UA's Department of Anthropology, led by Byron Cummings and Haury, becomes a leader in the field of Southwest archaeology.

1935

In Vail, at the southwestern end of the Rincon Mountains, the Shrine of Santa Rita is dedicated to the Takamine family by Charlie and Caroline Beech. Caroline had been married to Jokichi Takamine, a Japanese national (b. 1854, d. 1922) who had come to the U.S. in 1887 and in 1900 isolated and purified adrenaline, the first hormone to be isolated in pure form.

1935

Albert Steinfeld dies at 81 (children Harold, Viola, Irene). Son Harold takes over the business. Two years later, Albert's uncle and estranged business partner, Louis Zeckendorf, will die in New York City, at 99.

1935

Thirty-one miles of road have been paved in Tucson.

1930s middle

At UA, a lily pond is installed on the lawn of the President's House next to Park Avenue. The President's House is later torn down to make room for Gila Hall. In 2014, the pond remains.

1935

The "swamp cooler," the first form of "air conditioning," makes its appearance in Tucson. Water is dripped into pads on four sides of a box and a fan inside the box draws air through the moist pads and pushes it into the area to be cooled. When the humidity rises, as it does in July and August during Tucson's rainy season, the coolers work less well.

1935

Bill Woodin's "Desert House" on Wilmot is sold by the family (as Woodin remembers it). His mother then marries Melville Haskell, owner of the Rincon Ranch southeast of Tucson (now called the Rocking K—"what's left of it," says Woodin) as well as the Rincon Stock Farm on Fort Lowell Road, where Haskell raises quarter horses.

1935

For the first time, UA awards a PhD degree to a woman. The recipient is Florence Van Bibber, whose dissertation is entitled "Theories of Learning and Their Educational Implications." In 1916, UA had awarded an MA degree to a woman, Elizabeth Murphey, whose thesis was entitled "The Oregon Boundary Line." In 1934, it had awarded a master's degree to the woman who would become the author's mother, Mary Louise Phelps, whose thesis in psychology was entitled "The Effect of Steadiness Testing on the Variability of Respiration." Two of UA's first three BA recipients had been women, one a Mexican-American.

1935

The federal Public Works Administration provides funds for eight buildings at UA. Most are designed by Roy Place and are now in the National Register of Historic Places.

1936

Himmel Park is constructed in the Sam Hughes Neighborhood with assistance from the Works Progress Administration. It includes a public pool and ball fields.

1936

On Tucson's south side, the South Lawn Cemetery is established at 5400 South Park, on the site of an older burial ground. After 2007, this cemetery will be called Funeraria del Angel South Lawn, now part of the Dignity Memorial network.

1936

For years, Monte Mansfield has been promoting an underpass out of downtown north on Stone Avenue. It opens this year, constructed by the Southern Pacific Railroad..

1936

River Road, unpaved, is now in place north of the Rillito from Oracle Road to Swan. Along with Campbell Avenue, Dodge and Maple (now Alvernon), also unpaved, it provides dry-weather access to the Foothills region north of the river.

1936

The remains of the first St. Augustine Cathedral are demolished by the city. After being abandoned for the new cathedral on Stone, the building had had a checkered history, including being used for a time as a brothel. Efforts to preserve the building had been unsuccessful.

1936

The Arizona State Museum finally gets its own building west of Old Main on the south side of the street. Formerly, it had been in the Agriculture building and the football stadium.

1936

To draw tourists, civic leaders propose to the City Council to restore street names to those documented in Major David Ferguson's 1862 map:

- Congress Street was originally Calle de la Alegría (Street of Joy).

- Main Street (now Main Avenue) was Calle Reál (Royal Street). It was originally the primary thoroughfare in Tucson and part of the Camino Reál (or Royal Road) system that ran south to Mexico City, the capital of New Spain. Pennington Street was Calle del Arroyo (Gully Street or Wash Street) because it followed an arroyo. Larcena Pennington (b. Tennessee 1837, d. Tucson 1913), a member of a Tucson pioneer family, had been captured by Apaches in 1860 and left for dead in the Santa Ritas. She managed to survive 16 days in the wilderness and make it back to safety.

- Ott Street, which no longer exists, was Calle de la Plaza (Plaza Street), as it led into La Plaza de las Armas in Presidio San Agustín.

- Alameda Street was Calle de la Guardia (Guard Street), then Cemetery Street, since Tucson's cemetery was then located on its east end, at Stone and Alameda.

In addition, Speedway was to be named Calle Padre Kino, 22nd Street named Old Spanish Trail, and Sixth Avenue named Pioneer Boulevard. Streets south of Broadway would be named for Spanish female saints, streets north for Spanish male saints. Streets east of Sixth Avenue would be named for Arizona pioneers. All proposed changes are voted down except Calle Reál, which doesn't stick either.

1936

Herbert Bolton's massive biography of Kino, Rim of Christendom, *is published. Interest in Kino is reviving. His grave has still not been found.*

1936

North on Campbell Avenue just past the Rillito River, at the base of John Murphey's Catalina Foothills development, St. Philip's in the Hills Episcopal Church is completed, designed by architect Josias Joesler; George Ferguson, rector. A year earlier Murphey had started building on his Catalina Foothills Estates property.

1936

Homer and Cornelia Lininger buy the family compound on Alvernon near Broadway that had been built in 1931 by Mr. and Mrs. Quinsler of Massachusetts and turn it into a hotel called the Lodge on the Desert. Roads at this time are still unpaved past Country Club. The Lodge has been expanded and, owned now by Lodge Partners LLC, an Arizona investment partnership, it is still being operated as a resort hotel.

1936

Northeast of Old Main, a handsome red-brick "Women's Building" designed by Roy Place is completed. It has a pool, a gym, a room in the basement for dance classes, and other facilities for women's physical education. Quickly the campus comes to use it as something like a Student Union. In 1966, it is converted into a Student Union Annex. In 1969 it is demolished to make room for the Student Union Addition. The current Student Union complex occupies the site.

1936

UA's law school had been admitted to membership in the American Association of Law Schools in 1932. The author's father, Hal Warnock, had graduated from the law school at UA in 1935. Finding no jobs for lawyers in Tucson, Hal had decided to go to Washington, D.C., to try to get a job with the FBI. To get there, he joined a semi-pro baseball team on its way to play in a tournament in Wichita. His play attracted the attention of some big league scouts in the stands and, after a phone call to J. F. McKale, he signs with the St. Louis Browns, because they promised to take him up right away. On Labor Day, he is in uniform in the Browns' dugout watching the first Major League Baseball game he has ever seen. In the eighth inning, coach Rogers Hornsby puts him in to pinch-hit. He decides to swing at the first pitch, no matter where it is. He hits a double, and is batting 1.000 in the Big Leagues.

The author's mother has by now moved on to Oklahoma City to take a job she got there in the city clerk's office.

1936

This year's rodeo is the "biggest and best," with so many contestants it runs into Monday.

1936

The inhabitants of a one-square-mile area of Pima County along South Sixth Avenue south of Tucson vote 52-35 (out of about 350 eligible voters) to incorporate as a town in order to prevent the area from being annexed by the City of Tucson. The population of the area is primarily Mexican-American. The main highway from the south and west, Highway 80, runs through the area. The City of Tucson had been concerned about businesses and buildings along the road that were not up to code and about the encroachment of "tourist courts." The residents of South Tucson feared the expense of coming up to code and higher taxes. The vote to incorporate sets off a series of lawsuits and temporarily successful efforts to de-incorporate that are ended by the decision of the Arizona Supreme Court in *Colquhoun v. City* that decides that the incorporation is valid. Henceforth, South Tucson will have its own police force, among other things. In 1953, the new Town of South Tucson will itself annex county land to its south that includes a small Yaqui community and the dog track that had been operating at South Fourth Avenue and 36th Street since 1944. The town has plans for further annexation which the City of Tucson frustrates by annexing the areas that surround South Tucson. In 2014, the area referred to as Tucson's "South Side" includes the separate municipal-

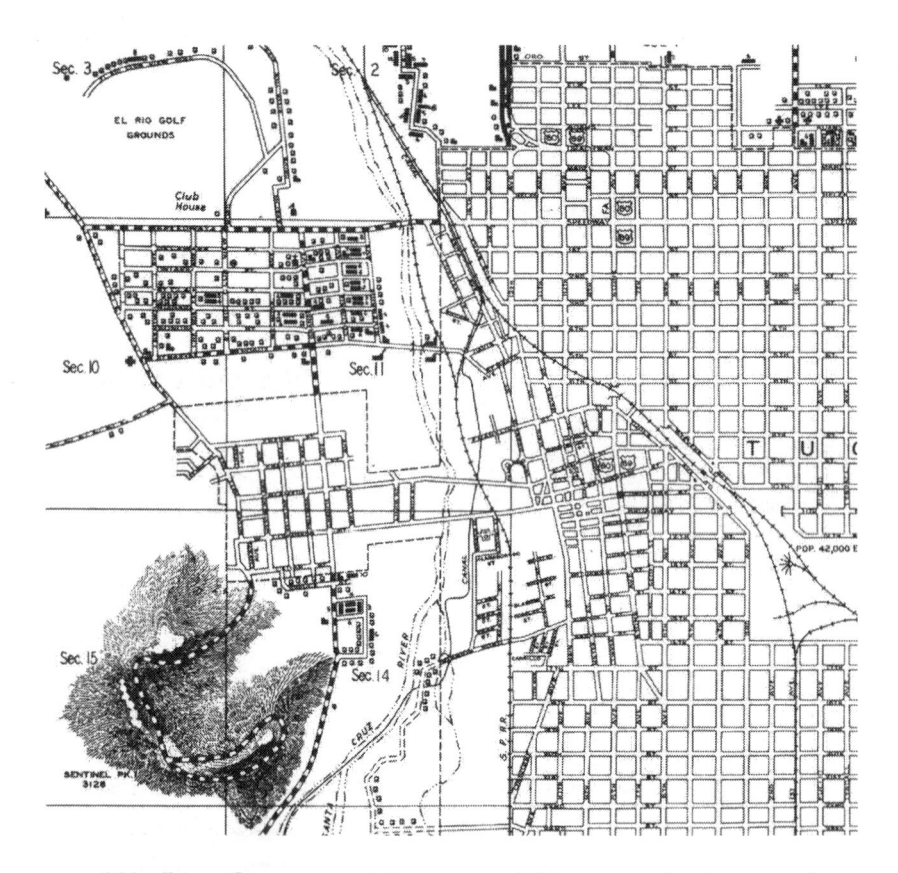

1936 Pima County map of Tucson area. This map, produced as part of a statewide project in which each county comprehensively mapped its roads, shows a new focus on automobile use, depicting roads by pavement type. The road to the top of "A" Mountain (Sentinel Peak) appears in place. Within city limits, there is less detail.

ity of South Tucson, whose police force continues to enforce speed limits along Sixth Avenue, but also the larger area of the City of Tucson south of 22nd Street and west of the municipal airport.

1936

The first aerial photographs of the area of Tucson are taken. They show a very large mesquite bosque (seven square miles) south of Martinez Hill. Birders on the ground have already identified over 100 varieties of birds there, many nesting.

1937–1939

Rawghlie C. Stanford, a Democrat, becomes governor, replacing Benjamin Moeur, a Democrat.

1937

Louise N. Grace (1868-1954) of New York, heiress to The Grace Shipping Lines fortune, begins to build a 15,000 sq. ft. house for herself on 200 acres of land west of Hacienda del Sol Road in John Murphey's Catalina Foothills development. The house, designed by Josias Joesler, comes to be known as Eleven Arches. When Ms. Grace is in town, the house will be a social center for the wealthy and well-connected. After her death, it will go through several owners. In 2014, the house remains, but the land has been mostly sold off.

1937

UA establishes the Laboratory of Tree-Ring Research to continue A. E. Douglass's pioneering work in dendrochronology. In 2013, the new Bryant Bannister Tree-Ring Building will be dedicated on the UA campus, made possible by a donation from Agnese Haury, widow of Emil Haury.

1937

With land purchases and financial support provided by Mr. and Mrs. Wetmore Hodges, archaeological excavation is begun by Carl Miller north of Tucson at Ruthrauff and La Cholla. It is continued the next year by Isabel T. Kelly at the major "Hodges" Hohokam site, leading to the excavation of 84 houses and a ballcourt that is dated to the colonial period, AD 500–900. Among southwestern Indians, ballcourts are unique to the Hohokam. Over 24 have been found in the Tucson Basin. One is thought to have existed in a large village now beneath downtown Tucson. Within a few miles of Hodges, over 30 other prehistoric sites will be located. Kelly moves on before completing her report on the excavation. At the urging of Emil Haury, work is done on the report in 1955 by James Officer, a graduate student in anthropology, and in 1978 the report is completed by Gayle Harrison Hartmann at the urging of Stephen M. Larson, past president of the Arizona Archaeological and Historical Society, who had purchased a home nearby. Preparation and publication of the report by the University of Arizona Press is supported by 36 private donors. The Hodges site and many others in the area will be obliterated in the 1970s by residential development, with the ballcourt now bulldozed and under a trailer park.

1937

Byron Cummings, the first head of Anthropology, is forced into retirement by financial exigencies at UA. He hands the program over to his student Emil Haury, who is already on his way to becoming one of the leading archaeologists of the 20th century.

1937

The Papago Tribe of Arizona adopts a constitution. By now, a larger reservation to the west has been created to add to the separate one created around San Xavier in 1874. Altogether, this reservation is second in size only to the Navajo Reservation. In 1986, the tribe will change its official designation to the Tohono O'odham Nation. The Nation will build its first casino in 1993.

1938

The author's parents take up residence in Tucson on North Second Avenue. In the year after his first year with the Browns, the author's father had been playing AAA baseball to get "seasoned." When he was hit in the leg by a pitch that broke a blood vessel, he decided to return to his original aspiration to become a lawyer. After he got a job as an inspector for the U.S. Department of Agriculture, he sought out Bunny in Oklahoma City and they married. Not long afterward, while stationed in Birmingham, Alabama, he received a call from Pop McKale who told him about an opening for a lawyer with the firm of Mathews, Bilby, and Shoenhair. He and Bunny packed up and returned to Tucson. He got the job. The firm has offices on the sixth floor of the Valley National Bank (formerly Consolidated National Bank) Building. In 1939, the firm will merge with a firm that is on the ninth floor—Knapp, Boyle, and Thompson.

1938

At Tucson's Rodeo Grounds on South Sixth Avenue, students from UA conduct the first intercollegiate rodeo.

1938

Old Main is declared structurally unsafe and condemned. In September 1942, it will be saved from demolition when it is repaired and rehabilitated by the U.S. Navy to serve as the Naval Indoctrination School.

1939–1941

Robert Taylor Jones, a Democrat, replaces Rawghlie Stanford, a Democrat, as governor.

1939

Broadway Village, Tucson's second suburban shopping center, is built at East Broadway and Country Club, developed by John Murphey (architect Josias Joesler) on the site of what had been Tucson's first Golf and Country Club.

1939

Ten private "ranch schools" are now in operation around Tucson, patronized almost entirely by families from elsewhere. For boys, there is the Evans School (far east side in the Tanque Verde area), Green Fields (northwest side near the Rillito), and the Southern Arizona School for Boys (near the entrance to Sabino Canyon). For girls, there is John Murphey's Hacienda del Sol. Added in 1940 will be the Potter School for Girls (across from the Arizona Inn; closed 1953) and Brandes School (on the north side of East Broadway near Craycroft, for asthmatics, named after the headmaster Rafael Brandes, an asthma sufferer), and in 1944 the Fenster Ranch School for kids with rheumatic fever and asthma (named after the founders, who had moved to Tucson for health reasons in 1941).

1939--1940

On the northeast corner of North Country Club Road and East 3rd Street, the chapel and convent of the Benedictine Order of Perpetual Adoration is constructed, Spanish Eclectic design, architect Roy Place.

1939

New Deal programs in the Public Works Administration assist with water infrastructure in Tucson and other cities. After a dam project for Sabino Canyon that had been proposed by the Army Corps of Engineers is not supported with sufficient local contributions, the Works Progress Administration helps to build infrastructure in the canyon.

1940

Tucson's population is 35,752 (Pima County 72,838), up from 32,506 (Pima County 57,676) in 1930. The water table in the Tucson Basin is at about 38 feet, still in the sandy gravel of the more recent alluvial deposits, which extends to about 45 feet, where the sandy clayey aquifer begins. The population of the state is still mostly rural, until after the coming war.

1940

Tucson Public Schools: high school enrollment (with change since 1930), 2,216 (an increase of 735); elementary, 9,526 (up 2,525).

1940

UA 2,922 (up 758), with 281 faculty (an increase of 99) and 35 buildings (11 new ones).

1940

During the 1930s, the Depression years, 52 residential developments were platted, down from 81 in the 1920s. To the east, they included New Deal Acres, Terra de Concini, Broadway Village, El Montevideo Estates, and San Clemente; to the north, El Cortez Heights, Miracle Mile, and Catalina Foothills; to the west, El Rio and Sentinel Peak Acres; and to the south, National City.

1940

The first parking meters arrive in Tucson.

1940

The City Directory for this year is published by the Arizona Directory Company of Tucson.

- It lists 60 physicians, eight sanatoria, and 77 attorneys (one of whom is the author's father), up from 36 lawyers in 1920.

- Thirteen auto dealers are listed (up from four in 1910) and 57 "Auto Camps" (none in 1920).

- Bottlers are now associated with specific brands: Barq's, Coca-Cola, Dr. Pepper, Nehi, 7-Up.

- About 40 cafes and restaurants are listed (up from 22 in 1920).

- Forty contractors are listed (up from 29 in 1910), 20 drugstores (up from five in 1910), 15 bakeries, many grocers and meat markets named for individuals, but also one called Time Market and a new one called "Safeway Pay'N Takit."

- The heading for Labor Unions does not list individual unions as had the Directory for 1930, but refers readers instead to the "Labor Temple" for further information (in 2014, the Labor Temple, on South Stone Avenue across from the Tucson Police Station, rents space to artists).

- Two "Broadcasting Stations" are listed, KTUC and KVOA.

- Thirteen Masonic orders are listed (including Masonic youth groups).

- As in 1930, the 40 "Miscellaneous Organizations" listed include quite a range: the Alianza-Hispano Americana, the Chinese Free Masons, the American Automobile Association, the El Rio Golf and Country Club, the Harvard Club, the National Guard, the American Red Cross, the YMCA, and the YWCA.

1940

The Carnegie Institution sells Tumamoc Hill to the U.S. Forest Service for one dollar. Grazing is still prevented but quarrying is allowed to resume, and destructive roads are built. The Tumamoc Ecological Reservation is retained.

1940

In a process that began in 1911, 2,774,370 acres of ancestral desert land west of Tucson have now been set aside as a reservation for Papago (later Tohono O'odham) Indians. The Indians living there make a precarious living as cattlemen, dry-land farmers, and government workers.

1940

Leighton Kramer died in Tucson in 1930 and his estate was probated in 1933. Dickson (b. 1896, d. 1985) and Sue B. Potter from Easthampton, New York, now buy from Hardy-Stonecypher Realty the portion of what had been Kramer's ranch just across Elm from the Arizona Inn, including the Rancho Santa Catalina house and the Wheeler well and 80-foot circular swimming pool on the property. The Potters add the Potter Place entrance on Elm Street, build a residence, and establish in Kramer's former mansion the

Potter School, a sporty horsey finishing/college prep school for girls grades 7–12 that operates into the early 1950s. In 1949, faculty will come from Smith, Vassar, Barnard, Scripps, Ohio Wesleyan, and Princeton Theological Seminary (David Sholin, later to become the pastor at Mountain View Presbyterian, an activist in the Sanctuary Movement, and president of Amnesty International). On the remaining Kramer Ranch grounds to the north, Catalina Vista is now platted. The development looks back to the "City Beautiful Movement" of 10 years earlier, with winding streets, parks, and houses limited by covenants to "Spanish, Mediterranean, Moroccan, Mexican, Indian, Early Californian" styles. Non-whites are excluded from this development and from others in Tucson, a practice that continues into the 1960s. There are not many sales in Catalina Vista until after World War II.

1940

The U.S. Border Patrol is moved from the Department of Labor to the Department of Justice. Because of World War II, its concern soon becomes enemy infiltration. Over the course of the war, staff is greatly increased.

1940

In November, Tucson hosts the world premiere of Columbia Pictures' *Arizona*, and a big event is mounted in town. The Mowry Mine in Patagonia and the Poston Mine in Tubac are featured in the film. West of the Tucson Mountains, a set is built for the film that is later used for other films and in 1960 is opened to the public as Old Tucson Studios and Theme Park. In the next decades, the Studios are used in many other films and TV shows, and "old West" entertainments are staged there for visitors. In 1995, the site is badly damaged in an arson fire. In 2014, restoration work continues. By the early 2000s, close to 70 films will have used some part of Tucson or Old Tucson as a set, considerably more than any other location in Arizona.

1941

A new superintendent is hired for the Tucson School District 1, Robert Morrow (b. 1903, Pawnee City, Nebraska; hired January 7). For the previous nine years Morrow had been director of the Arizona School for the Deaf and Blind. He will undertake, among other things, to educate children who otherwise would be unable to attend the public schools. Teachers are assigned to Comstock Children's Hospital, Tucson Medical Center, and the Pima County Preventorium. The preventorium is operated by the Pima County Health and Welfare Department for underprivileged children who have had contact with people infected with tuberculosis. Children from three to 18 years of age are in residential attendance. The preventorium has two sites, a winter camp located in an abandoned Civilian Conservation Corps camp 15 miles from Tucson in the Tucson Mountains, where the present Pima County Palo Verde Camping and Picnic Grounds are located, and a summer camp maintained in Oracle because of the milder climate. Counseling and special education are started in 1947. By 1949, Morrow has reported to the school board that the combined efforts of the counseling, testing, and guidance programs have brought "the number of pupils who drop out of school down to the lowest in the history of the school system" with tardiness and truancy reduced by 65 percent.

1941

In February the author is born at St. Mary's Hospital.

1941-1948

Sidney Preston Osborn, a Democrat, becomes governor, replacing Robert Taylor Jones, a Democrat.

1941

North of UA and south of Grant, Jefferson Park is annexed. Plans for an elementary school there have to be canceled when the United States enters World War II.

1941 December 3

Tucson Air Base, activated seven months earlier, is designated Davis-Monthan Army Air Field, with the mission of training bomber pilots. Monte Mansfield had traveled to Washington, D.C., to lobby for the designation. The first military aircraft assigned to the field are mostly obsolete Douglas B-18 (Bolo) twin-engine medium bombers. The remainder of the inventory consists of a small number of LB-30s, A-29s, and a few Stearman PT-17 biplane trainers. Other airfields in the area being used for military purposes are Ryan (southwest of Tucson) and Marana (west of the Tucson Mountains). Consolidated Vultee Aircraft Company goes into business at the city airport to modify B-24 bombers. Beginning in 1940 and extending through 1941, significant federal expenditures are made locally on roads, housing, runways, equipment, and other base requirements.

1941 December 7

The Japanese attack Pearl Harbor. At Davis-Monthan Army Air Field, base personnel are placed on 24-hour duty status and other precautions are ordered; 163 officers and 2,012 enlisted men are now assigned to the base.

1942

After Pearl Harbor, Davis-Monthan requests and receives authority to spend approximately $3.5 million for the expansion of the field. The scheduled projects include barracks, administration buildings, mess halls, officers' quarters, armament and supply buildings, hospital facilities, a theater, a chapel, and recreation buildings. B-17s and B-24s arrive in February and begin training. A bombing range is established south of Tucson on the east side of the Santa Cruz. Colonel Lowell Smith begins a long stint as base commander. Construction of facilities continues throughout the war. Crashes in the Tucson Basin are common.

1942

Blenman School opens in New Deal Acres. Covenants have had to be altered to permit a school there.

1942

The upper Santa Cruz Valley begins to be populated by "[r]etired captains of industry, eastern socialites, and young play boys and girls of inherited wealth" who patronize guest ranches such as the Rancho Santa Cruz, Kenyon Ranch, and Rex Hammaker's Rex Ranch near

Amado Siding. Some buy their own places (Sheridan, Landscapes of Fraud, *189).*

1942

The author's father, Hal Warnock, joins the U.S. Navy, going in as a lieutenant since he had taken ROTC at UA. My mother and I go with Hal to Phoenix, then Los Angeles, where Hal works in officer procurement. In 1944, he volunteers for combat duty and is sent to New York City and Norfolk, Virginia, for training with the amphibious forces. The author and his mother return to Tucson.

1943

On a ranch north of the Rillito and east of First Avenue, owned by J. Rukin Jelks (b. Tucson 1927, d. 2014), the Rillito Race Track for quarter-horse racing is founded by Jelks and three other Tucson-area horsemen—Bob Locke, Melville Haskell (b. Cleveland 1901, d. Sedona 1984; Great Lakes shipping, iron, coal), and Jake Meyer. In 1940, Jelks, Haskell, and others had founded the American Quarter Horse Association. The Rillito Race Track will become an important venue for quarter-horse and later for thoroughbred racing and in 1986 will be placed on the National Register of Historic Places. Horse racing still continues in January and February. Jelks's Sonoran Revival house and stables, built in 1940, still stand above the race track grounds and adjoining soccer fields. Jelks later ranches in Patagonia at the Diamond C, serves as chairman of the board of the Arizona-Sonora Desert Museum, and serves with Patronato San Xavier (see below: 1978), among other local activities.

1943

John Murphey's Hacienda del Sol School for Girls becomes a guest ranch resort.

1943

Rosemary Drachman Taylor, descendent of the Arizona pioneer who arrived in 1874, publishes *Chicken Every Sunday,* a novel closely based on her family's history in Arizona, mostly in Tucson. The novel is later made into a stage play and a 20th Century Fox movie.

1944 November

The author's father, Hal, gets leave from amphibious training in Norfolk, Virginia, to return to Tucson to see his newly born daughter, Martha. He returns to Norfolk, and in January is ordered to Long Beach to take command of Landing Ship Medium 156 in amphibious Group One, Flotilla One and sail for Guam in the South Pacific. My mother, Martha, and I are in residence just east of the UA campus, at 1019 East 4th Street, a site now occupied by the University of Arizona Aquatic Center.

1944 December 29

After new construction had prepared the way, the first B-29s arrive at Davis-Monthan. B-24 training soon ends. The B-29s are the new heavy bombers developed by the U.S. that will conduct more than 60 firebombing raids on cities in Japan. In August 1945, B-29s will drop the atomic bombs on Hiroshima and Nagasaki, since they are the only bombers capable of carrying the first atomic bombs. During the eight months pilots are trained on the B-29s at Davis-Monthan, there are 12 major crashes. Since 1941, there have been 26 major crashes of Davis-Monthan's bombers.

1944

The owners and funders of the original Desert Sanatorium, Alfred and Anna Erickson, donate the 300 acres of sanatorium land on East Grant at Craycroft for a new hospital that opens in November as Tucson Medical Center, Tucson's second hospital (after St. Mary's). A number of the Santa Fe-style adobe buildings of the original "Desert San" are preserved and are still to be seen on the north side of Grant.

1944

UA's polo team had been disbanded in 1942. This year its stable of cavalry horses is auctioned off.

1944

Arizona had legalized pari-mutuel betting in 1935 and this year Tucson Greyhound Park is opened at South Fourth Avenue and 36th Street. At first only 60 days of dog races per year are permitted.

1945

Rincon Market, opened originally in 1927, opens in a new location in the Sam Hughes District at the intersection of 6th Street and Tucson Boulevard, where it is still operating.

1945

The Tucson Arizona Boys Chorus for boys aged 6–11 is incorporated as a nonprofit educational organization. Its director is Eduardo Caso, an English tenor who had come to Tucson to recover from tuberculosis and founded the chorus in 1939. In the late 1940s and early 1950s, the author will sing with the Boys Chorus. Soon after the author's voice changes in 1955 and he stops singing with them, the chorus will begin to tour nationally and internationally, and in 1963 Tucson's "ambassadors in Levis" will perform at the White House Christmas tree-lighting ceremony. Caso dies in 1965. The chorus continues to perform nationally and internationally as well as locally, including at the annual Christmas performance at San Xavier Mission Church.

1945 June 19

The war in Europe ended on May 8 with the surrender of Germany. A little more than a month later, Davis-Monthan receives 135 German prisoners-of-war from Papago Park prison camp in Phoenix. The prison compound at Davis-Monthan, east of Craycroft on the base, is closed down on March 31, 1946.

1945 August 2

Squadron "B (N)" (Negro WAACs) is organized at Davis-Monthan Field with 118 enlisted women. On March 31, 1946, when the Strategic Air Command is created, it is disbanded and personnel transferred.

1945 September 9

World War II ends with the Japanese surrender. Not long afterward, Hal Warnock's group of LSMs lands on a beach in Japan and he becomes briefly part of the occupying force. In December, he returns home.

1945 September

At the end of the war, Davis-Monthan serves as the Separation Center for the 2nd Air Force from August to November, reaching its peak population of 10,300.

1945 December

The Tucson Municipal Airport is designated as a sub-base of Davis-Monthan Field. Base strength of 312 officers and 1,369 enlisted personnel is now less than half what it was in 1944.

1945

Ridership on Tucson's two bus systems greatly increased during the gas rationing of World War II. In 1945, seven million passengers are carried by the two systems. In the 1950s, ridership begins to decline. By 1965, it has declined 63 percent.

1945

Perennial flow on the Santa Cruz ends this year.

1946 March 31

The newly formed Strategic Air Command (SAC) assumes jurisdiction at Davis-Monthan. More B-29s arrive in May, then B-50s, which are upgraded B-29s designed specifically to carry atomic bombs. Housing demand in Tucson spikes.

1946

Many servicemen and servicewomen who had trained at nearby airfields, some with families, return to Tucson to attend UA and are temporarily housed in Polo Village, an installation of two-family military surplus Quonset huts north of Speedway on the east and west sides of the polo field. Also in use are four-family Temporary Dwelling Units east of Bear Down Gymnasium. The "temporary" Polo Village housing remains in use for 38 years. East Polo Village is removed in 1968 but the last Quonsets in West Polo Village field are removed only in 1984, to make room for the new Life Sciences building.

1946 July 1

Squadron "C" of the 248th Army Air Force Base Unit is organized at Davis-Monthan Field. The unit consists of several hundred black airmen from various stations throughout the United States.

1946

At Point of Pines on the San Carlos Indian Reservation, UA archaeologist Emil Haury establishes what will become the nation's premier archaeological field training school, operating until 1960.

1940s middle

In the Catalinas above the town of Oracle, the YMCA opens the Triangle Y Ranch Camp, which the author will attend for two summers during his elementary school years. The camp is still in operation.

1946

Tucson Gas, Electric Light & Power Company becomes a publicly held company.

1946

Roy Drachman establishes a real estate brokerage business. Born in Tucson in 1906, the first-born son of Emanual Drachman, he had lived for his first several years in an adobe house at 223 South Main that will be destroyed in the 1970s during urban renewal. In 1947, Drachman will partner with developer Del Webb, owner of one of the nation's largest construction firms, and begin to sell houses for Webb in Tucson's first large housing development (Pueblo Gardens, 700 units). Later he will co-develop with Webb the first shopping centers in Arizona, will put together the land deals that help attract Hughes Aircraft (becomes Raytheon) to Tucson, and will help found the Ramada Inn hotel chain. He dies in Tucson in 2002.

1946

With his father and brother-in-law, William A. Estes Sr. (arrives Tucson from Washington State in 1943) builds and sells his first house, in the Alvernon Way area south of Broadway. Estes Sr. will sell the firm and retire in 1973. In 1979, the firm will be reacquired by his son, William Estes Jr., and a partner. Estes Homes will build tens of thousands of homes in Tucson, Phoenix, and Sierra Vista, including Midvale Park in southwest Tucson and Ventana Canyon in northeast Tucson. In 1999 Estes Jr. will sell the company to KB Homes and devote himself to educational causes, dying in 2009.

1946

The high-end Aldea Linda residential development, now located north of 22nd Street between Swan and Craycroft, is founded by Air Corps veteran and recent arrival Samuel Goddard, later to be governor of Arizona (1965-67).

1946

Catalina Vista, the housing development north of the Arizona Inn, is annexed by the City of Tucson.

1947

Elbert Thompson Houston becomes mayor of Tucson, until 1950.

1947

Catalina Foothills Estates No. 2 is subdivided with (as was the case with John Murphey's Catalina Foothills No. 1) multi-acre lots and deed restrictions that include racial restrictions. By the 1980s, Catalina Foothills No. 10 is being built out.

1947

The Cleveland Indians Major League Baseball team chooses Tucson for its spring training. Owner Bill Veeck has a ranch east of Tucson. The team will train at Randolph Municipal Baseball Park (built 1937, renamed Hi Corbett field in 1951). The team hotel is the Pioneer Hotel, which has a whites-only policy. At this time, black baseball players (like Luke Easter, Larry Doby, Orestes "Minnie" Minoso) must find other places to stay when the teams are in town. Tucson resident Chester Willis often puts up players in his home. The Indians will return for spring training until 1992.

1947

The new Anglo residents in the Fort Lowell area east of town apply to establish a political entity separate from Tucson called "Rincon Village," but the Pima County Board of Supervisors declines to approve the application. In the years that follow, some farming continues in the area, despite the fall in the water table, on large parcels of land that had been acquired along the Rillito and Pantano Wash in the late 1930s. One is the Hill Farm of Dr. and Mrs. Donald Hill, who build a large house south of the Rillito designed by Josias Joesler that is still there in the Hill Farm housing development. The Adkins family is operating a steel tank manufacturing business on land they had acquired in 1928 that had been part of the old fort. In 2006 they will donate the land to the City of Tucson to become part of Fort Lowell Historic Park.

1947

East of Fort Lowell, the Tucson Country Club, Tucson's fourth golf course and the first one since El Rio opened in 1929, is established on a Hohokam agricultural site in the delta east of Pantano Wash and south of Tanque Verde Creek, just ahead of where these watercourses join to become the Rillito. This will be the last golf course built in Tucson until 1959 when another will be opened northwest of Tucson in Oro Valley, with the Forty-Niners Golf Course being opened shortly afterward far out east on Tanque Verde Road.

1947

The author, age six, is living at 1019 East 4th Street, a site now occupied by the UA Aquatic Center. He is able to walk a block from home and hang on the outfield fence to watch the UA baseball team play on a field that is now occupied by UA's Main Library. In the fall, he starts elementary school at Sam Hughes Elementary, opened in the Sam Hughes subdivision in 1927 in buildings designed by Roy Place.

1947

Stone Ashley, the mansion Florence Pond had built in 1930 at Wilmot and Speedway, is put up for sale.

1948 January 11

With the establishment of the United States Air Force by Congress, Davis-Monthan Army Air Field becomes the Davis-Monthan Air Force Base.

1948–1951

Dan Edward Garvey, a Democrat, replaces Sidney Preston Osborn, a Democrat, as governor. Garvey will be the last in a string of six straight governors who are Democrats, nine out of twelve since statehood.

1948

A school building boom begins in Tucson with bond issues passing in 1946 and 1948. One item supported is construction of a Vocational Building at Tucson High School. The high school goes on double sessions, which continue into the 1960s. Dunbar Junior High School is established in the Dunbar neighborhood for "colored" students.

1948

Reverend Paul David Sholin founds Mountain View Presbyterian (now St. Marks Presbyterian) on land donated by Linn Hazen, whose son Paul is a playmate of the author. Sholin had been born in Argentina in 1920, graduated from Princeton Theological Seminary, and requested placement in a multicultural city. In 1948–1949, Sholin also teaches theology at the Potter School for Girls.

1948

On Grant east of the new Tucson Medical Center, Grantwood Memorial Park is incorporated. It is now East Lawn Palms Mortuary and Cemetery and owned by Service Corporation International, based in Houston, "North America's leading provider of deathcare products and services."

1948

Because the military wished to separate the base and municipal facilities, the Tucson Airport Authority is created, a volunteer group of community leaders that includes Monte Mansfield, R. W. F Schmidt, Charles Broman (who will later serve as general manager of the airport), and Roy Drachman. The municipal airport moves from Davis-Monthan to its current location, on land leased from the city. The new airport is created with private money.

1948

Lebanese immigrant Frank Kalil, who had arrived in Tucson in 1909, had run business ventures in Tucson, Mexico, and Georgia, and who had returned to Tucson from Georgia in 1944 with his son Fred (Fred had worked at Davis-Monthan), starts a soft drink bottling company with Fred. Kalil Bottling Company now employs about 800 people and has distribution centers in Phoenix, Flagstaff, and El Paso, as well as in Tucson.

1948

Hayzel B. Daniels is the first African-American to graduate from the University of Arizona Law School and to be admitted to the state bar. Daniels had been a star running back for Tucson High School's football team in the 1920s after the new building opened—gaining over 300 yards in a game against Bisbee—but had been unable to travel with the team to Texas for games because he would not have been allowed to play there. He had chosen not to play football in college.

1948

The Blenman-Elm Neighborhood east of Catalina Vista and part of the Fort Lowell area northeast of the city are annexed by the City of Tucson. On Broadway, the eastern city limits end at Randolph Way and the pavement ends at Alvernon.

1948 August

At Davis-Monthan, a squadron is activated that uses adapted B-29s to refuel bombers in the air, the first such squadron in history. Also, the Aircraft Storage Depot adds reclamation and salvage to the storage mission. It grows over time into the 309th Aerospace Maintenance and Regeneration Group (aka "the Boneyard"), with over 4,000 aircraft in 2014, claimed by docents to be the second-largest air force in the world.

1940s late

Northwest of Tucson, Casas Adobes residential development is established by Sam Nanini, eventually to include a shopping center and Tucson National Golf Course. Ranches and guest ranches had operated on this land and north of it in the 1920s and 1930s, with citrus groves being developed on the south end in the 1930s.

1949

Consolidated Vultee closes down its aircraft modification operation in Tucson.

1949

Tucson General Hospital (15 beds) opens on north Campbell Avenue at Allen, formerly the site of the Harding Guest Ranch. The Arizona Cancer Center now occupies the site.

1949

Across from the UA Agriculture building, ground is broken for a Liberal Arts building where the Introduction to Humanities survey course will now be taught. The course has been required of sophomores in several UA colleges for the last 10 years. It had before been offered in the Humanities building designed by Roy Place and built in 1936. Many graduates now remember this Introduction to Humanities course as the most important one they took at UA. In May 1978, the Liberal Arts building will become the Social Sciences building.

1949

Fred Batiste joins the UA football team. He will be the first African-American athlete to play a game for UA.

1949

At Irving and 5th Street in what will come to be known as the Poets Square Neighborhood, construction is begun on what will be the first air-conditioned school to be built in School District 1 (using evaporative coolers). During the first semester of its existence, the school is named "Longfellow" after Longfellow Avenue that ran along its west side. On September 20, 1950, it will be renamed and rededicated as the Peter Howell School in honor of Peter E. Howell (b. Canada 1874, arrives Tucson 1900, d. Tucson 1952), a local businessman (Tucson Laundry and Dry Cleaners), active Mason, and school board member for 14 years. This year the author will move from Sam Hughes to the new elementary school and move with his family not long afterward to 4133 E. Poe Street, three blocks from the school.

1949

Between Country Club and Tucson Boulevard north of Fort Lowell Street, the Winterhaven subdivision is established with aspirations to a midwestern neighborhood ideal in architecture and landscaping. It will be developed into 1961. Homeowners are still decorating their homes extravagantly at Christmastime for the popular Festival of Lights.

1949

The first traffic lights in Pima County outside Tucson are installed, one of them at Broadway and Alvernon.

1949

For the last two years, Davis-Monthan supported between 5,000 and 6,000 personnel. This year its aerial refueling squadron supports the first round-the-world flight with no landings. The feat is accomplished by a B-50, *Lucky Lady II*. The flight is undertaken to demonstrate the reach of the Strategic Air Command.

1950

J. O. Niemann becomes acting mayor, until 1951.

1950

The City of Tucson now includes 8.76 square miles, up from 7.15 in 1930, with a census population of 45,454 in the city, 122,764 in the metropolitan area (the City Directory claims 253,000 in the metro area). Increases from 1941 are 8,636 in the city, 68,378 in the county. The city has 35,987 telephones, one for every 3½ residents of metropolitan Tucson.

1950

The School District 1 student population has increased to more than 18,000 (up from 11,000 in 1940, an increase of

64 percent), with 518 teachers, and a total district budget of $4,106,383 ($947,699 in 1940, an increase of 430 percent). UA enrollment is 6,227, with 468 faculty (up 187 since 1940) and 46 buildings (up 12).

1950

North of Grant and west of Campbell, Salpointe High School, a Catholic high school named after the Vicar Apostolic of the missions of Arizona during territorial days, opens with 100 students. The third high school in Tucson after Tucson High and Amphitheater, and emphasizing "vocational education," it grows substantially in facilities and number of students between 1954 and 1966, until the advent of Pima Community College reduces demand for vocational courses.

1950

The Tucson City Directory for this year is prepared by Baldwin ConSurvey Co. of Columbus, Ohio (the first non-local publisher of a Tucson directory), and Mullen-Kille Company, successors to Tucson's Arizona Directory Company, publishers of the 1940 Directory.

- The introduction notes with pride the fact that the city is served by US Highways 80 and 89, and close to 50,000 automobiles are now registered in Tucson.
- The Cleveland Indians have elected to do their spring training in Tucson. The author's father is able to arrange for the author to be a batboy at some of the games.

- Tucson now has "an alert Community Drama Movement" (three drama companies are listed, all led by Peter Marroney). At least five drama companies are active in Tucson by 2014.

- The first section of the Directory lists only businesses, now listed on pages that are colored yellow.

- 18 Automobile Dealers are listed, selling Buick, Cadillac, Chevrolet, Chrysler, Dodge, Ford, Nash, Oldsmobile, Plymouth, and Studebaker cars.

- Two new business categories appear, the "Tourist Court" and the "Trailer Camp," with already about 90 listed in each.

- Another new category that appears in the Directory is "Air Conditioning." "Refrigeration" services are offered for commercial, not domestic, purposes though one firm, Tucson Refrigeration and Air Conditioning Service, seems to cover both bases.

- The Directory says there are 100 churches in Tucson now, representing 35 different denominations.

- There are now five radio stations (up from two in 1940), and one of something called a "Drive In Theater."

- The Directory lists about 150 "Physicians and Surgeons" and 100 lawyers, one of whom is the author's father.

- 40 firms are listed under the heading Real Estate, 60 under Drug Stores, 40 under Taverns, and 200 under Cafes and Restaurants.

- A new firm called Dairy Queen is said to sell "ice cream," as is a business on Broadway east of Tucson Boulevard called the Hidden House. A bakery on South Sixth Avenue called Le Cave's has been in business at that location since 1935 and is still in business in 2014.

1950

The introduction to the City Directory says that enough water exists in the ground under Tucson to support a city of 250,000 and claims that "[i]f and when additional water is needed for Tucson, it can be obtained from other sources that already have been thoroughly explored...such as through construction of a dam on the San Pedro River near Charleston, Arizona." No worries.

1950

113 miles of streets in the city are now paved, more than triple the miles in 1935, when there were 31. Speedway is now paved to Country Club, and Broadway to Alvernon. In Pima County, 456 miles are now paved, 216 miles in the last decade.

1950

Northwest of the city, a new four-lane bridge across the Rillito is being built on a new alignment of Oracle Road (Florence Highway).

1950

The 27-mile highway to Mount Lemmon at the top of the Catalina Mountains (altitude 9,157 feet) is completed, 17 years after construction began. Since 1920, sporadic access to Mount Lemmon had been possible from Oracle up the north side of the mountains on a one-way 40-mile control road. The new road will be paved by the following year. It is named the Hitchcock Highway after the U.S. postmaster general who originally sponsored its construction, but is being referred to by residents as the Catalina or Mount Lemmon Highway. Mount Lemmon itself is named after Sara Lemmon, a 19th-century botanist who in 1881 apparently was the first European woman to ascend the peak. At the top now is the small community of Summerhaven, which gets electricity for the first time this year. In 2010, Summerhaven will have a population of only 40, but over 100 summer cabins will have been built in the area. During World War II, a ski facility had been constructed on Mount Lemmon. In 2014, Mount Lemmon Ski Valley is the southernmost ski area in the continental U.S., operating from December to April.

1950

Levy's builds a new department store on Pennington and Scott, moving from a much smaller store on Congress.

1950

Pueblo Gardens, a planned community and school, is developed around the 2000 block of East 33rd Street, southwest of the railroad tracks. More schools are now being built on the south side.

1950

The Gila Pueblo Archaeological Foundation is closed by its principal sponsor, Harold Gladwin. Its remarkable archaeological collection is donated to the Arizona State Museum at UA, which trebles its holdings.

1950s

Development jumps east on Broadway and Speedway. On Broadway, the frontage from Euclid to Country Club is built out using the latest modernist technologies: cantilevered overhangs, expanses of glass, integrated sculptural features. Along Speedway the urbanized area reaches Wilmot. On the southeast corner of Speedway and Wilmot, construction begins on the Harold Bell Wright residential housing development. Wright had died in 1944 in California but his home is preserved in the development.

1950s

A southwestern-themed art scene thrives downtown: Papago skirts, silver belts, Frank Patania's jewelry, Cele Peterson fashions, the Kaibab Shop, regional painters. Beginning in the 1920s and 1930s, the excitement generated by anthropological discoveries in the American Southwest had generated a national interest in Native American arts and crafts, particularly in works that were "authentic." Anthropologists and their family members had sometimes gotten involved in this trade, often to the advantage of both sellers and buyers of the works. Early traders were Malcolm Cummings, son of Byron Cummings, the first head of Anthropology; Clay Lockett; and John Tanner, who was appreciated by the Indians because he bought their works and did not take them on consignment. Fraud by other traders was not unknown.

1950

The Silver and Turquoise Ball has its beginnings this year when a group of Tucson's prominent women—Aurora Patania, Audrey Baird, Peggy Steinfeld, and Isabella Greenway—have a gathering at the Arizona Inn to thank the volunteers at the Tucson Festival Society. In 1993, a non-profit group independent of the Festival Society will be formed and in 2014, its "hostesses" will still be staging the elaborate Ball at the Arizona Inn annually at the end of the winter (also known as "the social") season. The proceeds of the Ball are dedicated to "promoting, supporting and encouraging the preservation of Tucson's historical traditions and diverse cultural heritage."

1950s

South of the old Canoa land grant south of Tucson, Carlos Ronstadt operates a feedlot for 3,000 head of cattle and farms 450 acres, using seven wells.

1951

Fred Artemas Emery Jr. becomes mayor of Tucson, until 1955.

1951 June

Tucson School District 1 reaches its largest geographic size through a final annexation of the southwest corner, an area that is at this time unorganized and contains no school. Enrollment is 19,866, Superintendent Morrow expects 21,400 by the end of the year. Annexing the Catalina Foothills is discussed but no action is taken.

1951

Groundwater pumping for agriculture in the lower Santa Cruz Basin is 1,110,000 acre-feet, up from 1,000,000+ in 1949, 672,000 in 1946, and 344,000 in 1941 at the start of World War II, over a 300 percent increase by 1951. Subsidence begins to be recognized as a problem.

1951–1955

Howard Pyle, a Republican, replaces Dan Edward Garvey, a Democrat, as governor. Pyle later breaks up a polygamous Mormon community in Colorado City, which turns out not to be a popular move. The polygamous practices of the significant Mormon community have been a troubling issue in Arizona since territorial times.

1951

Arizona's state legislature repeals the state's segregation law on March 30, 1951, and that fall, Robert Morrow desegregates Tucson School District 1, making it the first school district in Arizona to desegregate. The segregated Dunbar Junior High School is renamed John Spring, after one of the territory's most significant early educators. Tucson's newspapers support integration but not all citizens do. Children still attend neighborhood schools. Black teachers can now teach in any school but many remain on the west side. Tucson High had not been segregated when it opened in 1924, but some restrictions had been in place (separate homerooms, for example). Morrow had earlier eliminated those.

1951

Felix Lucero dies. Lucero was a veteran wounded in World War I who, it is said, pledged to create Christian art if he recovered. After the war, he had lived under the Congress Street bridge for a time. Not long before his death, on the west side of the Santa Cruz River north of Congress Street, he had completed his sculpture of the Last Supper, made from damp sand reinforced with river debris and covered with plaster. His sculpture, though frequently vandalized, still remains in place on banks of the Santa Cruz, in what is now called the Garden of Gethsemane.

1951

Richard Harvill is inaugurated as the 16th president of UA. Tucson and Arizona have begun to grow rapidly: The next year, Arizona will be the fastest-growing state in the country. Harvill recognizes the need to expand facilities and the importance of the research mission in higher education—and how much money will now be going to scientific research and development. Building upon already prestigious research programs at UA in areas like anthropology and astronomy, he embarks on a program to make UA a leading research university, developing areas like arid land studies and water research, and the Institute for Atmospheric Physics. A speaker at his inauguration urges, however, that we not lose our "cultural balance" and neglect "those studies generally grouped under the broad heading of the humanities," becoming "only seats of scientific development" because "the maintenance and development of our democratic institutions and democratic culture" will be important in "the event of a prolonged cold war." Celebrated at Harvill's inauguration are the donation of the Gila Pueblo collection to the Arizona State Museum and the loan by the Kress family of 25 European masterpieces to the UA Art Museum in perpetuity.

1951

With much fanfare, Jácome's, now run by Carlos Jácome's 10th child, Alex Jácome, opens a big new store across from Steinfeld's, on land Harold Steinfeld had sold them for the purpose (Alex Jácome and Harold Steinfeld are golfing buddies).

1951

Hughes Aircraft locates its operation in south Tucson on 32,000 acres of largely open land west of the airport, the land deal having been facilitated on an emergency basis by Roy Drachman, Monte Mansfield, and others. Hughes also buys from Mansfield a section of land in the Catalina Foothills, the last mile before the National Forest boundary on the east side of North Campbell. Del Webb is hired to do the plant construction for Hughes. The next year, Hughes Aircraft begins to manufacture in Tucson its Falcon, America's first air-to-air guided missile, produced in both radar-guided and heat-seeking versions. The missile enters service in 1956 and is used on

F-4 aircraft in the Vietnam War. It turns out to be ineffective in air-to-air combat and is replaced by the Sidewinder, manufactured by Raytheon (the successor to Hughes Aircraft), among others. In 2013, Raytheon Missile Systems, with 9,933 employers, is the second-largest employer in Tucson, not far behind the University of Arizona.

1951

The Roger Road Wastewater Reclamation Facility is completed on the Santa Cruz, with the capacity to treat 41 million gallons of sewage a day. In 2014, this plant treats 64 million gallons a day, with most of the treated wastewater discharged into the Santa Cruz River.

1951

Howell Manning Jr., grandson of Levi Manning and son of Howell Manning, is killed along with two workers from the Canoa Ranch when the truck Manning is driving on the Nogales Highway is struck head-on by a drunk driver. Howell Sr. had developed the Canoa land grant acquired in 1921 by his father Levi into the largest ranch in southern Arizona, a showcase operation with over 500,000 acres of public and private land. He now begins to sell off the ranch holdings and to descend into drink. He dies in 1966 at the age of 67. Sixteen months later his widow will sell the last remaining Canoa grant lands to the Duval Sierrita Mining Corporation.

1951

Out east, William Woodin Jr. builds a house on Sabino Creek. The big Sabino Vista development west of this house and Larrea Lane does not begin until 1978.

1951–1958

To accommodate the automobile, the city's Church Street Opening and Widening Project destroys a number of historic structures downtown, as well as a much-loved jacaranda tree.

1952

Zoning laws had been in place in Tucson to control development since the mid-1930s, not long after zoning laws first became legal in the United States (1927). Almost alone among realtors, Roy Drachman had been a proponent of such laws. Tucson had passed a zoning code in 1948, but Pima County had no such laws. In 1949, the state of Arizona had passed the County Planning and Zoning Act and this year, in an effort to control development outside of Tucson, the Pima County Board of Supervisors approves a new Pima County zoning plan. Many developers wish to avoid any kind of regulation and claim it will damage the economy, but even with the new zoning laws, the boom in home building that began in 1951 continues to 1956, with an average of 22 subdivision plats and 1,600 homes a year. One major developer in the 1950s and 1960s, Lusk Homes, promotes "Perfect Arizona Type" ranch-style homes, often constructed around shopping centers. Spanish-style names are favored at first (one of them is "Terra [sic] del Sol"). These are dropped in the 1960s. Two other building booms will follow, 1957–1966 and 1967–1973.

1952

The first Mexican-American since territorial days is elected to the school board. Robert Salvatierra Jr. defeats long-time member Fred W. Fickett. Salvatierra does not seek reelection in 1955, and there will be no Mexican-American on the board for another 20 years.

1952

The U.S. Border Patrol transfers officers from the Canadian to the Mexican border. Illegal immigration from the south is increasing. Large increases begin in the 1980s.

1952

On land west of the Tucson Mountains leased from Pima County, the Arizona-Sonora Desert Museum opens, founded as a non-profit corporation by William Carr, Arthur Pack, and others, with no state funding. To the surprise of many, the museum is an immediate success and eventually will be ranked by Trip Advisor as one of the top ten museums in the world. It makes the point that the American Southwest contains not one but several very different deserts, among them the Chihuahuan Desert that begins 60 miles east of Tucson and the Mohave Desert in California. The Sonoran Desert, by far the wettest and richest of these bioregions, extends not very far north of Tucson, but both the Chihuahuan and Sonoran Deserts extend many miles south into Mexico. All this is lost on the author, who is 11 and knows only Tucson and the California coast, where the family has gone on a summer vacation, crossing some remarkable sand dunes to do so.

1952

Between 1942 and 1952, the water table in the lower Santa Cruz Basin declines an average of 37 feet as the result of the removal of 7.6 million acre-feet of water. Subsidence becomes an issue there, as well as in the Tucson Basin. Twelve feet of subsidence is estimated by 2025 if overdrafts continue.

1953

Davis-Monthan base strength has grown to almost twice what it was in 1944: 1,121 officers and 6,283 enlisted personnel. This year, a jet-powered fighter with swept-wings, the F-86, appears in the skies above Tucson. It will see service in the Korean War. A six-engine jet-powered swept-wing long-range jet bomber called the B-47 also appears. It will be the mainstay of the Strategic Air Command into the 1960s, with a primary mission of delivering nuclear bombs to Russia, though it will also perform reconnaissance missions.

1953

On the far eastern side of Tucson, Wrightstown is annexed, an area of 48 square miles east of Pantano Road along Tanque Verde. A Wrightstown school is already in the area, built in 1914, and named for Fredrick and Dolores Wright, homesteaders who founded the school and donated the land on which the school is located.

1953

The rector of St. Philip's in the Hills Episcopal Church, George Ferguson, announces plans to build a church at 5th Street and Wilmot on property that had belonged to Harold Bell Wright and been donated to the church by owners of the current residential development. Like St. Philip's, St. Michael and All Angels will be designed by Josias Joesler and built by John Murphey. The original building is built of adobe. The first rector will be John Clinton Fowler, a native Arizonan who had attended public schools and UA in Tucson. Under his rectorship, which will last through 1986, the church will be involved in work to support the civil rights and the farm workers movements, and to oppose nuclear weapons and the Vietnam War.

1953

The Potters sell the Rancho Santa Catalina/Potter School for Girls property to the Catholic Sisters of Charity, who rename it Casa Elizabeth Seton and teach kindergarten and music there. The Sisters of Charity had first come to Arizona in 1933, and had had various ministries in association with Saints Peter and Paul Church and School that is several blocks away on Campbell, in a parish that had been founded in 1930 because of Tucson's expansion northeast. The Potters keep their large house at 5 Potter Place and before long begin to sell lots on the east and north side of Potter Place.

1953

Excavation for a new Tucson Newspapers building at Alameda and Stone reveals numerous skeletons and artifacts of people who had been buried in Tucson's first cemetery, the National (or Government) Cemetery. One skeleton had an arrowhead lodged in its breastbone. The cemetery had been closed in 1875 and later residences and small businesses had been built on the site.

1953

The author enrolls in junior high at Roskruge, on 6th Street kitty-cornered from Tucson High.

1953 October

The area for aircraft storage east of Davis-Monthan is increased to 1,290 acres by the purchase of 480 acres.

1953

A big school bond issue is passed for two new high schools and more elementary schools with almost no opposition.

1953

At Rillito Downs, North First Avenue and River Road, an oval track is constructed to permit thoroughbred racing as well as the quarter-horse racing that had gone on there in the "chute" since 1943.

1953

The area of Tucson's Birthplace west of the Santa Cruz River at the base of Sentinel Hill—the site of the original San Agustín Mission and Convento, later the site of Chinese truck farms and a brickworks—begins to be used by the City of Tucson as a landfill, and later a bus barn. The brickworks and landfill destroy an estimated 2/3 of the archeological remains of the mission and convento.

1954

City water is no longer being used to support agriculture in the middle Tucson Basin. Agricultural water use is now seen as a threat to the city.

1954

William Woodin Jr. succeeds Carr as director of the Arizona-Sonora Desert Museum. He will become the museum's longest-serving director, at 17 years.

1954

The U.S. Air Force's Air Defense Command begins to build a radar station on Mount Lemmon to track missile launches from White Sands Missile Range in New Mexico to the east and Vandenberg Air Force Base on the West Coast. In 1969, during the Vietnam War, the radar facility will be closed down.

1954

A flood wipes out most of the bridges in Sabino Canyon.

1954

Tucson begins a series of annexations, going from 8.76 square miles in 1950 to 14.02 square miles this year, up to 24.53 square miles by 1958.

1954

The U.S. Housing Act offers support for addressing "decay and blight" through "urban renewal."

1954

In the year of Steinfeld's "Suntennial," Big Bill Zeckendorf of New York, grandson of Arizona pioneer William Zeckendorf, and at this point "the largest urban developer in the nation," visits Tucson and speaks about its "bright future" in development because of its warmth and wide open spaces. By 1965 Zeckendorf will have been wiped out.

1954

In Maricopa County, Del Webb begins to develop Sun City, introducing the new development concept of a "retirement community," in which all residents are active retirees. The first homes are sold in 1960 and the idea takes off. Webb builds other Sun Cities throughout the Sun Belt into the 2000s, though none in Pima County.

1954

The TTT Truck Terminal is built on the Benson Highway at Craycroft. In 2014, it remains in business at a location one mile east on Craycroft and Interstate 10.

1954

In February, the first Tucson Gem and Mineral Show is held. The *Star* reports in 2014 that it brings $70 million to Tucson.

1954

Nan Lyons is elected to the school board, the first woman since early in the century. Since this election, women have served continuously on the board.

1954

The last remnant of the adobe wall of the Presidio San Agustín had been taken down in 1918. A parking lot is now planned for the site. Before construction, UA archaeologist Emil Haury excavates the site. He discovers a remnant of the wall of the northeast bastion and, under that, evidence of a prehistoric pit house. The parking lot is then constructed over the site.

1955 January 29

The Arizona Historical Society Building and Museum is dedicated at 949 East 2nd Street, near UA, on land leased from UA for 99 years. Dr. Robert H. Forbes of the UA College of Agriculture had gotten the state of Arizona to support the project. Needed matching funds are contributed by many supporters including the Vosburg, Steinfeld, Brophy, and Pogue families and Phelps Dodge Mining Company. George Chambers and John Murphey are successive heads of the finance committee. The Arizona Historical Society is the descendent of the Society of Arizona Pioneers, founded in 1884.

1955

Don Hummel becomes mayor (until 1961), and pursues annexation. Later, during the administration of President Lyndon Johnson, Hummel will serve as the assistant secretary of the U.S. Department of Housing and Urban Development.

1955

Tucson Gas and Electric announces plans to build a big generating station southeast of Tucson at Alvernon and Irvington. At first, the station burns diesel and natural gas, adding coal in the 1980s, and later methane from the local landfill.

1955

The Tucson Home Builders Association is formed in support of residential development in Tucson. The association begins to sponsor an annual Parade of Homes which showcases different models, among them the Inspiration, the Idea House, the Riviera, the Monterrey, the Lanai, the Triumph II, the Imperial, the Arizonan, and Perfect Arizona

Type homes. Advertised house prices range from $6,500 to $40,000, with most around $15,000–$17,000. High-end features are burnt adobe and brick construction, gravel or "chunk marble" roofs, exposed beam ceilings, sliding glass doors, vinyl-tile kitchen floors, and brick terraces. In the next seven years, numerous residential developments will appear around Tucson, among them Painted Hills (west on Speedway in the Tucson Mountains), Casas Adobes (west of Oracle and Ina), Oracle Foothills Estates (east off North Oracle Road), Flecha Caida Ranch Estates (North Pontatoc Road), Carlos Terraces (northeast of Grant and Craycroft), Indian Ridge Terrace (north of Tanque Verde Road east of Pantano Wash), Green Hills (East Speedway a half mile past Wilmot), Beauty Built Homes (south of Broadway east of Swan), and Cielito Lindo (Drexel and Alvernon).

1955 fall

The author becomes a freshman at Tucson High School.

1955

To commemorate the 75th anniversary of the arrival of the railroad in Tucson, the Southern Pacific donates to the City of Tucson a locomotive that is placed in Himmel Park—No. 1673, a Mogul 2-6-0 configuration built in 1900 in upstate New York by the Schenectady Locomotive Works. It had logged over one million miles, primarily in southern Arizona.

1955

A new jet-powered swept-wing eight-engine long-range bomber appears in the skies over Tucson, the B-52. It has a longer range and much greater carrying capacity than the B-47 and will soon supplant it in the Strategic Air Command. The B-52 remains in service with the U.S. Air Force, though not at Davis-Monthan, and is expected to serve into the 2040s.

1955

Margaret Sanger (b. New York 1879, the 6th of 11 children), a sufferer from tuberculosis, moves to Tucson, which she had first visited in 1934. Now married to Noah Slee, of 3-in-1 Oil, the well-known advocate of birth control for women and founder of what became Planned Parenthood will live at 65 Sierra Vista in Catalina Vista until her death in 1966, which comes not long after the decision of the U.S. Supreme Court in *Griswold v. Connecticut* that legalizes birth control.

1955

On the east side, the "University Ruin," a significant Hohokam site from the Classic Period, AD 1150–1450, had been given to the UA Department of Anthropology in 1933 by Dorothy Knipe from land she and her husband had homesteaded between Tanque Verde and Sabino Canyon Roads. A caretaker's house for a visiting scholar had been built on the site that is still there in 2014. Digs supervised by Julian Hayden were conducted there in 1940 and 1941 under the auspices of the National Park Service and the Civilian Conservation Corps. The site, which had been badly picked over, still gives evidence of a platform mound. This year, a residential development, "Indian Ridge," begins to be developed around the site by Lusk Corporation. It will be built out in 1964. The Arizona State Museum conducts further excavation in 2010–2103. The ruin still belongs to UA.

1955–1959

Ernest McFarland, a Democrat, becomes governor, replacing Howard Pyle, a Republican. Earlier, McFarland had been majority leader of the U.S. Senate but had been defeated for reelection by Barry Goldwater.

1955

Voters approve a bond election for the schools for a combined total of $8,585,000. Seven elementary schools, one junior high school, and a new high school (Sunnyside, on Tucson's far south side just north of the municipal airport) are constructed, with additions made to 10 other schools.

1956–1958

The city's only high school, Tucson High, on 6th Street and Euclid, is attended by students from all of Tucson's many ethnic groups. When Pueblo High School is completed in 1956 on Tucson's South Side, at South Twelfth Avenue and 44th Street, its students, who move from Tucson High as a body, are predominantly Hispanic. Pueblo's name was chosen by the students. When Catalina High School is completed in 1957 north and east of Tucson High at Pima and

Dodge, the students who move to it are predominantly Anglo, as is the student body of Rincon High School, which is completed further east in 1958, on Swan and 5th Street. Catalina and Rincon are named according to the new school board policy to name schools after mountain ranges. School board head Deb Secrist had wanted to name the two new schools "Abraham Lincoln" and "George Washington." Later high schools are named after desert plants, e.g., Cholla and Saguaro. Elementary and junior high schools are being named after teachers. A de facto racial segregation of high school populations takes hold, except at Tucson High, where the mix persists. The author's Tucson High School class of 1959, which is continuing a practice of regular "Keep the Connection" get-togethers, remembers this mix as one of the most important benefits of their high school education.

1956

The Tucson Fire Department now has seven stations in the city. In 2014, it will have 21.

1956 April 29

At Davis-Monthan, an on-base drag strip for racing is officially opened on a portion of unused runway that had been made available to the Tucson Junior Chamber of Commerce. The author is about to get his learner's permit.

1956

The new Pima Verde Shopping Center is completed on the northeast corner of East Pima Street and North Craycroft Road. Small businesses occupy the building in 2014.

1956

East of the Chemistry and Physics building, the first pay parking lot at UA appears.

1956

Tucson acquires a wing of the Arizona Air National Guard. Its fighter aircraft will be housed at the Tucson Municipal Airport. In an innovative move, the Airport Authority has issued revenue bonds to allow construction of a new Tucson control tower to replace the wooden one that had been in use since World War II.

1957

Two new bond issues for schools are defeated. Schools go on double sessions. The 1958 bond issue is more carefully prepared and promoted by the board and it passes.

1957

North of town, the Amphi Plaza Shopping Center at North First Avenue and Fort Lowell Road is thriving. In 2014, the buildings are mostly vacant.

1957

On East Pennington Street, Tucson's first rooftop parking area is constructed on top of the Latimer Building.

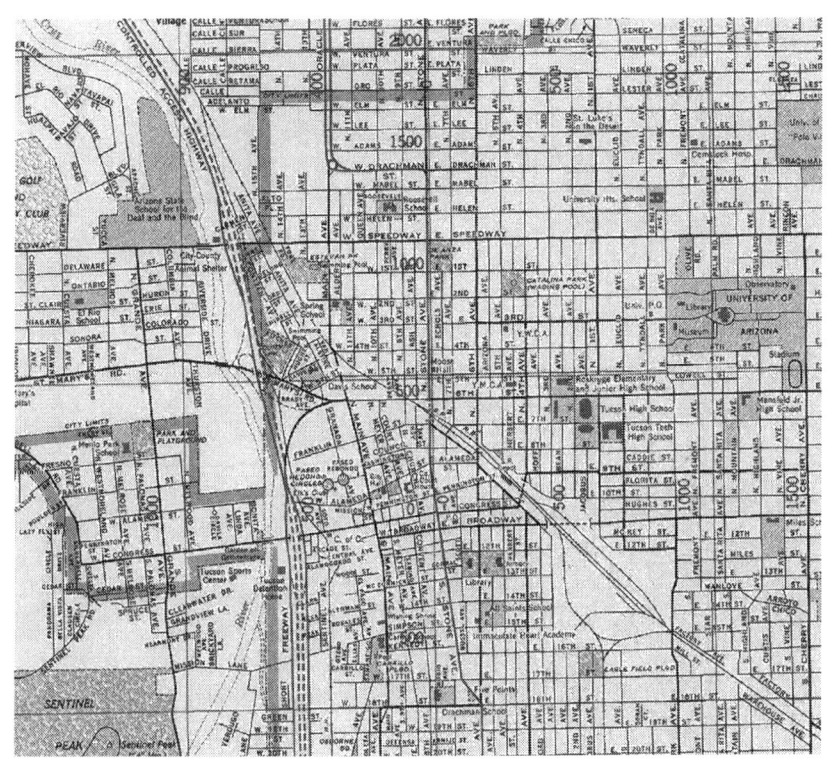

1956 Gousha map of Tucson (paid for by Shell Oil Company). This map is in the modern road-map style, which comes into wide use in the 1940s. Color and thickness denotes a road's importance. A standard symbology is employed for attractions and specialized areas such as parks and schools. Note the first part of what would later become Interstate 10 under construction. Barrio Viejo is still in place. © Successors to H. M. Gousha Corporation. Acquired from online David Rumsey Map Collection under Creative Commons license BY-NC-SA 3.0. Reuse allowed with attribution.

1957

On Stone just north of the Pioneer Hotel, Porter's Western Store installs a new glass front. Porter's will later move to 828 North Stone to make way for Union Bank.

1957

Tucson City Water acquires five private water companies and doubles in size from 1955. The question of whether to raise rates is contentious in the 1950s, with Republicans generally against it.

1957

Brownie Cote buys the 640-acre ranch that lies east of Tucson at the base of the Rincons, owned by Jim Converse since 1908 and operated as a cattle and dude ranch. In 2014, Cote's son Bob and Bob's wife Rita operate it as the Tanque Verde Guest Ranch, a "world class resort."

1957

Betty and Lloyd Golder, recently relocated from Chicago, buy the 4,800-acre Rancho Vistoso that lies several miles north of Tucson on the west side of Oracle Road. Two years later, their son, Lloyd Golder III (b. 1925, d. 2013), will buy from Roberta Nicholas the adjoining 18,000-acre Rail N Ranch that runs along the east side of Oracle Road. This land is now the site of Catalina State Park, Miraval Resort & Spa, SaddleBrooke, and the Rail N Ranch development.

On the west side of Oracle is the Rancho Vistoso housing development.

1958

Fifty-six miles southwest of Tucson, on land leased from the Tohono O'odham Nation, Kitt Peak National Observatory opens under director and UA professor of astronomy Aden Meinel. Kitt Peak will eventually house 24 optical telescopes, among which is the world's largest solar telescope, and two radio telescopes, "the most diverse collection of astronomical observatories on Earth," according to its website.

1958

With partial funding from the Atomic Energy Commission, UA gets a TRIGA nuclear reactor, the first nuclear reactor at an educational institution. Designed for research and instruction, it is a pool-type reactor that can be installed without a containment building. In the Metals and Materials Science building on 2nd Street it operates safely until it is decommissioned and removed in 2014.

1958

This summer, under the auspices of the American Field Service student exchange program, the author is able to go to Buenos Aires, Argentina, and live with an Argentinian family for two and a half months. The family speaks no English and he finally learns to speak Spanish, though with an Argentinian accent. He returns to Tucson with a sense of having much to learn and to unlearn about the way things stand in the world.

1958

Monte Mansfield sells his Ford dealership to Holmes Tuttle.

1958

Just east of El Conquistador Hotel on Broadway between Country Club and Alvernon, construction begins on El Con Mall. Leon Levy and Harold Steinfeld had fought rezoning the area for business. After losing that fight, Levy tries to talk Steinfeld into coming to the mall as a second anchor but Steinfeld declines. Levy then opens his second store on the north end of the mall. The hotel continues to have financial problems and 10 years later it is razed.

1958

On November 16, an unusually heavy snowstorm maroons the author and some Tucson High School classmates in Summerhaven on Mount Lemmon. They stay overnight in the handsome two-story Mount Lemmon Inn. In the Santa Ritas, the same storm catches some Boy Scouts hiking to Old Baldy. Three scouts die on the mountain. One of them, Mike Early, is a classmate of the author. Despite an assiduous search, their bodies are not found until December 4.

1959–1965

Paul Fannin, a Republican, is elected governor, replacing Ernest McFarland, a Democrat. He will serve three terms.

1959

Just south of Canoa, the Tubac Golf Resort begins to be developed by a California group on the site of one of the first Spanish land grants, made to Don Torbirio de Otero in 1789 and held in the Otero family until 1941. The original Otero hacienda is preserved as part of the resort. A few years earlier, the town of Tubac, site of the first Spanish presidio in Arizona, had begun to become an art colony.

1959

Tucson Rapid Transit gets its first air-conditioned buses.

1959 March

The Duke and Duchess of Windsor, formerly King Edward VIII of England and Wallis Simpson, an American, do Tucson this month while in residence at the Arizona Inn with their pugs. They observe spring training at Hi Corbett field and are given a tour of Davis-Monthan.

1959

The author graduates from Tucson High School (enrollment 5,400), and at the end of the summer flies out of Tucson on a DC-6 to attend Amherst College in Massachusetts (enrollment 1,000, all males). He will not return to Tucson to live until 1990.

1959 September 20

At the invitation of Mary Jeffries, the Reverend Martin Luther King, Jr. comes to Tucson to speak at the popular Sunday Evening Forum. Jeffries had organized the Forum in 1940 at the University Methodist Church and over the years attracted many significant speakers. The Forum is now being offered at the UA Auditorium, and UA vice-president Robert Nugent introduces King to a full-house. Jeffries has told King that there is a multi-racial church in Tucson, Southside Presbyterian Church. After his speech, King visits the church at the invitation of Southside's pastor, Rev. Casper Glenn. Most of Southside's congregants are Papago Indians. After King tells Glenn he has never visited an Indian reservation nor had a chance to get to know any Indians, Glenn takes him to Sells where he meets and speaks with tribal leaders, including chairman Enos Francisco Sr. King mostly listens and asks questions. He flies back to Atlanta that evening. His visit to Tucson has not been without controversy. Some residents have claimed King is a Communist.

1959

Phelps Dodge (now Freeport McMoRan) Sierrita open-pit copper-molybdenum mine begins to operate 20 miles south of Tucson, reserve life to 2080. Next door, ASARCO's Mission Mine begins to be developed, reserve life to 2033 (begins using CAP water in 2009).

1959–1960 school year

The peak elementary school district enrollment is 29,429 and the peak high school district enrollment is 8,807 for a total of 38,236. Total enrollment in 1940, just before Robert Morrow took office, had been 9,000. In the 1949–1950 school year, the peak enrollment in the elementary school district had been 12,981 and in the high school district had been 3,893 for a total of 16,874. The Tucson District 1 budget almost quadrupled in the last decade, from $4.6 million to $16.6 million.

1960

The City of Tucson's population is 212,892, up from 45,454 in 1950, an increase of 360 percent. Annexation since 1952 had added over 60 square miles to the city (9.6 to 70.9). Further annexation begins to be resisted by developers and residents because it means higher taxes. The increase in population from 1951 is 167,438 in the city, 124,444 in the county. The increase in population in Pima County in this decade is four times the increase in the previous decade.

1960

The Tucson Basin's water table is at about 80 feet, more than double its depth in 1940, and falling.

1960

Total enrollment, with increase since 1950: Tucson District 1: 27,585 with 7,908 at Tucson High School (Libby Coyner, Arizona State Archives). UA 12,518, +6,291 (a 100 percent increase); 907 faculty, +439 (a 94 percent increase); 65 buildings, +19 (a 41 percent increase). Tucson's Indian School on South Twelfth Avenue and Ajo Way, run by the Presbyterian Mission since 1888, and at this location since 1907, closes its doors. Four years later, it is demolished.

Started originally for Pimas and Papagos, it had begun in the 1930s and 1940s to accept students from other tribes.

1960

The City Directory for this year is published by Mullin-Kille Company of Arizona, whose home offices are in Chillicothe, Ohio.

- It lists 200 physicians, about the same number of lawyers, 35 liquor stores, 100 "taverns," 20 automobile dealers, 180 "Trailer Courts," and 100 "Motels," with 15 listings for "Automobile Parking," a new one.

- Also new are the three television stations, KGUN, KOLD, and KVOA-TV, with several firms now listed for distribution and repair of televisions.

- 20 firms are listed as being in the business of "Advertising," a large increase.

1960

The leading radio station in town is KTKT, located in the basement of the Arizona Land Title building downtown. The station has recently introduced a format of "Color Radio," which includes R&B music by black artists, played by DJ Frank Kalil. The 50's had seen the first Spanish language radio station, KEBT.

1960

Dense urban development begins in the Fort Lowell area with the Glenn Aire subdivision, 28 acres east of Swan between Fort Lowell and Glenn. The first subdivisions east of Pantano wash are platted. To the north in the Catalina Foothills and up Oracle Road, residential development continues.

1960

El Con shopping center opens. Federated Department Stores, an East Coast consortium, buys Levy's, keeping Leon Levy as manager. Harold Steinfeld declines to sell his store: It will be his last chance to do so. Levy's downtown store is operated by Federated for a few more years, then closed. Desperation is setting in as to how to save downtown.

1960

Making a commitment to use the space for "research and education," UA buys Tumamoc Hill from the U.S. Forest Service for one dollar. For the same price, the Forest Service had bought it from the Carnegie Foundation in 1940.

1960

Southwest of Old Main, UA's College of Law moves into the first building specifically designed for it. This is one of the first buildings to "jump" across the rock wall built around the west campus in the 1930s.

1960

The bids for the first phase of the Titan II Intercontinental Ballistic Missile site construction project are won by three companies (Jones-Teer-Winkelman Construction

Combine) for a total bid of $27,700,000. The Titan IIs use liquid rocket propellants that are for the first time "storable" in the missiles, an important innovation in ICBM technology that allows the missiles to be kept in underground silos ready for immediate launch instead of having to be fueled before launch. The propellants are, unfortunately, highly toxic.

1960

The Poetry Center at UA is founded through gifts by Ruth Stephan, an Illinois native who began visiting Tucson in the 1940s. Robert Frost reads at the dedication on November 17. Congressman Stewart Udall and UA president Harvill also attend. The center will develop one of the premier poetry libraries in the country and Frost is the first of many major poets and writers who will read at the Poetry Center over the years, some of whom are faculty in the creative writing program at UA or graduates of that program. The list includes all national poet laureates during the Poetry Center's life. Early on, visitors would sometimes stay in a small house on Highland called the Poet's Cottage, as, in 1990, did the author and his wife when they were being interviewed by the English Department at UA, where, they noted, many of the notable visitors had left poetic graffiti on the walls and door frames.

1960

The Lunar and Planetary Observatory, referred to by old-timers as the "Loony-Lab," is opened at UA, directed by nationally respected astronomer Gerard Kuiper, recently arrived from the University of Chicago. At this time, very little is known about the moon and planets: Astronomers have been studying the physics of stars and the cosmos, not the physical features of planets. UA's telescopes on Mount Lemmon will now be used by the Lunar and Planetary Lab (LPL) to do the first survey of the moon and then to develop landing sites for a hoped-for moon landing. In 1965, the National Aeronautics and Space Administration pays for a new Space Sciences building at UA for the LPL scientists. The moon landing takes place in 1969. From 1973 on, LPL will be involved—as an instrument maker, operator, or principal investigator (such as when Peter Smith is PI for the Pathfinder mission in 1997 that will return the first pictures taken on the surface of Mars)—in almost all major missions that use spacecraft to explore the solar system. LPL will also continue ground-based telescope research in, for example, its Catalina Sky Survey that Congress will authorize in 1998, that by 2014 will have discovered 5,800 new near-Earth asteroids. LPL does research only until 1972, when a Department of Planetary Sciences is established at UA as the teaching arm of LPL in a new field that reaches across physics, chemistry, astronomy, geology, atmospheric science, and other disciplines. Only graduate students are admitted in Planetary Sciences until the 1980s when a program for undergraduates is begun. After 2008, UA will operate on Mount Lemmon Arizona's largest public observatory, the UA Sky Center, offering tours during which viewers can use the telescope there; its 61-inch mirror was used for the moon surveys.

1961

Lewis Davis becomes mayor of Tucson, until 1967.

1961

On a secluded plot John Murphey had reserved for the purpose high in the Catalina Foothills, John and Helen Murphey complete a 15,000-square-foot house for themselves that they call Casa Juan Paisano, designed by Mexican architect Juan Worner Bas, whom they had met on a trip to Mexico City in 1952. The house combines modernist and colonial architecture in a style Worner Bas describes as "Mexican Colonial," which he says integrates grand Aztec with delicate Arabic elements. Murphey also commissions Worner Bas to build an annex to Josias Joesler's Broadway Village Shopping Center at Broadway and Country Club. The Murpheys now become the patron of Worner Bas, as they had been of Josias Joesler, who had died in 1956.

1961

On Tucson's far east side, Otto Small (b. Poland 1910, d. Tucson 1964 in a car accident) completes the first of the 160 houses that will be built in his Desert Palms development between Speedway/Wrightstown and Camino Seco/Harrison Roads. The development, which lies only a couple of miles short of Saguaro National Monument and the Rincon Mountains (now Saguaro National Park East), is built out by 1968.

1961

The Fluor Corporation of Los Angeles, California, submits a low bid of $35,643,500 for Phase II of Titan II Intercontinental Ballistic Missile site construction.

1961

Lorna Lockwood, who had received her BA and her law degree from UA, becomes the first woman Arizona Supreme Court justice and goes on to become the first woman in the United States to serve as chief justice of a state supreme court.

1962

A Titan II ICBM site subcontractor declares bankruptcy, electrical workers go out on strike, a federal mediator is called in—but the eighteen Titan II sites surrounding Tucson will get built.

1962

In a largely undeveloped area in the northeast Catalina Foothills, Skyline Country Club begins to be developed by Oklahoma attorney-investor Leonard Savage and John Bender as "a quiet alternative to Palm Springs."

1962

During the renovation of St. Augustine Cathedral, Bishop Salpointe's remains are found and relocated to Holy Hope Cemetery.

1962 March 11

Martin Luther King Jr. visits Tucson again at the invitation of Mary Jeffries. This time, he preaches at the 11 a.m.

service at Catalina (United) Methodist Church on Speedway at the invitation of the minister, Dr. Hayden Sears. Sears is criticized by some members of his congregation for issuing the invitation. Later in the day, King visits the Tucson Press Club Forum and that evening again speaks at the UA's Auditorium (now Centennial Hall). He tells the packed house about the progress that has been made in the civil rights movement and work that is yet to be done. Some of that work, it is clear, is in Tucson.

1962 June

Tucson's urban renewal plan is defeated by voters. Growth continues in and around Tucson, but voters have stopped supporting bond issues.

1962 December 31

Davis-Monthan base strength declines about 20 percent from its levels during the 1950s, to 867 officers and 4,608 enlisted personnel.

1963

On Broadway east of downtown, a renovated and redesigned underpass beneath the Southern Pacific Railroad tracks is dedicated.

1963

A new terminal opens at Tucson Municipal Airport, with flights to and from Mexico. Major remodeling takes place in the 1960s and 1970s. In the fall, the author, having graduated from Amherst College, leaves from this new terminal to "read" English for two years at Oxford University in England.

1963

Richard and Jean Wilson acquire a large Santa Fe-style house and land northwest of the intersection of Oracle and Ina Roads that from 1937 to 1943 had been the occasional residence of avid polo player John DuBlois Wack of California. The Wilsons begin to restore the house and acquire surrounding land. Eventually, after resisting the offers of developers, they create what is now the 49-acre Tohono Chul Botanical Gardens and Park, formally dedicated in 1985, whose mission is "to enrich people's lives by connecting them with the wonders of nature, art and culture in the Sonoran Desert region."

1963

Harold Steinfeld sells the Pioneer Hotel to investors who want offices for a new bank, Union Bank. The hotel no longer turns a profit.

1963

Reverend David Sholin, pastor at Mountain View Presbyterian, who in recent years has been working with church members to build a program that helps blacks and other minorities buy homes in racially restricted areas of Tucson, goes to Washington, D.C., to take part in Dr. Martin Luther King's March for Jobs and Freedom. When he returns, 300 of his 2,000 parishioners leave the church.

1963

The Pima County Juvenile Court Building opens on South Freeway. It continues to be referred to by locals, including the author, as "Mother Higgins," after Clara Higgins, the woman who with her husband, Patrick, had run the county's detention facility for juveniles from 1920 to 1947 (Patrick died in 1932). The new facility houses 26 boys and 12 girls. In 2014, the Pima County Juvenile Court facility, on East Ajo Way since 1967, has 162 beds.

1963

The U-2 long-range photo-reconnaissance airplane appears in the skies above Tucson. It will be flying out of Davis-Monthan until 1976.

1963

Eighteen Titan II missile sites have now been activated at individual sites around Tucson. Each missile's warhead yields the equivalent of nine million tons of TNT, twice the explosive power of all the munitions used by all sides in the whole of World War II, in missiles that are launchable in under 15 minutes from the time the order is received and will arrive at their destinations 30 minutes later, with no possibility of recall. At 5th Street and Wilmot, the church sign for St. Michael and All Angels now carries the legend "It's a sin to build a nuclear weapon."

1963

The Harrenstein House with its striking rounded six-domed concrete rooftop is completed near the intersection of Orange Grove and North First Avenue. Paul Harrenstein is a civil engineer who has consulted on nuclear bomb shelter design. A bomb shelter is built underneath the house. The house remains a private residence.

1964

Florence S. Reynolds becomes principal at Pueblo High School, the first female high school principal in Arizona.

1964

At the urging of Edward Spicer, UA anthropologist and authority on the Yaqui (who call themselves "Yoeme") a federal reservation called New Pascua is created for Yaqui Indians southwest of Tucson on the north side of the Tohono O'odham reservation. The Yaqui are indigenous to a region in northern Mexico, not to the Tucson Basin, but in 1978, they are recognized by the U.S. government as a "created tribe," and in 1994 as a "historical tribe," making them eligible for a reservation. Southwest of Tucson, the tribe has operated the Casino of the Sun since 1994, and, since 2011, the Casino del Sol. The Yaqui will continue to conduct their distinctive Easter ceremonies at Capilla San Ignacio de Loyola (785 W. Saguaro Street at Old Pascua SW of Grant and Oracle), Capilla de San Martin de Porres (on west 39th just off South 10th Avenue), Capilla del Señor de los Milagros (South 16th Avenue and West 44th Street), and

Capilla Cristo Rey (7529 S. Camino Benem, at New Pascua, off Valencia Road).

1964

The Green Valley golf course and retirement community has been planned on the west side of the Santa Cruz and I-19, 25 miles south of Tucson. The Green Valley News *community newspaper begins to publish now but the development will not take off until the early 1970s, after it has changed hands. In 2014, 20,000 people are estimated to live in Green Valley, 35,000 in the winter months, 98 percent of them white. Across from the development, on the east side of I-19, the town of Continental (from the Continental Farms that were in the area between World War I and 1948) is appearing. Both Green Valley and Continental are in the north part of the San Ignacio de Canoa land grant.*

1964

A youth mariachi group called Los Changuitos Feos (the Ugly Little Monkeys) is started under the sponsorship of the Catholic Youth Organization of All Saints Parish, likely the first youth mariachi group in the United States.

1964

The Tucson Audubon Society, which had been meeting intermittently since 1949, becomes a chapter of the National Audubon Society.

1964 March

With Governor Paul Fannin's signature, the Arizona Atomic Energy Commission is created to try to benefit from federal Project Plowshare funds. Plowshare, the brainchild of physicist Edward Teller and sponsored by the Eisenhower administration, was an effort begun in 1957 to develop peaceful uses for atomic explosions. From 1961 to 1973, Plowshare conducted thirty-five underground nuclear explosions in the United States. None was conducted in Arizona, though many different projects were considered by the AAEC, including using nuclear explosions to help dig the Central Arizona Project canal. Plowshare effectively ended in 1973 without fanfare and without successes.

1964

A new jet that is both a fighter and a bomber appears in the skies over Tucson, the F-4 Phantom. The F-4 will fly many missions in the Vietnam War.

1964

UA's Optical Sciences Center (OSC) opens, with support from the UA Foundation and the U.S. Air Force, which will supply many of the first graduate students. The Air Force has been working to develop cameras for its reconnaissance airplanes and, since the launch of the Sputnik satellite by the Soviet Union in 1957, for spy satellites. The developer of the OSC and its first director is Aden Meinel, formerly director of the Steward and Kitt Peak Observatories. In 2005, OSC will become the College of Optical Sciences, offering graduate and undergraduate courses. In 2006, the striking Meinel Building will be completed on the campus at the corner of Cherry Avenue and University Boulevard, on the site of the first ROTC stables.

1965–1967

Samuel Goddard, a Democrat, replaces Paul Fannin, a Republican, as governor.

1965

South of Tucson in Sahuarita, on the old Continental Farms site on the Santa Cruz, farmer Keith Walden converts his cotton crop to pecans.

1965

Ridership on Tucson Rapid Transit buses has declined 65 percent from its peak in 1945. TRT will be purchased by the city in 1969. The suburban and exurban (Green Valley) developments now being built can be reached only by car.

1965

Don Diamond (b. NYC 1918) had attended the Brandes School (for asthma sufferers) before high school, and later, UA (1947-49). He had later returned to New York City and joined the commodities trading firm in which his father was a partner, retiring from the firm at the age of 37 and returning with his wife Joan to Tucson, where, foreseeing the continuing growth of Tucson, he began to buy up large lots of land around the city. Over the next 50 years, he would develop many properties in Tucson, elsewhere in Pima County, and in Colorado and Texas, including exclusive enclaves, master-planned developments, and multi-builder neighborhoods, as well as office, retail, industrial, and hospitality properties. He establishes Diamond Ventures, Inc. in 1988.

1965

Tucson's population has grown by more than 600 percent since 1940 (from 35,752 to over 220,000). From 1940 to 1965, 3.3 million acre-feet of water are pumped out of the aquifer under the Tucson Basin. Pumping for domestic uses rises from 7,000 acre-feet in 1940 to more than 54,000 acre-feet in 1965, and for agriculture from 42,000 acre-feet to 141,000 acre-feet. From 1947 to 1951, the overdraft in middle and upper Santa Cruz River Basins (Tucson and Nogales) had averaged 55,000 acre-feet per year. With the passage of bond issues in 1952 and 1958, the city had added new wells at Valencia Road, after which the *cienega* south of Martinez Hill had dried up entirely. In the 1960s, the city begins to use effluent in agriculture.

1965

The Immigration and Nationality Act of 1965, promoted by President Kennedy and signed by President Johnson at the Statue of Liberty after Kennedy's assassination, abolishes the "National Origins Formula" in favor of a preference system based on skills and family relationships, with a limit of 170,000 visas per Eastern Hemisphere country and 120,000 per Western Hemisphere country, with immediate relatives and "special immigrants" exempted.

1965

On Stone just north of Congress, the Tucson Federal Savings Tower is built; the architect is Lew Place, son of Roy. It is Tucson's tallest building at the time (21 stories).

1965

J. Knox Corbett Lumber and Hardware Company, in business since before statehood, closes its doors. Its office building is still standing just north of the Sixth Avenue underpass. Many other lumber and hardware companies are now in business in Tucson supporting its rapid expansion.

1965

William R. Mathews, who had controlled the *Arizona Daily Star* for the last 35 years, sells it to the William A. Small family, publishers of the *Citizen* since 1936. The Smalls survive a federal anti-trust challenge, but in 1971 William Small Jr. will sell the *Star* to the Pulitzer Publishing Company and in 1976 will sell the *Citizen* to Gannett. For the first time since statehood, Tucson will not have a locally owned daily newspaper.

1965

Having completed his course of study at Oxford, the author begins study at the New York University School of Law. He lives in law school housing in Greenwich Village.

1965

Tucson Parks director Gene Reid opens a petting zoo in Randolph Park. By 2014, this zoo will have come to hold more than 500 animals, including elephants and giant anteaters, and Randolph Park will have been renamed Reid Park.

1965 April

A major bond election take place, the first after voters defeat a number of proposals in 1963. This one succeeds and makes possible, it is said, "Tucson's participation in the national urban renewal movement designed to rejuvenate our inner cities. The city would acquire blocks and blocks of crumbling adobe houses and buildings to make room for the construction of the Community Center, which would include a large sports arena, a music center, and a smaller live theater, and a large parking garage. The bonds would also provide financing for a new city hall building, a new police station on South Stone Avenue; several new firehouses and parks and miles of new streets, water lines, and sewer lines." Roy Drachman leads the "citizens' committees" of business leaders that successfully promote passage after defeat of the proposals three years earlier. The county later asks for and gets the committees' support for bond issues that finance the "building presently housing the offices of the board of supervisors (and of many other county departments and agencies), the building containing the Pima County court system, and the building known as the County Morgue..., a new and enlarged wastewater treatment plant...and land for the present downtown Holiday Inn." Tucson School District 1 also asks for and gets support from the committees for buildings and improvements.

1965

Electronics firm Burr-Brown Research Corporation moves into the first building at what will be its 250,000-square-foot facility north of the municipal airport. The company had been started in 1956 by Page Burr and Tom Brown to try to take fuller advantage of the invention of the transistor. Brown had handled manufacturing in Tucson, and had bought out Burr and run the company during its very rapid growth after 1959. In 2000, Brown will sell the company to Texas Instruments in a stock deal worth $7.6 billion.

1965 December

Department of Defense cutbacks halt $3.9 million worth of scheduled construction projects at Davis-Monthan Air Force Base. There are 768 officers and 5,563 enlisted personnel now assigned, a slight decrease from the already decreased levels of 1962.

1960s middle to late

Pueblo High develops a program to teach Spanish to Mexican-Americans, recognizing that the usual "foreign-language" Spanish classes do not work for them. Later in the 1960s, Maria Urquides, Henry Oyama, Adalberto Guerrero, and Rosita Cota research and co-author a National Education Association report called "The Invisible Minority" on the status of Mexican-American students in American high schools. That report leads to congressional hearings at which the four District 1 teachers testify. The first federal legislation funding bilingual education follows.

1966

Father Kino's grave is found in Magdalena, Sonora, by a team of Mexican anthropologists that includes Arizona State Museum archaeologists. A memorial to Kino is constructed in the plaza at Magdalena in 1971. The governor of Sonora commissions an equestrian statue of Kino and three castings are made. One is placed outside Magdalena, Sonora; one is in Trent, Italy (Kino's birthplace); and one is in Tucson on the Kino Parkway at 15th Street. In 2014, in front of the Arizona History Museum in Tucson, a copy of a statue of Kino that had been sculpted by Belgian-American artist Suzzane Silvercruys a year before the discovery of the grave to be placed in the U.S. Capitol building can be seen, along with a statue of Rough Rider and mining executive John Greenway. The Jesuits have begun to seek Kino's beatification, the step before sainthood.

1966

Charles Ares is hired to become the new dean of the College of Law and to give it national standing. The previous fall, Ares had been a professor at the New York University School of Law and the author had taken Ares's course in criminal law and found it the best of his first-year courses.

1966

A new baseball stadium is completed at UA to replace the one that had been constructed in 1929, the first year the author's father had attended UA and played on the baseball team.

1966

Congress passes the U.S. Demonstration Cities and Metropolitan Development Act. A large "Model Cities" grant is received by the City of Tucson to address "blight" in six square miles in downtown (Barrio Viejo).

1966

Congress also passes the National Historic Preservation Act intended to coordinate and strengthen protection of historical and archaeological sites in the U.S. from destruction by federal projects. It then creates the National Register of Historic Places, to be overseen by the National Park Service, and State Historic Preservation Offices. Listing in the register makes properties eligible for grants, loans, and tax incentives. The Act makes possible the highly significant archeological work that follows in the Tucson Basin over the next 50 years, much of it in advance of development and road projects.

1966

Helen d'Autremont (b. 1889) dies in an accident in a car in which she was a passenger. She and her husband Hubert had come from Duluth to Tucson in the '30s seeking health for a child of theirs who suffered from severe respiratory problems. A family of means, they had acquired a large tract of land northwest of Grant and Swan to what is now Wyatt Drive, land that by 2014 will have been almost entirely developed. Hubert died in the late 40's. Helen had remained very active in civic work in Tucson and was one of the largest contributors to Tucson charities, usually anonymously. She founded an interracial low-cost housing development, helped to found the Amerind Foundation, and provided financial assistance to UA students, among many other works. In 1986, she will be inducted into the Arizona Women's Hall of Fame.

1966

Pima College is approved by the Arizona state legislature as a junior college. The first classes will be offered in 1969. The first building—now the West Campus—opens in 1970 west of the Santa Cruz between Speedway and Anklam Road. In 1972 the college is renamed Pima Community College.

1967–1975

Jack Williams, a Republican, becomes governor, replacing Sam Goddard, a Democrat. He will serve three terms.

1967

"Jim" Corbett Jr. becomes mayor, in office until 1971. He had earlier served in the Arizona House and on the Tucson City Council. In 1878, his grandfather had opened what might have been the first hardware store in the Territory of Arizona, a store later merged with the lumber store of his great-uncle J. Knox Corbett. Jim's uncle was Hi Corbett, after whom the baseball field in Randolph Park had been named.

1967 October

A UA study sponsored by the Arizona Atomic Energy Commission is produced by the UA Hydrology and Water Resources Office, among others, entitled "Potential Site Investigation for Nuclear Energy

Crater Experiment and Water Management in Arizona." Governor Williams authorizes a study which identifies 14 sites for possible nuclear detonations, nine on the Navajo Reservation, one on the San Simon River on the Mexican border southeast of Tucson, setting 1970 as the date for the first one in a water development project to be called Project Aquarius. Enthusiasm (and promotion by the Williams administration and the AAEC) is high to begin with but is eventually tempered (as it will be in all Plowshare projects) by a growing appreciation of the problems of residual radioactivity, also a problem in the copper mining, gas storage, and geothermal products proposed. Plowshare peters out nationally in 1973 with no nuclear detonations having taken place in Arizona.*

1967 December

Davis-Monthan base strength—1,140 officers and 7,985 enlisted personnel—has returned to the levels of the 1950s.

1967

Recent arrival in Tucson, Marian Lupu, becomes the unpaid director of the Tucson Council on Aging, established after the passage of the federal Older Americans Act of 1965. The Council will become the Pima Council on Aging, which Lupu will direct for 40 years. Her efforts and advocacy will build PCA into an important resource for seniors.

1967

J. Carlos McCormick, who earlier had served on the staff of President John Kennedy and gone on to become the president of the Alianza Hispano-Americana, is convicted of embezzling money from the organization and sentenced to prison. The next year, McCormick's conviction is reversed by the Arizona Supreme Court but the Alianza, a mutual-aid group founded in Tucson in 1894 that had grown into an international organization, now begins to fade away. It had reached its peak membership at the end of the 1930s.

1967–1968

El Conquistador Hotel on Broadway between Country Club and Alvernon is demolished, causing great sadness in many circles. It had opened in 1928 in the open desert east of downtown and never been financially successful. The desert around it has by now been entirely developed.

1968

The complete restoration of the St. Augustine Cathedral on Stone that had been ordered by Bishop Francis J. Green in 1966 is completed, coinciding with the centennial of the completion of the original adobe church of St. Augustine on Church and Broadway. The remodeled church preserves the towers and the facade installed in 1928 that had been modeled after one on the cathedral in Querétaro, Mexico.

1968

A dirt track for car racing opens southeast of Tucson. The track is paved in 1993, closed in 2010, and reopened in 2013 under new ownership as Tucson Speedway.

1968

The City of Tucson acquires El Rio Country Club to become a municipal golf course.

1968

Out east, northeast of the intersection of Wilmot and Speedway, the former half section that had been the site of the Florence Pond mansion, Stone Ashley, is subdivided. The Stone Ashley House itself later becomes El Dorado Lodge, then the Palm Court Restaurant, then the Charles Restaurant, and then a restaurant called Stone Ashley. Since 2004, it has been the home of the Mountain Oyster Club (established 1948). In 2014, most of the remaining Pond land is occupied by El Dorado Hospital, El Dorado Country Club Estates, three banks, several commercial office complexes, and apartments.

1968–1974

Urban renewal takes place in Tucson. If we don't count the removal before statehood of the notorious area west of Stone between Congress and Maiden Lane (no longer there) known as the Wedge, "renewal" had begun in the late 1950s with the Church Street widening that destroyed a number of historic structures in the Presidio Neighborhood. The renewal that begins now will destroy what remains of the original St. Augustine Church at Church and Broadway, abandoned in 1897. Also destroyed will be the large Jacobs House at Meyer and Alameda, the Cosmopolitan Club on Ochoa, Ronquillos Bakery on Court, the Blue Moon Lounge on

Congress, and the Ying On Club and the Chinese Chamber of Commerce Buildings on South Main, among many other residences and businesses. Preserved by the city are the "Fremont" House on South Main (now more properly called the Sosa-Carrillo-Fremont House and now a museum run by the Arizona Historical Society) and the Fish-Stevens Houses on North Main (now the home of the Tucson Museum of Art). The house of Mariano Samaniego on Ochoa is incorporated into the new La Placita buildings. The facade of the old San Augustín Church is preserved and is now to be seen on the entrance to the Arizona Historical Museum at Park and Second Avenue. Before demolition, archaeologists from the Arizona State Museum record 211 buildings and excavate throughout the site, which had been occupied since shortly after the founding of the presidio in 1775.

1968

The author begins a clerkship in the United States Court of Appeals for the Ninth Circuit with Chief Judge Richard Chambers, who sits part of the year in San Francisco and part of the year in Tucson. While Judge Chambers is sitting in Tucson, the author rents a room on the second floor of a run-down building on Franklin Street at Meyer without quite knowing why he finds this part of town so appealing. He knows almost nothing of the history of the area and he is not alone.

1968

Robert D. Morrow retires, with 54,000 students in Tucson School District 1, up from 9,000 in 1940, the year before he took the job; 55 of District 1's schools had been built or started during his tenure. School budgets: $18,900,000 in 1960, $33,000,000 in 1968. Morrow had desegregated the district's schools in 1951, before the *Brown* decision. Upon his retirement, an investigation into de facto segregation in the district begins.

1968

In the year that Martin Luther King is assassinated, the black students at UA who have formed a Black Student Union begin active civil rights protests that will continue through 1971. The UA and President Harvill are not spared the unrest sweeping the country because of racial discrimination and later the Vietnam War.

1968

The Colorado River Basin Project Act is signed by President Lyndon Johnson. This is the act that leads to the Central Arizona Project canal that brings water to Tucson from the Colorado River.

1969

University of Arizona Athletic Director Dick Clausen hires Willie Williams as Arizona's head track and field coach. Williams may have been the first African-American to be hired as a head coach at a Division I school.

1969

Tucson Awareness House is started by a group of local teachers and community leaders concerned about drug and alcohol use in recent years by young people in the community. This becomes Amity, still active in 2014.

1969

At the new El Con shopping center, Federated Department Stores builds a big store for Levy's on the center's west end. In July 1970, Steinfeld's leases the old Levy's space. In 1971, JC Penney builds another big store in the shopping center. In 2012 the Levy's space is razed and replaced by a Walmart.

1969

The City of Tucson takes over the Tucson Rapid Transit bus system and with the help of federal money begins to make improvements that dramatically increase ridership. In 1975, after a contest, the new company is named Sun Tran.

1969

In the skies over Tucson, the swept-wing jet fighter known as the F-100 Super Sabre is now flying out of Tucson's Air National Guard base next to the Tucson Municipal Airport. The Guard's mission is to provide combat-ready fighter pilots and homeland protection. In 1977, the F-100 will be replaced by the A-7 Corsair.

1969

The author decides not to continue in the law and not to return to Tucson. He goes to Laramie, Wyoming, to see what will develop. After several months, he begins teaching literature and composition courses for the Department of English at the University of Wyoming.

1969

Frank Boice sells the 25,000-acre Empire Ranch east of the Santa Ritas to Gulf American Corporation, a land sales company with significant operations in Florida. Pima Country requires Gulf American to build infrastructure before it will rezone the land for development. The infrastructure is not built and neither is a residential development. In 2000, the Las Cienegas National Conservation Area is established on the land ("cienega," also "cienaga," means "marsh" in Spanish).

1969

The interstate highway through Tucson—I-10—is completed. The formerly thriving businesses along US 80, the Benson Highway, will now struggle to survive.

1969 December

Davis-Monthan base strength—1,288 officers and 6,817 enlisted personnel—increases again and now exceeds the levels of the 1950s by about 10 percent.

1970

Tucson's urbanized area population is 262,933, a 23.5 percent increase from 1960 (City Directory claims 350,000). The city area has increased from 70.9 square miles in 1960 to 97.1 square miles.

1970

Total enrollments, with change from 1960: Tucson School District 1 57,346 (minority enrollment is 18,957, 33.1 percent), with 12 public high schools, 89 elementary and junior high schools, and 23 parochial schools. Pima Community College enrolls 3,543; the University of Arizona enrolls 26,021, an increase of 13,506, with 1,579 faculty, up 672, and 97 buildings, up 32.

1970

This year's City Directory is published by R. L. Polk & Co. of Dallas, Texas.

- It notes that at this point the city is now served by I-10, the new interstate highway that, like the Southern Pacific line, connects Los Angeles to New Orleans.

- It also notes that in 1959, the "Tucson Industrial Development Board" had been formed that has now become the "Development Authority for Tucson's Expansion (D.A.T.E.)."

- The Directory claims 238 churches of "nearly every denomination."

- It lists 12 AM radio stations, two FM radio stations, four TV stations, 14 theaters (7 of which are "drive-in"), 11 hospitals, 28 hotels, and 146 "motels," with 26 guest ranches in the vicinity.

346   *Tucson: A Drama in Time*

- "Tucson Municipal Airport" is now "Tucson International Airport," with flights to and from Mexico.

- The Directory notes that Davis-Monthan Air Force Base is now home to the 12th Strategic Aerospace Division, with the 390th Titan Missile Wing in charge of two squadrons of Titan II ICBMs (total of 18) in silos around Tucson, and home also to the 100th Strategic Reconnaissance Wing, flying U-2 missions. Davis-Monthan is also home to the Tactical Air Command's 4453rd Combat Crew Training Wing which trains pilots to fly the F4C Phantom II fighter-bombers, now in service in Vietnam, and rescue helicopters. It is still serving as the Military Aircraft Storage and Disposal Center for aircraft that are out of service.

- As cultural amenities, the Directory lists the Tucson Symphony, Tucson Civic Chorus, Tucson Boys Chorus, and the Tucson Festival Society which is in charge of events like the Fiesta de los Vaqueros (the Festival Society lasts into the 1980s). It might also have listed the activities of UA's Poetry Center, founded in 1960, now a growing archive and national center for poets and lovers of contemporary poetry. It might have mentioned Tucson's active ethnic and acoustic music scene, and its active scene in crafts and painting, including the silver jewelry of the Patania family, the work available at Tom Bahti Indian Arts, the increasingly well-known work of Ted DeGrazia, and the western painting and sculpture of the sort sponsored by the Mountain Oyster Club. All of the above remain important presences in Tucson in 2014.

1970

Southeast of Tucson, the Sonoita-Patagonia Creek Preserve becomes a National Historic Landmark. The area had been preserved from the pressure on its water resources that had been experienced by the Santa Cruz River Basin.

1970s

U.S. and Mexican governments agree to the "twin plants" system that supports growth of maquiladoras *(large assembly facilities that employ relatively cheap Mexican labor) in Nogales, Sonora. Growth on the Mexican side puts more pressure on Santa Cruz water.*

1970s

Open-pit mines in the Sierritas south of Tucson achieve peak production, and usage of pumped groundwater increases.

1970

UA students briefly occupy the offices of Old Main and the ROTC Building protesting the Vietnam War.

1970

As the water table in the Tucson Basin falls to more than 90 feet below ground level, the Great Mesquite Bosque on the Santa Cruz south of Martinez Hill, formerly home to many species of birds and even fish, disappears entirely.

1970

The Tucson School District school board approves a resolution that asks the Tucson City Council to stop putting low-income housing units in minority population areas, believing that the practice has increased de facto segregation and racial isolation.

1970

The county's transportation plans from 1965 have been roundly opposed by significant portions of the public and now the proposed Butterfield Expressway that would have passed through Barrio Historico, dividing Tucson at that point and destroying the El Tiradito shrine, is voted down. In 1972, El Tiradito is put on the National Register of Historic Places.

1970

South of downtown, on 22nd Street and South 5th Avenue, Garcia's Cleaners and Laundry is established. In 2014, it is expanded and still in business as Garcia's Cleaners and Shirt Laundry.

1970

The old bridge on West Congress that crosses the Santa Cruz River is replaced.

1970

On Fourth Avenue between the underpass and University Avenue, a street fair is mounted by the motley collection of the avenue's merchants which include a grocery named the Food Conspiracy Co-op. In 2014, the Food Conspiracy is still there, along with Antigone Books, a number of restaurants, and other enterprises. Two street fairs a year are now staged along the avenue, before Christmas and before Easter, with many of the wares being offered by off-street merchants. The Tucson Modern Streetcar tracks now run south down the avenue from University Street to the Fourth Avenue tunnel and into downtown.

1970 December 21

The Pioneer Hotel catches fire. Before it is extinguished, 29 people are dead, including Harold Steinfeld and his wife, Peggy, who die in their penthouse residence of smoke inhalation. The building survives, but four years after the fire, the Pioneer Hotel is in foreclosure. The demise of the hotel is seen as contributing to the demise of Tucson's downtown generally. A black 16-year-old, Louis Taylor, is convicted of starting the fire. He is released in 2013, after 42 years in prison, with questions having arisen as to whether the fire had been started by arson. In 2014, the hotel building houses business offices and apartments.

1971

Lewis Murphy becomes mayor of Tucson, until 1987, which will make him the longest-serving mayor of Tucson.

During his administration, Tucson's population will nearly double and 63 square miles will be annexed by the city.

1971

The Sisters of Charity sell Casa Seton in Potter Place north of the Arizona Inn to John S. Greenway, son of Isabella and John Greenway and then the owner of the inn (Isabella Greenway had died in 1953). Two weeks after the sisters leave Casa Seton, the 83-foot well that had been dug on the land in 1907 by J. B. Wheeler goes dry.

1971

The new University of Arizona Medical Center opens on the west side of Campbell, built between Helen and Elm on land that had been occupied by the UA's polo field, Polo Village East, and by houses in Murphey's Old World Addition, a number of them designed by architect Josias Joesler. In 2014, one of the houses in the addition remains, on the corner of Campbell and Mabel.

1971

At UA, a new Student Union building is completed that doubles the square footage of the old one.

1971 November 5

The Tucson Convention Center that had been built as part of Tucson's urban renewal project opens to much fanfare. La Placita Village is about to break ground on the area that had been the plaza for the first St. Augustine Church.

1971

Two new Valley National Bank branch office buildings are under construction on East Broadway Boulevard, one on the northwest corner of East Broadway and North Country Club and another further east at Kolb. In 2014, the distinctive building at Country Club is occupied by Chase Bank and the one at Kolb is occupied by small businesses.

1971

The Jerry Lewis Cinema out east on Broadway near Kolb Road is near completion. In 2014, it is the Gaslight Theater, featuring melodramatic entertainment, music, and free popcorn, with the Gaslight Print Shop and Costume Shop nearby in the old Valley Bank building.

1971

Student protests and marches continue at UA, now focused on the Vietnam War, though civil rights issues remain part of the mix at UA as elsewhere in the United States. UA president Richard Harvill thinks about arresting protesting students but decides not to do so after being advised by Charles Ares, dean of the Law School, that this would violate the First Amendment of the U.S. Constitution. Instead, the campus police are directed to take photographs of protesters.

1971

At UA, English professor Charles Scruggs takes over direction of an International Film Series that had been running under the auspices of the English and French Departments since 1953. The weekly series is open to the public and the only venue in Tucson where independent and foreign films can regularly be seen. It is often sold out and runs until the 1990s. In 2002, Peggy Johnson opens the non-profit Loft Cinema on Speedway, which begins to fill the gap. The once-a-year-in-the-spring Arizona Film Festival begins in Tucson in 1991 and, sponsored by various community partners, is still taking place in 2014. The Loft is thriving, still led by Peggy Johnson.

1971 December

Davis-Monthan base strength is 1,153 officers and 7,500 enlisted personnel, about what it was in the 1950s, down slightly from what it had been in the preceding two years. The F-4 Phantom fighter-bombers that have been based at Davis-Monthan are moved to Luke Air Force Base in Phoenix this year and replaced at Davis-Monthan by the A-7 Corsair, an attack aircraft, one of which crashes just south of UA a few years later. The pilot manages to avoid the campus and comes down under his parachute in the UA Mall. South of the campus several people are killed.

1972

Collective merchant income downtown reaches an all-time low.

1972

Old Main is placed on the National Register of Historic Places. A historic preservation ordinance is passed by the city, emerging from a "Comprehensive Planning Process." "Infill" begins to be promoted to combat "sprawl."

1972

John Schaefer had replaced Richard Harvill as UA president last year. This year his Athletic Director, Dave Strack, hires Fred Snowden to coach the men's basketball team. Snowden is the first African-American head coach of a team at a major university and the second at a Division I school. Snowden begins recruiting black players. Attendance at Bear Down had been dismal in recent years. In the middle of Snowden's first year, the McKale Center arena is completed, which seats almost 14,000, as opposed to the 3,000 in Bear Down. Snowden's teams soon fill McKale. Snowden himself receives hate mail and death threats. In the late 1970s, UA's teams move from the Western Athletic to the Pacific 10 Conference. In 1982, after three losing seasons that follow this move, Snowden leaves coaching. The coach who replaces him, Ben Lindsey, is replaced the next year by Lute Olson.

1972

A gift to the Astronomy Department from the estate of Grace Flandrau, an author and frequent winter visitor to Tucson, is used to build the Flandrau Science Center & Planetarium, which opens in 1975.

1973

A new Superior Courthouse, the fourth one in Pima County and the one still being used in 2014, begins to be built just south of the old pink one designed by Roy Place and completed in 1929.

1973

The *Arizona Daily Star* moves from its location on North Stone where it had been since 1954 to facilities on South Park that will house their huge new Goss Metroliner offset press (175 feet long, 1000 tons). The first papers from the new press come out on the night of August 19. In 2014, the press is still running strong, though print journalism has begun to struggle.

1973

At the old Prison Camp on Mount Lemmon, David Giles founds the Southwest Indian Youth Center to provide intensive residential services for adjudicated Native American youth exhibiting extremely challenging behaviors. In 2014, its successor, Intermountain Centers for Human Development (ICHD), still led by David Giles, provides behavioral health support services in many different settings for children and adults of all ethnicities diagnosed with serious mental illness, serious emotional disabilities, developmental disabilities, and substance use problems. It also serves youth aging out of the child welfare system and families of their clients. ICHD is among the top 200 employers in Tucson.

1973

Steinfeld's downtown store closes. After the fire at the Pioneer Hotel that killed Harold Steinfeld and his wife, management had been taken over by his nephews, Lee and Jim Davis.

1973–1974

After a federal investigation, 28 TUSD schools are found "racially identifiable" (that is, more than 50 percent minority): Borton, Carrillo, Cavett, Davis, Drachman, Government Heights, Holladay, Lawrence, Manzo, Menlo Park, Mission View, Ochoa, Pueblo Gardens, Richey, Robison, Roosevelt, Rose, Safford, Tolson, Tully, University Heights, and Van Buskirk Elementary Schools. Also identified are Safford, Spring, Utterback, and Wakefield Junior High Schools, and Pueblo and Tucson High Schools.

1974

The Pioneer Hotel, opened in 1929, closes. Steinfeld's downtown store building is demolished by eastern real estate investor Allan Elias, who in 1970 had started buying up properties in Tucson. He will also buy the Pioneer Hotel building and convert it to offices.

1974

The Carl Hayden Hospital that is downtown on Congress next to the El Paso and Southwestern Railroad terminal closes permanently. In 1979 the handsome building is demolished and a large federal office building is constructed on the site. The El Paso and Southwestern Railroad terminal next to it survives and in 2004 will be listed on the National Register of Historic Places.

In this photograph, which looks southwest from the intersection of Church and Alameda streets, seen in the foreground is the third Pima County Superior Courthouse (1929) and in the background the fourth one, completed in 1974 on a site directly south of its predecessor, along Church Street between Pennington and Congress Streets. The new courthouse is a nine-story concrete and glass structure that matches the two other county buildings built on the site and resembles Tucson's new City Hall to the right of it (behind which a piece of Sentinel Peak can be seen). To the left, in a very different style, is Tucson's tallest building, an office building built at about this time. The courthouse is the final component of the government complex developed as part of a now seen-to-be-unfortunate "urban renewal" in Tucson 1968–74. The tree-filled open space to be seen behind the old courthouse and east of City Hall is Presidio Park, a piece of ground that had lain within the walls of Presidio San Agustín, the founding fort of Tucson (1775). Presidio Park now contains a number of historical statues and since 1974, it has been the focal point of the Tucson Meet Yourself Festival. This photograph was taken by Kelly Presnell of the Arizona Daily Star on May 3, 2013, but the appearance of the block hadn't changed much since 1974.

1974

The Fenster School, established in 1944 for children with lung conditions and later a regular college preparatory school, takes over the campus of the Southern Arizona School for Boys that had been in operation since 1930 on Sabino Creek. In 2014, the Fenster School announces it will close down for a year because of declining enrollments.

1974

The Tucson Meet Yourself (TMY) festival is founded by University of Arizona folklorist and anthropologist Dr. James "Big Jim" Griffith. The festival, which takes place downtown over three days in October, aims to represent the actual variety of cultures and ethnic groups in Tucson in food, music, arts, and other cultural practices. At the 2012 festival, 60 different cultural groups, ethnicities, and nationalities are represented. In 2011 Big Jim is recognized by the National Endowment for the Arts as a "National Heritage" treasure. In 2014, TMY continues under the direction of UA research professor Maribel Alvarez with the mission, says TMY's website, of continuing "to research, document, interpret and present the living traditional arts and expressions of everyday life of the folk and ethnic communities of the multi-national Arizona-Sonora region."

1974

Northwest of Tucson, around the Canyon del Oro wash, in an area that had been ranched early on by Mariano Samaniego, among others, Oro Valley is incorporated as a separate municipality. The area had begun to be developed in the 1950s.

1974

At Davis-Monthan, a new base exchange facility is opened where members of the military can shop.

1975–1977

Raúl Castro, a Democrat, is elected governor (b. Cananea, Mexico, 1916, comes to Arizona in 1926), replacing Jack Williams, a Republican. Earlier Castro had been a Pima County Superior Court judge and U.S. Ambassador to El Salvador and then Bolivia, appointed by President Lyndon Johnson.

1975

The Sunshine Climate Club, the Tucson booster organization started in the 1920s, is incorporated into the Tucson Chamber of Commerce.

1975

The Arizona State Museum begins a project to translate and publish the records of the Spanish Colonial period in northwest Mexico, under the direction of Jesuit scholar Charles Polzer.

1975

The Tucson Botanical Gardens, founded in 1964 by horticulturalist and collector Harrison Yocum, moves into the historic home and nursery of Rutger and Bernice Porter on North Alvernon near Grant Road, still TBG's home in 2014. Rutger Porter and Bernice Walkley had come to Tucson at the end of the '20s from the west and east coasts, respectively, married in Tucson in 1931, and opened the Desert Garden nursery.

1975

The Tanque Verde Swap Meet is established by the Chapin family on the corner of Tanque Verde and Grant Roads. In 1986, it will move to a 30-acre site on South Palo Verde Road, where in 2014 it is still operating Thursday through Sunday, still owned by the Chapin family.

1975

The Mountain Oyster Club moves from the Pioneer Hotel, where it had been since 1965, to the historic Jácome House on Franklin and Stone, then owned by accountant, rancher, and club member C. T. R. Bates. The club, started in 1948, had met originally in the Santa Rita Hotel.

1975

Tucson Rapid Transit, now owned by the city and renamed Sun Tran, begins building transit centers throughout the city, using better fuels, making it easier to pay fares, and providing access for people with disabilities.

1975

Park Mall opens on the south side of East Broadway with Tucson's largest office building having been built across the street at 5151 East Broadway.

1975

The remarkable "Ramada House" is built in the Catalina Foothills, designed by architect Judith Chafee, who since 1970 has been on the faculty of the School of Architecture at the University of Arizona. The house will later be placed on the National Register of Historic Place. Chaffee will design other remarkable contemporary southwest residences in Tucson before her death in 1998.

1976

South of Davis-Monthan Field and the aircraft storage facility there, the nonprofit Pima Air and Space Museum opens, with 46 airplanes on display. In 2014, it has nearly 300 aircraft and occupies a campus of 127 acres.

1976

The top-rated radio station in town is now KCUB, a country station, replacing KTKT in this spot. This year KCUB is named by Billboard magazine as the Grand International Station of the Year.

1976

The Tucson Community Food Bank (TCFB) opens, supported by Mayor Lew Murphy, among others. In 1977, Charles "Punch" Woods becomes president/CEO, retiring 25 years later. In 2014, TCFB, on Country Club Road south of 36th Street, runs many programs devoted to food security for southern Arizonans, including a market for nonprofit agencies, a Food Box program with pantries all over Tucson that is funded by the Arizona Department of Economic Security, and a Food Resource Center that offers educational programs on nutrition, food production, and desert gardening.

1976

At Congress Street and Interstate 10, the handsome depot of the El Paso and Southwestern Railway which opened in 1913 to bring freight north from Douglas, is purchased by Alan Norville. It will be remodeled to house a Big Yellow Restaurant and later Carlos Murphy's Mexican restaurant.

1976

In the Fort Lowell area, Pima County establishes an official Historic District of 126 acres extending on both sides of Fort Lowell Road from Beverly to Pantano Wash. In 1978, the Fort Lowell Multiple Resource Area will be placed on the National Register of Historic Places and in 2014, a museum is being operated in the old commanding officer's headquarters by the Arizona Historical Society.

1977-1978

Governor Raúl Castro is appointed by President Jimmy Carter to be U.S. Ambassador to Argentina. He leaves office and is replaced by Wesley Bolin, also a Democrat.

1977

Downstream of Tucson on the Santa Cruz River, in an agricultural area made possible by groundwater pumping, the town of Marana is incorporated. Beginning with 10 square miles, it has in 2014 grown through annexation to over 120 square miles.

1977

Tucson's urban renewal efforts are coming to be seen as a disaster. The Tucson Convention Center is not attracting enough business; the shops in La Placita are not being patronized. Downtown remains moribund except when workers in the big new government buildings are coming and going.

1977

The Ina Road Wastewater Reclamation Facility is completed to handle waste from Marana and Oro Valley, capacity 25 million gallons a day.

1977

In October, major floods occur again in the Tucson Basin.

1977

In the early 1970s, city leaders had recognized that the fourteen miles of the Santa Cruz River channel that ran through Tucson had become a trash heap, with flooding a continuing problem despite the significant decline in the water table. The U. S. Army Corps of Engineers had been asked to study how to beautify and control the channel. In November, work finally begins toward that end.

1977

Democratic council members who had supported a water rate increase are recalled by voters.

1978 January

In southeast Tucson, a new Arizona State Prison Complex opens on Wilmot Road, with 384 nonviolent first offenders, ages 18–25.

1978

Last year, a relatively slow-flying straight-winged jet attack aircraft called the A-10, whose mission was close-air support of ground troops, had appeared in the skies over Tucson. A-10 pilots train on the Barry M. Goldwater gunnery range in southern Arizona west of Tucson. In 2014, the A-10 remains in service at Davis-Monthan with the Air Force and the F-16 remains in service with the Arizona Air National Guard that is based at Tucson International Airport.

1978

In the school desegregation lawsuit that had started in 1968 against the Tucson School District 1, the decision is delivered by United States District Court Judge Frey. His first order affects only schools in northwest Tucson. After the plaintiffs object to this, schools in other areas are included. Communities' preferences for "neighborhood schools" are clashing with de facto segregation. Neither side sees busing as a solution. In 1979, while on vacation, Judge Frey dies of a heart attack, thought to be brought on by the strain of the case. The case is taken over by Judge Mary Ann Richey, who orders busing and the creation of seven elementary "new schools," in which teachers and staff are required to resign and re-apply for their jobs after showing that they are willing and able to embrace the program. She also orders the creation of two elementary "magnet schools," Borton and Holliday, that will have smaller classes and extra programs.

1978–1987

Bruce Babbitt, a Democrat, replaces Wesley Bolin, a Democrat, as governor. Babbitt is twice reelected but leaves office to run unsuccessfully for president of the United States. In 1993, he will be selected by President Bill Clinton to be secretary of the interior.

1978

Northeast of Tucson, east of Sabino Canyon Highway and north of Cloud Road, Sabino Vista residential development begins to be built, construction to take place in several phases.

1978

A local group incorporates a nonprofit corporation, Patronato San Xavier, "to be used solely and exclusively for historical, research, scientific and educational purposes concerned with the restoration, maintenance and preservation of Mission San Xavier del Bac." The group is led by attorney James M. Murphy and includes Emil W. Haury, Dianne Bret Harte, Jane H. Ivancovich, Watson Smith, and Bernard I. Fontana. The church had been made a National Historic Landmark in 1960.

1978

Sun Tran purchases Roy Laos's bus company, which had been serving south and west Tucson since the 1930s. Tucson now has a single transit system.

1978 October

Following several years of deteriorating relations between teachers and the current school board for Tucson School District 1, and within the board itself, the teachers strike. Wilbur Lewis, the second superintendent to follow Robert Morrow, resigns in December.

1979

Tucson Gas and Electric sells the gas operation to Southwest Gas and becomes Tucson Electric Power.

1979

Northeast of Tucson in the Catalina Foothills, on a site that incorporates the buildings of the Double U Guest Ranch where the movies *Arizona* and *Billy the Kid* were filmed, Canyon Ranch of Tucson opens its doors, a luxurious "health and wellness" resort and spa conceived by former developer Mel Zuckerman and his wife, Enid. For a couple of years the enterprise just hangs on but by 2014, it has become a significant employer in Tucson and has opened facilities in Miami Beach; Lenox, Massachusetts; and Las Vegas.

1979

Ofelia Zepeda, a Tohono O'odham woman, co-founds the American Indian Language Development Institute (AILDI). The institute has the aim of rescuing endangered Native American languages, or, in the language of their mission statement, "to provide critical training to revitalize and promote the use of indigenous languages across generations." In 1982, having received a PhD in linguistics from UA, Zepeda will edit and publish with the University of Arizona Press *When It Rains: Papago and Pima Poetry*, a collection of poems written in both English and O'odham. In 1983, she will publish *A Papago Grammar*, and later collections of her own poetry written in English and O'odham, the first such collections by an O'odham poet in her own name, and will be awarded a MacArthur Grant. In 2014, AILDI is still offering its 4-week summer institutes at UA and has been widely imitated elsewhere. Zepeda has been its director since 2005.

1979

Paul McCartney of the Beatles buys 151 acres in the foothills of the Rincons off Tanque Verde Road, near Redington Pass and, years before, Emilio Carrillo's La Cebadilla Ranch.

1980

Tucson's urbanized area population is 330,537, an increase of 25.7 percent since 1970, with an increase in population of 68,573 in the city and 180,220 in Pima County. The city is now 99.5 square miles, with the urbanized area 125.1 square miles. Total platted lands are 231.8 square miles. Land around Tucson is no longer being seen as an unlimited resource. Urban infill begins.

1980

Total school enrollment: Tucson Unified School District 55,654 (A decline of 1800 from the 1970 total. It had reached its highest enrollment of 63,488 in 1973.), 21,164 of whom (38 percent) are minority students, 3,000 of whom are African-American. Tucson has 14 high schools, down two from 1970, and 103 elementary and junior high schools, up 14 from 1970. The private St. Gregory School for middle and high school students is established this year on North Craycroft near Old Fort Lowell.

1980

Enrollment at Pima Community College is 19,935, an increase of 16,442, over 500 percent. UA's enrollment is

30,960, an increase of 4,839, with 1,774 faculty, an increase of 195, and 130 buildings, an increase of 33.

1980

This City Directory is published, as was the 1970 Directory, by R. L. Polk of Dallas, Texas.

- It notes that I-19 south to Nogales has been joined to I-10, and lists 22 hotels and 146 motels (both about the same as 1970), hundreds of "Mobile Home Parks" (which in the 1970s had been called "Trailer Courts and Parks"), and 30 guest ranches in the area (an increase of four from 1970).

- It claims 318 churches (+80 since 1970) broken down as 273 Protestant, 23 Catholic, three Jewish, two Greek Orthodox, seven Mormon, and 10 "Other." It lists a big new hospital, the University Medical Center.

- It claims 31 theaters, of which 12 are drive-ins.

- It notes that the Development Authority for Tucson's Expansion (D.A.T.E.) has been replaced by the Tucson Economic Development Corporation (T.E.D.) and announces the imminent location of an IBM facility in Tucson.

- As cultural amenities, it lists a new Tucson Opera, the Tucson Ballet, the Arizona Theatre Company, and especially the new Tucson Museum of Art, built on the sites of the homes of E. N. Fish and H. S. Stevens downtown, calling the new museum "a city's pledge fulfilled."

- The Directory notes the "excellent facilities" provided by the large Tucson Convention Center that has recently been built south of the museum.

- The Tucson International Airport has recently acquired facilities to handle air freight.

- At Davis-Monthan, the 12th Strategic Aerospace Division has become the 12th Air Division. The Tactical Air Command's 4453rd has been replaced by the 355th Tactical Fighter Wing, flying the new A-10 attack fighter. The 18 Titan II ICBMs surrounding Tucson are being managed out of Davis-Monthan, which, says the Directory, employs 8,000 military and 3,000 civilian personnel.

- It also notes that 90 miles east of Tucson at Fort Huachuca is the U.S. Army's Electronic Proving Ground that has just had the army's Military Intelligence added to its mission and employs 17,000 military and 3,000 civilian personnel.

- Kitt Peak, 50 miles west of Tucson, is said to have the world's largest solar telescope.

- Among the listings in the classified section are five for a kind of business that hadn't appeared in the 1970 Directory: "Computer Equipment Manufacturers."

1980

Jácome's department store, which had been hanging on downtown, closes after 67 years in business in Tucson.

1980

At Sunrise Drive and Swan Road, the Sunrise Village Center opens with the first major grocery store in the Foothills. The shopping center is thriving still, with a number of other businesses in place, including a Starbucks.

1980

In southeast Tucson, IBM opens a plant and lab on 931 acres it had purchased on Rita Road southeast of Tucson. At its high point, 5,000 people work at IBM Tucson. In 1990, its General Products Division is phased out and operations are reduced. In 2005, 2,000 employees are working at the site on storage and other products. In 2013, it is the 49th-largest employer in Tucson, with 914 employees, running an Executive Briefing Center and managing the UA's Science and Technology Park at the site.

1980

A new four-engine straight-wing turbo-prop-powered airplane appears in the skies over Tucson, the EC-130H, called Compass Call. Its mission is electronic warfare, disrupting enemy communications and radar. In 2014, it remains in service at Davis-Monthan, along with a newer version of it, the EC-130E Hercules, which has the mission of providing command and control of tactical air operations over battlefields or in enemy territory.

1980

UA's cactus garden, now much reduced in size from its early beginnings, is named in honor of Joseph Wood Krutch.

1980

Use of groundwater in the Tucson Basin reaches its peak.

1980

Arizona passes the Groundwater Management Act that creates Irrigation Nonexpansion Areas (regulating new agricultural areas but allowing existing ones to continue with current practices) and Active Management Areas (to encourage conservation and discourage new wells and increased pumping). Active Management Areas don't reach the private water operators in Tucson (UA, Winterhaven, Flowing Wells, Amphitheater). Tucson Water begins to report annually on subsidence and groundwater depletion in the city's well fields (with 1,000 well sites in the Tucson Basin and more than 270 in Avra Valley). Water awareness begins to increase in Tucson and reduced-flow water fixtures and drip irrigation become the norm. Effluent (recycled water) begins to be used for golf courses, school yards, and parks. Over 1976–1996, per capita use by Tucsonans is one of the lowest in the Southwest, 163 gallons per day.

1980

Fort Lowell residents Edward (Ned) and Rosalind Spicer form the Old Fort Lowell Neighborhood Association. In

1981, the City of Tucson will establish a Historic District for the 18 acres south of Fort Lowell Road that are in the city limits, and in 1982, the San Pedro Chapel built by the residents of "El Fuerte" will be made the first City of Tucson Landmark. In 1984, the City of Tucson will adopt an "Old Fort Lowell Neighborhood Plan" for the roughly square-mile area as a way of trying to guide development. In 1993, the city will annex the area north of Fort Lowell Road up to the rivers and the city and county Historic Districts will become one. Development continues in the Fort Lowell area in 2014 in the area of what had been a significant Hohokam settlement.

1980s

North of Tucson, several golf course resorts are developed: in the Catalina Foothills, La Paloma (1980, Mehl brothers) and Ventana Canyon (1984, Bill Estes) in the area of the Flying V guest ranch that had operated at the mouth of Ventana Canyon since the early 1900s, and in Oro Valley, Rancho Vistoso (1983, Lennar, 8,000 acres, 8,500 homes, master-planned), Hilton El Conquistador (500 acres off North Oracle Road, 45 holes of golf, tennis), and Saddle-Brooke (1986, Robson, master-planned retirement community on the northwest flank of the Catalinas).

1981

Near Fort Lowell, Tom Doucette begins construction of the Hill Farm subdivision on land between the old fort and the Rillito that the Hill family had sold to the Akins Company. About 90 houses and a lake are planned in the area of a mesquite bosque that had grown up along old irrigation ditches. After forming his own company, Doucette will go on to build several developments in Tucson: the houses at David and George Mehl's La Paloma development (1984), the Lambert Lane subdivision in Oro Valley (1987), the Country Club subdivision (near Tucson National golf course) and Salida Del Sol and Estates (Swan and Sunrise) (both in 1990), the Presidio at Williams Center (on east Broadway) and River Park (near the Tucson Racquet and Fitness Club)(both in 1996), Mission Arbor (2001, near Mission Road) now called Mission Harbor), The Woods (near Agua Caliente wash), Paseo Estrella (2005, near Starr Pass), and Desert Mosaic subdivision (c. 2008, near Grant and Silverbell Road).

1981

In southwest Tucson, where Midvale Farms had been, Midvale Park is incorporated. Midvale Park will be a large master-planned community of 3,350 homes developed by Bill Estes and KB Homes.

1981

The Pima County Health Department finds serious soil and water pollution on the south side in an area south of 22nd Street and north of Los Reales Road, east of I-19 and west of Del Moral Boulevard, the result of dumping since 1952 of the industrial solvent and carcinogen trichlorethylene (TCE), primarily by Hughes Aircraft. The county closes down many polluted wells. Two years later, the U.S. Environmental Protection Agency will place a large part of this area on its Superfund cleanup list. Lawsuits against the City of Tucson and Hughes continue into 2006.

1981

The Tucson Poetry Festival is started in Tucson, the goal of which is "to expand the audience that typically goes to poetry readings and workshops, and to do it in a way that's appealing, free, and open to everyone interested," in the words of its 2014 director, Ander Monson.

1981

Reverend David Sholin of St. Mark's Presbyterian is appointed chairman of Amnesty International.

1981

Sandra Day O'Connor, who had grown up on a ranch east of Tucson near Duncan, Arizona, and later served in the Arizona legislature, is the first woman appointed to serve as a justice of the Supreme Court of the United States, appointed by Ronald Reagan.

1982

In July, a storm blows the roof off the old Southern Pacific Railroad Warehouse on Stone and Franklin. The building will soon be gone. By 2014, only the concrete foundations will remain on the spot.

1982 October 1

Deactivation of 18 Titan II ICBMs around Tucson begins, to be completed in 1984. Davis-Monthan serves as the storage facility for deactivated Titan IIs. By 2006, they have all been destroyed, except for a training missile to be put on display at the Titan Missile Museum south of Tucson. Tucson's missile complex is the only one of the three Titan II complexes not to have experienced serious accidents with the missile's highly toxic liquid propellants.

1982

Year-round dog racing is legalized in Arizona. In 1987, Tucson's dog track at South Fourth Avenue and 36th Street will be purchased by Joseph Zappala and Robert Consolo Jr., who in 2014 are still the owners. In 1991 off-track betting will be legalized throughout Arizona. Evidence of animal cruelty haunts the enterprise, but it continues.

1982

The first Tucson International Mariachi Conference is held and is a popular success. The 32nd occurred in 2014.

1982

The Sanctuary Movement begins in Tucson when Reverend John Fife of Southside Presbyterian Church declares his church a sanctuary for "the Oppressed of Central America" and warns "Immigration" not to "profane the Sanctuary of God." In 1980 the number of immigrants from Central America seeking asylum had begun greatly to increase but most applications were being denied. The Sanctuary Movement will spread to other states and other churches and develop an affiliation with Amnesty International, now being directed by Reverend David Sholin of Mountain View Presbyterian, and also be supported locally by Father Foster of St. Michael and All Angels Episcopalian. The movement remains active until 1988. In 2014, it is revived at Southside, whose pastor is now Alison Harrington, to shelter an undocumented family with a U.S.-born son who had been law-abiding, tax-paying citizens in the United States for 14 years.

1982

Craycroft Road had been extended through the grounds of Old Fort Lowell to River Road in 1970. This year a bridge is built connecting Craycroft Road to the Catalina Foothills. Swan Road, which lies along the western boundary of the Fort Lowell Neighborhood, had ended at the Rillito until 1971 when a bridge was extended across it into the Foothills. By 2014, there are 11 bridges north across the Rillito (on Craycroft, Swan, Alvernon, Dodge, Campbell, First, Stone, Oracle, La Cañada, La Cholla, and I-10), five bridges across the Pantano (on Tanque Verde, Speedway, Broadway, 22nd Street, and Golf Links/Houghton), and one across Tanque Verde Wash (Sabino Canyon Highway).

1982

The U. S. Army Corps of Engineers, part of whose mission is to "reduce risks from disasters," begins to apply a cement to stabilize the channels of the Santa Cruz and the Rillito. The destructive flood of 1977 had led to this measure upon the recognition that floods in these watercourses cause damage not by overflowing the river's banks but by channel erosion.

1982–1983

Steinfeld's best year is 1982, followed by its worst year, 1983. The cause, according to Steinfeld's descendant Lee Davis, now managing the business, is the economy gone bad, the Tucson Mall and Foothills Mall openings, mines shutting down, and the devaluation of the Mexican peso.

1982–1983

More elementary schools are made into magnet schools, along with Safford Junior High School and Tucson High School. The TUSD school board decides not to ask that the federal court's desegregation order be dissolved, believing that more progress will be made if it remains in place.

1983

St. Martin's Soup Kitchen is organized by two Tucsonans, Gordon Packard and Nancy Bissell. A lawsuit by the neighborhood where the soup kitchen is located forces it to shut down but Packard and Bissell go on to open the Primavera Men's Shelter. In 2014, with a mission of providing "pathways out of poverty through safe, affordable housing, workforce development and neighborhood revitalization," the Primavera Foundation's facilities and programs serve about 7,500 poor and homeless people a year, including veterans, with the help of 1,600 volunteers, 12,000 financial supporters, and 80 community partners.

1983

In October, major floods occur again in the Tucson Basin, worse than in 1977. Significant damage occurs in Marana, but soil-cemented banks in Tucson withstand the peak discharge. The Santa Cruz River no longer has the ability to shift its channel on its way through the city. Between major floods, however, the channel will aggrade with new deposits, which might make future floods dangerous.

1983

The Educational Enrichment Foundation is founded by Tucson's community and business leaders to support TUSD's schools because public funding of public education has become inadequate.

1983

Upon a complaint by a group called the Tucson Jewish Community Council, the TUSD board votes to disapprove a course being offered to teachers by UA's Near Eastern Center and to bar materials from district classrooms that include a number of resource materials covering Middle East history and cultures, as well as maps, videos, and a novel entitled *My Enemy, My Brother*. The council, which is supported by the Anti-Defamation League and the American Jewish Committee, alleges that these materials are anti-Israel and pro-Arab. A citizen had complained to the board that his son had been shown a map of the Middle East that didn't have Israel on it. It is later noted that this was a map of the Ottoman Empire. Censorship efforts of this kind are being mounted

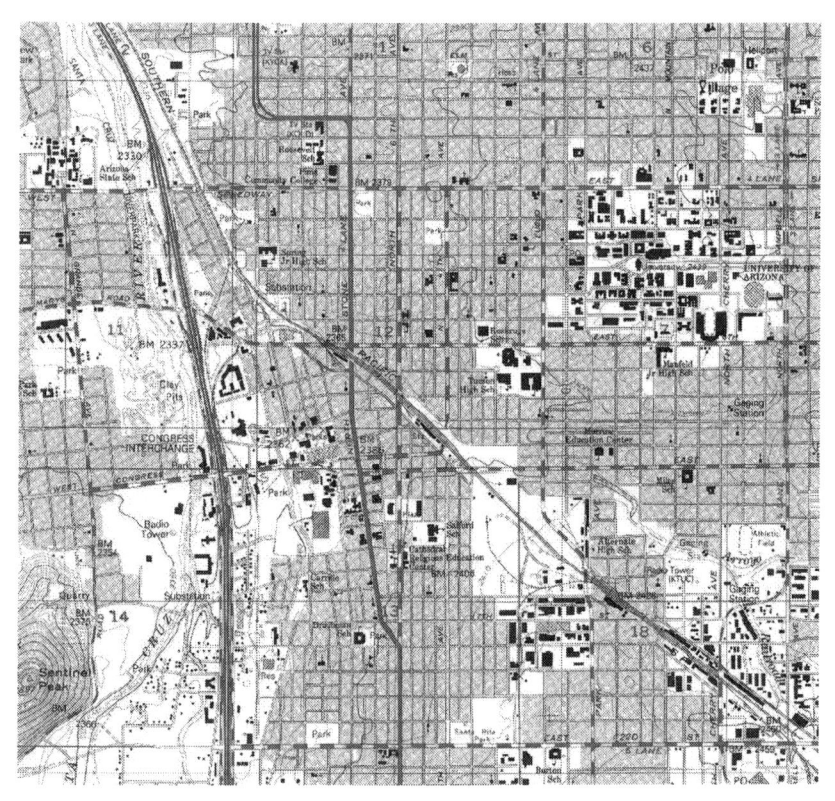

1983 USGS topographic map. This map shows a combination of topographic and symbolic road features. Elevations and the outlines of important buildings are shown to a high level of accuracy. Areas with dense urban development are denoted in pink on the original map. The University is now the dominant feature. Downtown makes a comparatively slight appearance. Barrio Viejo is no more.

across the country though this is not yet widely known. In 2014, the renamed Center for Middle Eastern Studies at UA is again offering outreach courses, programs, and resources for TUSD teachers on this subject.

1983

In the western Catalina Foothills northwest of Tucson, Sierra Tucson opens—a private luxury facility for the treatment of addictions and "co-occurring disorders." In 1996, the Miraval luxury health and wellness resort will open nearby.

1983

The Angel Charity for Children, Inc. is established this year by Tucsonan Louise Thomas to help non-profit agencies serving the needs of children in Pima County. Each year, the charity sponsors gala fund raisers, selects a beneficiary or beneficiaries, and partners with business and individuals in Pima County to fund grant applications. By 2014, its average yearly gifts will reach three-quarters of a million dollars.

1983

The Arizona Historical Society revives a secular version of the Fiesta de San Agustín (Tucson's patron saint, whose day is August 28). In territorial days, the fiesta had been a raucous 10-day affair—George Hand's diary describes it. The fiesta was first moved from the *placita* by the church to the Military Plaza, then to Levin's Park. Its particularly festive aspects became a victim of the moral reforms that took hold in Tucson and Arizona at the end of the 19th century, though the saint's day continued to be celebrated in San Agustín Cathedral. By the turn of the century, the fiesta had been consigned to the outskirts of town and was no longer being touted as an attractive feature of local culture. It was ended by the prohibitions on drinking and gambling instituted after the turn of the century.

1983

Tucson Weekly, an "alternative newsweekly," is founded by Doug Biggers, who had received a degree in English and Creative Writing this year. Downtown, Biggers will later help restore the Rialto Theatre and block, listed in the National Register of Historic Places in 2003, and in 2013 debut *Edible Baja Arizona*, a beautifully produced magazine that celebrates the foodways of Tucson and the borderlands.

1983

Native Seeds/SEARCH, a seed conservation organization, is established in Tucson by Gary Nabhan and his wife, Karen Reichhart, and Mahina Drees and her husband, Barney Burns. The organization has flowered and is still "working to strengthen food security in the Greater Southwest by conserving our region's unique crop diversity and teaching others to do the same."

1983

Tucson Water begins using recycled water for golf courses and parks and for the first time is not relying entirely on groundwater from the Tucson Basin.

1984

John Murphey's widow, Helen, commissions Juan Worner Bas to help design St. Philip's Plaza, a retail shopping center at the southeast corner of Campbell and River Road.

1984

Steinfeld's, run by descendant Lee Davis, opens a new store at Tucson Mall. It lasts 10 months. Before the year is out, Steinfeld's has closed its specialty stores in Casas Adobes to the north and Green Valley to the south and gone entirely out of business, after over 100 years in Tucson.

1984

Construction begins on a Kolb Road extension through Davis-Monthan Air Force Base, despite Davis-Monthan's long-standing opposition to the project. Many city dignitaries are present at the opening ceremony.

1984

Tucson's Roger Road wastewater treatment plant becomes part of the Tucson Reclaimed Water Treatment Plant. From 2008 to 2011, the combined discharge from the Ina Road and Roger Road plants will be 5,355 acre-feet per year. At the Cortaro Road gauging station, the flow in the Santa Cruz becomes about 40–60 cubic feet per second for much of the year. The flow in the Santa Cruz is again perennial in this stretch, and unmanaged riparian vegetation returns as far as Marana.

1980s middle

Hughes Aircraft reaches its highest level of employment, at 9,000.

1985

The Amity Foundation, which began in 1969 as Tucson Awareness House, begins to develop programs to help incarcerated juvenile drug users, female offenders, couples, and families. In 2014, it has programs in California, New Mexico, and Arizona. Its principal residential facility in Tucson is the 60-acre Circle Tree Ranch on East Tanque Verde Road.

1985

For a new city library, the City of Tucson buys the land on Stone Avenue downtown on which the last Steinfeld's and Jácome's stores had stood. The Joel D. Valdez Main Library will open at the site, which is just east of the old presidio wall, in 1990.

1985

The Tucson Historic Preservation Foundation is established to try to develop funds to save historic buildings. It becomes dormant in the 1990s but in 2008 is restructured by Demion Clinco and a new board is created.

1985

The Davis-Monthan 50 is founded, a group of local businesspeople to lobby for the continuation of the base. One prominent founding member, who will be active until her death in 2013, is Dorothy Finley, a beer distributor.

1985

The Steward Observatory Mirror Laboratory begins operations under the east stands of the UA football stadium. Very large mirrors for optical and infrared telescopes will be made there using a honeycomb technique developed by the lab's first director, UA professor Roger Angel, and a new method of polishing the big mirrors. The lab had initial support from UA, the National Science Foundation, and the U.S. Air Force. It is still under the east stands and is still the place where "the largest and most advanced Earth-based telescope mirrors in the world" are produced, two of which were installed in the early 2000s in the Magellan Consortium's telescopes at its Las Campanas Observatory in Chile.

1985

Major remodeling at Tucson International Airport doubles its size. This year the Arizona Air National Guard that is based at the airport begins to train pilots in the sleek, nimble, and loud F-16 Fighting Falcon, whose mission is air superiority, that is, defeating other airplanes in the sky.

1985

Dickson Potter dies. All the houses now on Potter Place except a large one owned by Susan Small had been built before this date. The Small House is built in 1989–1990, as are the townhouses in Potter Park Court that are built on the site of what had been the Potters' house. The author will buy one of the townhouses in 1991. By 1991, the large elegant green-tile-roofed house in Potter Place that had been Leighton Kramer's Rancho Santa Catalina, then the Potter School for Girls, and then Casa Elizabeth Seton, owned by the Arizona Inn since 1971, is closed up and being used by the Arizona Inn for storage.

1986

Unisource Energy Tower is completed at Congress and Stone and is the tallest building in Tucson at 23 stories, 330 feet. In 2012, Unisource will move to a new building at Broadway and Sixth Avenue downtown. The tower is renamed One South Church.

1986

Learjet moves its headquarters to Tucson. Three years after this, Learjet will move its production facilities and headquarters again, to Wichita, Kansas.

1986

The Campus Historic District is created at UA. It includes 17 buildings in several different architectural styles built between 1891 and 1937, almost all of them in red brick, many of them designed by architect Roy Place, who over the years designed 50 buildings on the UA campus. Included in the District are Old Main and Place's 1927 library that had been placed on the National Register of Historic Places earlier. Also included are the olive groves and the berms and basins of the earlier flood irrigation system used west of Old Main.

1986

A Savings and Loan Crisis begins this year that by 1995 results in the failure of a third of the savings and loan associations in the United States, among them Pima, Catalina, and Home Federal Savings and Loan Associations in Tucson.

1987

Beginning in the 1960s, after the completion of Interstate 10, the formerly glamorous "Miracle Mile" had become a locus of prostitution and other illicit activity. The Tucson City Council now changes the name of the north-south leg of Miracle Mile to Oracle Road thinking this might help address the problem. Council member Tom Volgy opposes the name change as merely cosmetic. By 2008, efforts are being made to revitalize the area and a movement is afoot to restore the "Miracle Mile" name.

1987

Tom Volgy becomes mayor, until 1991. Volgy was born in Hungary in 1946 and in 1971 had become a professor of political science at the University of Arizona, also serving on the City Council.

1987-1988

Evan Mecham, a Republican, becomes governor, replacing Bruce Babbit, a Democrat, who left office to run for president of the United States.

1988-1991

Rose Mofford, a Democrat, replaces Evan Mecham, a Republican, as governor after a grand jury indicts Mecham and his brother for perjury, fraud, and misuse of campaign funds; and Mecham is then impeached by the Arizona State House, convicted by the Arizona Senate of obstruction of justice, and removed from office. Later, in his criminal trial, he is acquitted on all six felony counts.

1987

Sun Tran's first off-street terminal, named after transit pioneer Roy Laos, opens on Irvington on Tucson's south side. The Ronstadt Center downtown will open in 1991, and the Tohono Tadai Transit Center will open on the northwest side in 1994.

1987

The 860 acres of Tumamoc Hill are designated a National Historic Landmark by the U.S. Department of the Interior. The Desert Lab had been so designated in 1976.

1988

Downtown along the railroad tracks at the site of the old Steinfeld's and Toole Avenue warehouses, an arts district has begun to emerge. Sixteen years later, the Tucson Historic Warehouse Arts District Master Plan will be adopted by the City of Tucson. The Warehouse District is now seen as a larger area around the tracks defined roughly as lying between Toole on the south and 6th Street on the north, Sixth Avenue on the east and Stone Avenue on the west. The goals of the development are to provide an "incubation, production and exhibition" area for artists in a diverse and mixed-use space that is walkable and bikeable.

1988

On Sunday November 20, a group called "Street Smart," that has been meeting all year in the lobby of the Congress Hotel, conducts a demonstration in opposition to the Arizona Department of Transportation's plans to build an "Aviation Parkway" to connect with I-10. The west end would bisect Tucson's downtown area, destroying the emerging Arts District, among other things. About 160 people form a human chain that reaches from The Shanty on Fourth Avenue through the tunnel to the Congress Hotel. The protest makes statewide news. The plan for the western end of the parkway is later abandoned. In 2014, an alternative proposal, developed originally by another group called "The Citizens' Transportation Alternative," is still in play, though funding is a problem.

1988

Inspectors from the Soviet Union arrive by helicopter at Davis-Monthan airbase in Tucson to oversee destruction of the ground-launched cruise missiles stored there. The GLCMs will be destroyed under the Intermediate Nuclear Forces treaty signed by Mikhail Gorbachev and Ronald Reagan in 1987, the beginning of the end of the Cold War.

1989

A law is passed by the Arizona legislature restricting provision of official government information to English only, claiming authority in Article 28 of the Arizona Constitution which declares English to be "the official language of the State." In 1998, the law is declared unconstitutional by a unanimous Arizona Supreme Court. In 2006, Proposition 103 is generated by the legislature which amends the state constitution to require "all official actions of the government to be conducted in English," with certain exceptions, including one for "actions necessary for tourism, commerce, or international trade." Proposition 103 is passed by Arizona voters by a three to one margin.

1989

The law firm of the author's father, Hal, which has become the oldest and largest in Tucson, merges with the larger Phoenix firm of Snell and Wilmer and moves west across Stone Avenue to offices in the One South Church Building, Tucson's tallest, built in 1986. In 1991 Hal will leave the firm but continue to practice law until his death in 1997.

Until the end, he received through the mail requests for his autograph from readers of the Encyclopedia of Baseball.

1989–1990

The author and his wife, Tilly, teach this year as visiting professors at Northern Arizona University in Flagstaff.

1989

The author of *Desert Solitaire* and *The Monkey Wrench Gang*, Edward Abbey, dies in Tucson and is buried by friends outside the city in a location that still has not been found.

1990

Tucson's population is 405,371, up 22.6 percent since 1980. The city includes 156.04 square miles, with 495 square miles in the "urban area."

1990

Having resided elsewhere since he graduated from Tucson High School in 1959, the author returns to Tucson with his wife Tilly (b. Columbus, Georgia). Both join the Department of English at the University of Arizona in a newly formed graduate program called Rhetoric, Composition, and the Teaching of English.

1990

The City Directory for this year, published by Cole Publications of Lincoln, Nebraska, is different from earlier ones in format and intended audience, offering only printouts of census data that are intended to be useful in marketing, not general information for residents.

1990

Total school enrollments: TUSD 56,938, of whom 27,181 (47.7 percent, up from 38 percent in 1980) are minority students. Next year, minorities will become the majority in TUSD schools. Tucson now has 17 high schools, up three since 1980; 110 elementary schools and 30 junior high schools, an increase of 37; 57 parochial schools, an increase of 24; and nine "private academic" schools, same as 1980.

1990

Pima Community College's enrollment is 28,766, +8,781 from 1980, an increase of 43 percent. UA's enrollment is 35,735, + 4,939, an increase of 16 percent, with 1,652 faculty, down 122 from 1980, and 154 buildings, up 24.

1990

Tucson Electric Power Board votes to build a wholly owned coal-fired generating plant 250 miles north of Tucson in Springerville, Arizona.

1990

City wells pump 70 billion gallons (215,000 acre-feet) from the aquifer in the Tucson Basin to service 800,000 residents (cf. 1.6 billion gallons to service 25,000 residents in 1922).

1990

The Central Arizona Project (CAP) delivers the first water to Tucson, the canal running 336 miles from Lake Havasu on the Colorado River (the entire course of the Santa Cruz River is 184 miles). Construction, which had begun in 1973 after President Johnson signed the enabling legislation in 1968, is now complete. The construction costs of $4 billion are to be repaid to the federal government over time by CAP users. Fourteen pumping plants must lift the water 2,900 feet from the river. Unfortunately, when CAP water is delivered directly to Tucson homes in 1992, it comes out brownish orange. In 1995, voters in Tucson pass a Water Consumer Protection Act that prohibits use of CAP water in residences unless it matches the quality of the groundwater, an impossibility. The rate of groundwater use continues upward. Recharge of groundwater with CAP water had always been a part of the CAP agenda and Tucson Water begins recharging a significant portion of its CAP allocation into a recharge basin in Avra Valley west of Tucson.

1990

The Pima County Board of Supervisors votes 3–2 to allow rezoning of 5,600 acres of the Rocking K Ranch east of Tucson at the foot of the Rincon Mountains to allow Rocking K Development to build 10,000 homes, four golf courses, three resorts, and some commercial and industrial properties. The collapse of the real estate market some years later causes some renegotiation, restructuring, and a scaling back of the plans, but in 2014 development is still being contemplated by the company.

1990

Los Descendientes del Presidio de Tucsón is founded by Arnold Smith, a descendant of a Presidio soldier. Its mission is preserving the culture of Tucson. Four levels of membership, with actual descendants of Presidio soldiers occupying the first level, descendants of the Mexican period (September 1821 to June 1853) on the second level, descendants of "pioneer" families (to February 1912) on the third level, and such as your author on the fourth level.

1990

The U.S. Congress establishes the 1,210-mile Juan Bautista de Anza Natural Historic Trail to commemorate Anza's two remarkable expeditions from Tubac to San Francisco in 1774–1777. Tumacácori and its mission church are made a National Historic Park. The site of Kino's first mission in what is now Arizona, at Guevavi, is now included in Tumacácori National Historic Park but the mission church exists today as only a low mound of eroded adobe bricks. The area had been mapped in 1917 by Byron Cummings, Robert Forbes, H. O. Jaastad, and others. Partial excavations have been conducted over the years, the latest begun in 2014 by archaeologists from Archaeology Southwest and the Arizona State Museum.

1991–1997

J. Fife Symington, a Republican, replaces Rose Mofford, a Democrat, as governor.

1991-1999

George Miller becomes mayor. Before being elected mayor, he had served 14 years on the Tucson City Council.

1991

The City Directory for this year is published by R. L. Polk and Co.

- It claims 35 movie theaters (no drive-ins), 15 AM and 12 FM radio stations, and for television three network, one educational, one independent, and "cable" stations.

- There are 453 churches (up 135 since 1980), with 330 Protestant (up 57), 40 Catholic (up 17), five Jewish (up two), and 78 "Others."

- This Directory notes that "government" is the major employer in Tucson at 54,000, with 10,000 at UA and 8,500 at Davis-Monthan.

- It also says that Tucson is becoming a center for high-tech companies, naming "A.Research, National Semiconductor, Burr-Brown, Environmental Air Products, TEC, and others."

- Thirty "Nursing Homes" are listed and 26 golf courses claimed.

- Automobile dealers in Tucson are now selling Isuzu, Honda, Toyota, Mitsubishi, and Mazda cars, along with the American and European brands. One of the most successful dealers in town is Jim Click, a nephew of the Tuttle who had bought Monte Mansfield's Ford dealership in 1958. Click had come to Tucson to take over Tuttle's Ford dealership in 1971 and by now has become the dealer for a number of different makes, foreign and domestic. This year he is joined by his father, who had been a Chevrolet dealer in Altus, Oklahoma, retired to Tucson, and then "unretired" to join the son's firm.

- At Davis-Monthan, the 355th Tactical Fighter Wing with A-10s is all that remains. East of Tucson, Fort Huachuca has become the headquarters of the U.S. Army Strategic Communications Command, now housing the Counter Intelligence Corps, with 11,000 total employees.

1991

Southeast of Tucson in the foothills of the Rincon Mountains, Pima County buys the Posta Quemada Ranch. The ranch had been owned since 1932 by Charles C. Day of Philadelphia and family and is the site of an old Butterfield Stage station and of Colossal Cave.

1991 April

The last ground-launched cruise missile being stored at Davis-Monthan is destroyed under the terms of the Intermediate Nuclear Forces Treaty signed in 1987. The Soviet Union dissolves at the end of this year.

1992

Hughes Aircraft acquires General Dynamics' missile business and relocates engineering and manufacturing functions and employees to Tucson from locations in Arkansas and California. This acquisition adds major production programs for the Tomahawk Cruise Missile, Standard Missile, Rolling Airframe Missile (RAM), Sparrow Missile, Stinger Missile, Advanced Cruise Missile (ACM), and the Phalanx Close-In Weapon System (CIWS). Because of the company's emphasis on tactical missiles, it changes its name to Hughes Missile Systems Company, later Raytheon Missile Systems Company, with, at that time, a focus on anti-missile missiles. The company, whose origins were at MIT in 1922, is still based in Massachusetts.

1992

Conservators, many of whom are at the top of their profession internationally, begin a five-year restoration of the interior of San Xavier Mission Church.

1993

The Colorado Rockies Major League Baseball team begins spring training at Hi Corbett field, replacing the Cleveland Indians.

1993

At the headwaters of the Santa Cruz River, the Ki-He-Kah Ranch in the San Rafael Valley sells off some 160-acre parcels. Owners are permitted by law to subdivide into 2.5-acre lots, making low-density residential development a threat in the valley for the first time. In 1994, some local non-absentee landowners form the San Rafael Valley Land Trust and start searching for a way to preserve large land holdings. In 1998, their leader, Bob Sharp, whose in-laws, the Greene family, had owned land there since 1903, sells to the Nature Conservancy and in 1999 the San Rafael State Natural Area is formed.

1994

15 miles south of Tucson, the town of Sahuarita is incorporated at the site of what had been Continental Farms and a World War II bombing range and is now the site of the Walden family's large pecan operation.

1994

Arizona passes a law giving public funding to independently operated "charter schools." The first charter school in the United States had opened in 1992. Arizona soon leads the nation in the number of them. In 2013, Arizona has more than twice as many as the state in second place, California.

1994

At the Clearwell site in the Tucson Mountains, Tucson Water builds two 30,000,000 gallon roofed reservoirs for potable water.

1994

Starting in 1987, at a site on the northwest side of the Catalina Mountains some 30 miles north of Tucson, a structure called Biosphere

2 had begun to be built. Funded by Texas investor Ed Bass, the facility had been constructed on a 40-acre campus to be a closed, self-sufficient ecological system. Biosphere 1 was Earth. In 1991, eight crew members had been sealed inside the structure. Problems and difficulties of various kinds had soon emerged and this year the seals had been broken by two of the original crew who had left early and were concerned about those who had remained. Bass will obtain a court order this year to oust the key managers and seize the premises. In 1995, Biosphere II, no longer considered to offer the prospect of a self-sufficient ecosystem, will be turned over to Columbia University as a research facility. In June 2011, Mr. Bass will donate the facility to the University of Arizona along with $20 million to support research. In 2014, UA continues to operate the facility for research and science tourism.

1995

In 1961 Hinchcliffe Court on Granada, Arizona's first winter resort, had been bought by Marietta Franklin and Gladys Carrol, relatives of Selim Franklin and owners of the Franklin House on Main just east of Hinchcliffe Court. This year, as a benefit for the Tucson Museum of Art on Main Avenue, Tucson artists upgrade and rehabilitate the bungalows. The bungalows of Hinchcliffe Court remain attractive rentals today.

1995 general overview map of Tucson (public domain). This map offers an early example of digital map design. Text is smooth, regular, and precisely placed, and features show the new capabilities of graphic design software, with masking around text, vector construction of roads, and a drop shadow under the legend.

1996

The City of Tucson opens Dell Urich Golf Course where the Randolph South Golf Course had been. Flood control funds had been used to give the course a major workover involving the creation of large basins. The city now has three municipal courses other than the two at Randolph (now Reid) Park: Silverbell (on the road northwest to the old Silverbell Mine), Fred Enke (in the southeast near Davis-Monthan, named after a longtime UA coach), and El Rio (on West Speedway not far from the Santa Cruz).

1996

At UA, ground is broken on the Mall for a major classroom building that will be built underneath the Mall and used primarily for first- and second-year classes. The new Integrated Learning Center (ILC) will be connected underground to the Main Library by an Information Commons with ranks of computer terminals and study rooms. Under current president Peter Likins, the ILC will be named in honor of Manuel

Pacheco, UA's first Hispanic president, who had served from 1991 to 1997. The large Main Library building—built in the 1980s with the assistance of the Friends of the Library, a development group the author's mother, Bunny Warnock, had helped found—is the only one on the Mall not made of red brick.

1996

The Southern Pacific Railroad is purchased by the Union Pacific Railroad.

1996

The University of Arizona Press and the Southwest Center publish a beautiful book by Bernard Fontana, anthropologist and authority on New Spain, called *A Gift of Angels*. It contains the story of the San Xavier Mission Church with full-color illustrations of its remarkable interior, recently restored by some of the world's best conservators.

1996

Casa Santa Clara is opened, a six-bed sober living facility for men being released from prison, created by Nick Jones, a Vietnam veteran and ex-inmate, and Mark Harris, pastor of the Oasis Church. In 2014, it becomes Old Pueblo Community Services, which operates 10 transitional living facilities with 300 beds, and offers services for both men and women, including Veterans Assistance Programs and a Community Recovery Program for less than affluent residents.

1996

Fairfield Homes announces plans to develop 3,186 acres of the Canoa Ranch south of Green Valley with over 6,000 homes, two golf courses, hotels, shopping centers, and a private airstrip, but the rezoning request is denied by Pima County supervisors.

1996

East of Tucson, the Central Arizona Project begins the first water recharge project in Pima County using spreading basins. In 2010, one of these, the Avra Valley Recharge Project, will be sold to Metro Water, the water company operating in northwest Tucson.

1997 May

The Haunted Bookshop, next to Tohono Chul park, closes, unable to compete with bigger stores. Many come in to buy mementos.

1997–2003

Jane Dee Hull, a Republican, replaces Fife Symington, a Republican, as governor after Symington resigns following his conviction on seven counts of bank fraud. In 1999, Symington's conviction is overturned by the U.S. Court of Appeals for the Ninth Circuit. Before Symington can be retried, he is pardoned by President Bill Clinton.

1998

Tucson Electric Park opens on Tucson's south side near I-10. The Arizona Diamondbacks and Chicago White Sox baseball teams do their spring training here in the "Cactus League," with the Colorado Rockies still at Hi Corbett Field.

1998

The Barraza-Aviation Parkway is completed. It runs west-northwest for five miles from the South Palo Verde Overpass to Broadway just east of the downtown underpass. Original plans called for it to bisect the downtown area all the way to Interstate 10.

1998

Unisource becomes the Arizona-based parent company of Tucson Electric Power.

1998

The city purchases the railroad depot property from the Union Pacific Railroad, which had bought the Southern Pacific two years ago. Restoration of the main depot building and the three adjacent buildings to their 1941 modernized Spanish Colonial Revival architectural style is completed in 2004, and artists' studios and compatible businesses begin to be supported in the surrounding area, now called Tucson's Historic Warehouse District.

1998

The Tucson Basin's water table is at about 105 feet, 25 feet deeper than in 1960. To treat effluent and add to the recharge, the 17.3-acre Sweetwater Wetlands is established this year, after several years of study and preparation, as a managed riparian area in abandoned agricultural fields next to the Roger Road Reclaimed Water Treatment Plant. Native and some non-native (e.g. salt-cedar) plants thrive there and many birds return, though far fewer than had inhabited the seven square miles of the Great Mesquite Bosque near Martinez Hill that had died out completely in 1970 because of the fall in the level of the water table.

1999

Bob Walkup becomes mayor (until 2011). He had worked for Hughes Aircraft Company and been chair of the Tucson Economic Council.

1999

After a sales tax increment is approved by voters, a Rio Nuevo board is established to revitalize downtown by creating Tucson Origins Heritage Park, among other projects. One proposal that has been considered is to discharge CAP water upstream of Tucson to create flow again in the Santa Cruz River and create a *Paseo de las Iglesias* of restored river and riparian vegetation that would extend from San Xavier to the San Agustín Mission site at the base of Sentinel Hill, the Birthplace of Tucson. The proposal is defeated in part because of the fear that pollutants might leach into the water from the landfill the city had operated for years, starting in the 1950s, on the west bank of the river at the base of Sentinel Peak.

1999

An Arboretum is established on the UA campus that features desert-adapted plants from around the world (like the carob from North Africa, the bottlebrush from Australia, and the neem from India) and a number of Heritage Trees and Great Trees of Arizona (like the silk floss tree south of the Engineering building and baobab at the southwest corner of the Administration building). A sycamore tree on the east side of Flandrau is grown from seeds that went to the moon on the Apollo 14 flight in 1971. The Arboretum's office is in Herring Hall, UA's second building, remodeled starting this year to house UA's Herbarium (plant archive)

2000

The City of Tucson's population is 486,699, up 20.1 percent since 1990.

2000

No City Directory had been published since 1992 and no directory other than the telephone book had been published after that time until 1997, when the Polk Cross Reference Directory was published. Mountain Bell had published its phone directories until 1984, and then, as Mountain Bell and US West, until 1989, with US West publishing the phone directories from 1990 to 1997.

2000

Total school enrollments, with change from previous decade:

- TUSD: 53,602, a decline of 3,336 (–6 percent). Of the total, 40,208 (75 percent) are minority.
- Pima Community College: 28,446, a decline of 300 since 1990.
- UA: 34,490, a *decline* of 1,245, with 1,624 faculty, down 28, and 172 buildings, up 18.

2000

Tucson Electric Power builds a solar generating station near its coal-fired plant in Springerville, 250 miles northeast of Tucson.

2000–2003

Major archaeological work is done at the Mission San Agustín and Mission Gardens sites, in the Presidio Neighborhood, and in other areas downtown as part of Rio Nuevo's Tucson Origins Project.

2001

Fifteen miles south of Tucson in the Santa Cruz River floodplain, the Central Arizona Project completes its Pima Mine Road Recharge Project facilities and spreading basins that are permitted to recharge 30,000 acre-feet annually.

Northwest of Tucson near Tangerine Road and I-10, the Lower Santa Cruz Recharge Project had been completed in 2000. Because of its excellent infiltration rate, its annual permitted capacity was increased to 50,000 acre-feet.

2001

Use of recovered CAP groundwater has begun, and use of fossil groundwater begins to be reduced again.

2001

The Pima County Board of Supervisors updates the Pima County Comprehensive Land Use Plan, integrating the land-use policies and principles of conservation developed in the Sonoran Desert Conservation Plan (SDCP), including the Conservation Lands System (CLS). The CLS, which covers approximately two million acres in eastern Pima County, identifies lands necessary to achieve the biological goals of the SDCP, while also delineating areas suitable for development.

2001

Pima County purchases 4,800 acres of Canoa Ranch and begins restoring land and buildings with voter-approved bond money. Plans call for a visitor center, gift shop, museum, and interpretive and environmental education sites.

2002

A major new Student Union building is completed at UA, replacing the one that had been built in 1951 as a memorial to World War II. The new building continues to house the bell salvaged from the battleship *U.S.S. Arizona*, sunk in the Japanese attack on Pearl Harbor, which is rung on special occasions.

2002

The Mission Gardens site in Tucson's Birthplace at the foot of Sentinel Peak is bought by Pima County, and a new volunteer group called Friends of Tucson's Birthplace (FOTB) begins restoring the garden with heritage plants from the Hohokam era through the time of Father Kino and the Spanish. The FOTB group supports a reconstruction of the Mission San Agustín and *convento* east of the garden but the issue is controversial because of a lack of specific information about the buildings. Beginning in the 1950s, almost all archaeological evidence of the buildings had been destroyed by city activity on the site.

2002

Mel and Enid Zuckerman and Jerry Cohen, founders of Canyon Ranch, establish the nonprofit Canyon Ranch Institute to translate the "health and wellness philosophy and expertise" of Canyon Ranch to communities beyond Canyon Ranch, hoping to reach lower-income groups.

2002

The Concourse Renovation Project begins at Tucson International Airport, to be completed in 2005.

2003–2009

Janet Napolitano, a Democrat, is elected governor, replacing Jane Dee Hull, a Republican.

2003

In June, the Aspen Fire takes hold in the forest on the Catalina Mountains. It will remain uncontrolled for a month, burn 84,750 acres, and destroy 344 structures, including many businesses in Summerhaven. The handsome Mount Lemmon Inn burns to the ground. Evacuations on the mountain are timely and there is no loss of life. The fire tops the ridge to the south and residents of Tucson can see it coming down the face of the mountain. It does not reach Tucson's city limits but does raise concerns about the effect on the burned-over hillsides and watershed during the rainy season.

2003

The neighborhood of Binghampton on the Rillito around Dodge applies for status as a Rural Historic Landscape.

2004

The Arizona Water Settlements Act is signed by President George W. Bush. It finalizes an agreement between the U.S. and Arizona for Central Arizona Project repayment obligations, settles water disputes between the Gila River Indian Community and all parties (including New Mexico parties), and settles pending litigation by the Tohono O'odham Nation. The director of the Arizona Department of Water

Resources will be allocated water to be held in trust that can be re-allocated for municipal and industrial purposes after 2010.

2004

In an effort to restore and rejuvenate the Rialto Theatre downtown, the Rialto Theatre Foundation is established by Doug Biggers, earlier the founder of *Tucson Weekly*. In 2014, the Rialto continues to offer well-attended concerts by live artists.

2005

Downtown on Congress and Stone, the Fox Theatre opens after a $14 million restoration. It closed in 1974 and sat empty for nearly 25 years. In 2014, it is thriving as a venue for concerts, shows, and events.

2006

Pima County takes over the Tucson Public Library. The "Carnegie Free Library" had become the "Tucson Public Library" on January 7, 1957. In 1990, after Pima County got more involved in library operations, the name was changed to the Tucson-Pima Public Library. By 2014, the Pima County Library had 27 branches offering a wide range of community services in many settings supporting literacy for all ages.

2006

Sun Tran receives a delivery of low-floor, handicapped-accessible biodiesel buses and now 100 percent of its buses are using cleaner-burning technologies: compressed natural gas, biodiesel, or hybrid.

2007

UA's Poetry Center moves into the new Helen Schaefer Building that has been built for it north of the main campus on Helen Street west of the UA Foundation building. Besides sponsoring readings and maintaining its extraordinary library, it has begun to sponsor programs for emerging writers, a *corrido* (Mexican ballad) contest, and other community programs.

2007

UA opens a branch of its medical school in Phoenix occupying three buildings of the old Phoenix Union High School, built in 1912, from which the author's mother had graduated in 1929.

2008

On East Speedway, Magic Carpet Golf closes after 40 years. The rebar-and-concrete characters are scattered throughout the city.

2008

Arizona's voters approve a constitutional amendment banning same-sex marriage.

2008

Restoration of the West Tower at San Xavier is completed under the auspices of Patronato San Xavier and architect Bob

Vint, preservation architect at San Xavier for the last 19 years. Restoration of the East Tower will begin seven years later.

2009–2015

Governor Janet Napolitano, a Democrat, leaves office in the middle of her second term to become the secretary of the U.S. Office of Homeland Security, appointed by President Barak Obama. Secretary of State Jan Brewer, a Republican, replaces her as governor. In 2014, Napolitano becomes chancellor of the University of California at Berkeley.

2009

The first Tucson Festival of Books is offered on the UA Mall over two days in March during UA's Spring Break. It is an astonishing success, attracting 50,000 visitors its first year, 70,000 its second year, over 100,000 in the years that follow, and signing up many community sponsors. Its founders are Bill Viner, a local home builder, and his wife, Brenda; John Humenik, the editor of the *Arizona Daily Star*; Frank Farias; and Bruce Beach. All proceeds are directed toward improving literacy rates in southern Arizona, with Tucson's community literacy umbrella organization, Literacy Connects, being an important beneficiary.

2009

After allegations of mismanagement, the state legislature takes oversight of Rio Nuevo away from the City of Tucson and gives it to the governor.

2009

The *Tucson Citizen*, the oldest continuously published newspaper in Arizona, ceases publication. Some Citizen staffers go on to establish the online *Tucson Sentinel*, still in operation in 2014. The *Arizona Daily Star*, which Lee Enterprises of Wisconsin had purchased from Pulitzer in 2005, also continues in operation.

2009

At 22nd and Alvernon, Tucson's last drive-in theater, the DeAnza Drive-In, closes.

2010

Don Diamond, who has been acquiring real estate and developing properties in and around Tucson since 1965, has also over that time been active with his wife Joan in philanthropic work, supporting the University of Arizona in various ways, as well as many local non-profits and service organizations, and the Jewish community. This year the ribbon is cut on one of their biggest philanthropic projects, the Diamond Children's hospital at the University Medical Center. A daughter, Deanne, had died of complications from asthma at age 14.

2010

The U.S. Census reports Tucson's population as 520,116, an increase of 6.9 percent since 2000, with the population of the metro area being just under a million (69.7 percent white,

5.0 percent black or African-American, 2.7 percent Native American, 2.9 percent Asian, 0.2 percent Pacific Islander, 16.9 percent from other races, and 3.8 percent from two or more races). Hispanic or Latino of any race are 41.6 percent of the population. Non-Hispanic whites are 47.2 percent of the population, down from 72.8 percent in 1970.

2010

Total enrollments, with change since 2000:

- TUSD K-12 about 51,000, a decline of about 1,000. It will close nine schools this year, with declines projected to continue at about this rate to 2022.

- Pima Community College 35,365, an increase of 6,899.

- UA 39,086, an increase of 4,598.

2010

Arizona's legislature drafts House Bill 2281 which bans "programs of instruction" that "are designed primarily for pupils of a particular ethnic group" or that "advocate ethnic solidarity instead of the treatment of pupils as individuals." An amended version adds prohibitions of classes that "promote the overthrow of the United States government" or "promote resentment toward a race or class of people." The superintendent of public instruction or the State Board of Education will determine if a program is in violation of this law and will be entitled to withhold 10 percent of the school budget from schools determined to be in violation. Classes required by federal law for Native American students are exempted. The law is signed by Arizona governor Jan Brewer, a Republican, in May.

2010

Use of groundwater recovered from recharge had begun in 2000. By now it exceeds the amount of fossil groundwater being used. Use of recovered groundwater continues upward and the use of fossil groundwater continues to decline.

2010

Austin's Old Fashioned Ice Cream, opened in 1959 and known for its pickle ice cream, wonderful shakes, and diner fare, closes at its location on Broadway just west of Country Club. It does not survive much longer in its new location.

2011

Jonathan Rothschild, a lawyer and Tucson native, is elected mayor. He inaugurates a literacy initiative, a program to cut red tape for businesses and increase incentives, a tree-planting program, a program to increase fitness of Tucson's citizens through walking events, and a program to end veteran homelessness.

2011

Superintendent of public instruction Tom Horne, a Republican, declares TUSD's programs in Mexican-American Studies to be out of compliance with House Bill 2281. When Horne is elected attorney general, his successor, John Huppenthal, a Republican, orders an audit of the program by the Arizona Department of Education. The audit finds "no observable evidence...to suggest that any classroom within Tucson Unified School District is in direct violation of the law." Supporters of the program point to the much higher graduation and college attendance rates of students who participate in the program. Huppenthal dismisses the audit and threatens to withhold 10 percent of the district's funding. Next year, the TUSD board will vote to cut the Mexican-American Studies program and will remove certain books from the district's classrooms and libraries, among them William Shakespeare's *The Tempest* and Luis Alberto Urrea's *The Devil's Highway*. There are no plans to investigate any other ethnic studies programs in the city or the state.

2011

The Regional Water Assessment Task Force—formed in 2010 by the mayor of Tucson and the Pima County Board of Supervisors under the aegis of the Pima Association of Governments—issues its first report on measures needed to promote water sustainability in the region.

2011

A non-profit called Living Streets Alliance begins operation. They envisage streets as "living public spaces that connect people to places and each other" and begin work of various kinds to make Tucson more "walkable" and bicycle friendly. They find significant support in the community and are beginning to thrive by 2014.

2011

On February 12, a Mass celebrating the completed restoration of Saint Augustine Cathedral that had begun in 1968 is led by the bishop of Tucson, Gerald Kicanas.

2011

In August, not usually thought to be prime time for attracting visitors to Tucson, the Tucson Audubon Society offers its first Tucson Bird and Wildlife Festival. It is a success and is still going strong.

2011

The Colorado Rockies, Arizona Diamondbacks, and Chicago White Sox all move their spring training to new facilities built in Phoenix, and Major League Baseball is gone from Tucson. Tucson had also housed a AAA baseball team, on and off, since 1969, and efforts continue to recruit a Minor League Baseball team for the city, but as of 2014, the efforts have not borne fruit. Tucson Electric Power agrees to change the name of Tucson Electric Park to Kino Veterans Memorial Stadium.

2012

The first Kino heritage plants are planted by the Friends of Tucson's Birthplace in the four-acre Mission Garden that is to be developed at the base of Sentinel Peak on the exact site of the garden for mission San Agustín. The garden will represent the agriculture of many of the cultures that have inhabited the spot for the last 4000 years.

2012

A jaguar is photographed in the Santa Rita Mountains by an automated wildlife camera, confirming a photograph the previous year of what appeared to be a jaguar's tail. Beginning in 2003, the Northern Jaguar Project, run by Diane Hadley out of what had been the Solomon Warner House at the base of Sentinel Peak, had begun work in collaboration with local ranchers to create a large jaguar refuge in northern Sonora. By now the project has acquired over 20,000 acres for the purpose. Its long-term aspiration is a return of the jaguar to the United States.

2012

In spite of the fact that the city and county have not been able to come to terms, Pima County begins to move forward with construction of a new Consolidated Justice Court Building on north Stone Avenue at Toole. The site is discovered to be over Tucson's original cemetery, and an unanticipated cost is incurred to move 1400 sets of remains. Voters had approved a $76 million bond issue for the joint project in 2004. The courthouse will open in January 2015, with costs having increased to over $142 million.

2013

The federal judge overseeing TUSD's desegregation order requires TUSD to offer "culturally relevant" Mexican-American Studies classes to comply with the order. The district begins to offer these classes again, but state officials say they will be making announced and unannounced visits to these classes and teachers will have to submit substantial

The new Pima County Consolidated Justice Court under construction, begun in 2012. Justice Court, which adjudicates lesser matters—misdemeanor crimes and smaller civil matters—had been separated from Superior Court when the new Superior Courthouse was completed in 1974. Justice Court, which has been conducting its business in the historic pink courthouse, will move into the new building when it is completed. Photo by Mamta Popat, Arizona Daily Star, April 25, 2013.

paperwork to the Arizona Department of Education to be sure House Bill 2281 is being complied with.

2013

The Tucson/Pima County Community Food Bank reports that in its service area 26.9 percent of children—about one in 4—go hungry, lower than the Arizona average of 29.9 percent, higher than the national average of 22.4 percent; 29.7 percent of children in its service area live below the poverty line. This year the Food Bank distributes over 27 million pounds of food, enough for 63,394 meals a day.

2013

Tucson becomes part of the "25 Cities" effort to end homelessness, especially of veterans, in 25 selected cities. The effort by federal and local agencies and local supporters is coordinated in Tucson by the Tucson Pima Collaboration to End Homelessness.

2013

On East Broadway east of Tucson Boulevard, El Parador Restaurant closes after 40 years.

2013

East of the Green Valley exit on I-19 south of Tucson, Pima County's historic Hacienda de la Canoa is dedicated in the Raul M. Grijalva Canoa Ranch Conservation Park. The main historic structures are the Manning Houses, but the emphasis of the site, according to the promotional video, is on honoring all the peoples who lived on and worked this land.

And where are we in 2014, as I write what will be the last entries in this account?

2014

The U.S. Census estimates that Tucson is still growing, by about 160 people per month.

2014

Tucson Electric Power builds a large new multi-story headquarters on the southwest corner of Sixth Avenue and Broadway, former site of the Tucson Fire Department's Station No. 1.

2014

In the Refugee Act of 1980, Congress had codified the U.S. policy of accepting as immigrants people trying to escape persecution in their homelands. Since 1978, over 60,000 refugees have made their homes in Arizona, mostly in Phoenix and Tucson. Over that time, significant populations have arrived from Afghanistan, Bhutan, Bosnia, Burma, Burundi, Cambodia, Croatia, Cuba, Ethiopia, Iran, Iraq, Kosovo, Romania, Somalia, the Soviet Union, Sudan, and Vietnam. Since 1978, the largest numbers have come from Vietnam and, more recently, Iraq. Very few refugees have been accepted from Central American countries, and none, it seems, from Mexico or El Salvador. In Tucson, the

Columbus/Grant area has a concentrated population of refugees from Africa, the Dodge/Flower area refugees from Bhutan.

2014

About 15 percent of Arizona's population has been born outside the United States with 38 percent born in the state. About 20 percent have been born in the midwestern United States and 9 percent in California. At statehood in 1912, about 30 percent of Arizona's population had been born outside the United States, with 31 percent born in Arizona.

2014

Tucson Weekly is acquired by 10/13 Communications, based in Reno, Nevada, which also buys *Inside Tucson Business*. The company had already acquired *Foothills News, Desert Times,* and *Marana News* from Tucson West Publishing, Inc., and also, in 2007, the *Explorer*, a paper distributed on Tucson's northwest side. 10/13 Communications owns a number of other "hyper-local" publications in the Phoenix, Dallas, and Houston areas. The publications in the Tucson area will be known as Tucson Local Media and remain part of the national Association of Alternative Newspapers but 10/13 says it will be emphasizing marketing and implementing an "innovative distribution model" that employs digital and mobile media.

2014

Tucson and its surroundings have attracted more than a few writers over the years. The travel writers, the first of

2014 screenshot from OpenStreetMap.org. This screenshot of a web map of central Tucson, automatically generated on-the-fly from crowdsourced GIS data, shows the power of modern web-based atlases. As with all material on the web, a tradeoff is that unless an active effort is made to archive different versions of this constantly changing data over time, historical research will become much more challenging. Some drama in time may be lost.

whom was Father Kino, if we don't include the makers of petroglyphs and pictographs, were passing through. The writings of some of these travelers—J. Ross Browne, Martha Summerhayes, John Gregory Bourke, John Van Dyke—have contributed to this account. Beyond this, a goodly number of noted and notable writers have found Tucson to be a place for them to stop awhile and write. Among this goodly number (in alphabetical order and with apologies in advance for those this writer did not think or know to mention) are Edward Abbey, Beth Alvarado, Patrick Baliani, Kate Bernheimer, Sherwin Bitsui, Charles Bowden, Karen Brennan, Susan Briante, Laynie Brown, Phil Caputo, Chris Cokinos, Barbara Cully, Ann Cummins, Alison Hawthorne Deming, Marvin Diogenes, Elizabeth Evans, Vivian Gornick, Joy Harjo, Jim Harrison, Tony Hoagland, Robert Houston, J. A. Jance, Fenton Johnson, Barbara Kingsolver, Joseph Wood Krutch, Ken Lamberton, Mary Levy, Nancy Mairs, Farid Matuk, Cormac McCarthy, CB McKenzie, Larry McMurtry, Jane Miller, Tom Miller, Scott Momaday, Ander Monson, Manuel Muñoz, Gary Paul Nabhan, Tenney Nathanson, Steve Orlen, Simon Ortiz, Jonathan Penner, Buzz Poverman, Boyer Rickel, Alberto Rios, Richard Russo, Aurelie Sheehan, Richard Shelton, Leslie Silko, Johanna Skibsrud, Luci Tapahonso, Erec Toso, John Updike, Luis Urrea, David Foster Wallace, Frances Washburn, Peter Wild, Joy Williams, Joshua Marie Wilkinson, Harold Bell Wright, and Ofelia Zepeda.

2014

UA, now occupying 356 acres (almost nine times the 40 acres at its beginning in 1885), is the #1 employer in Tucson, at 11,047.

- UA's enrollment this year is expected to reach 41,800, a record high, over 1,200 times what it was when UA opened.

- UA is ranked among the top 20 public research universities in the country and in certain areas where rankings are maintained—in anthropology, optics, space sciences, biosciences, creative writing, and management information sciences, for example—it is ranked in the top five.

- A number of strong interdisciplinary fields have emerged at UA that are not traditional "departments," among them:
    o Environmental Studies (which does work in Geography and Geophysics, Biology, Arid Land Studies, and Agriculture, among others)
    o Cognitive Science (which works in Psychology, Philosophy, Linguistics, Neuroscience, and Evolutionary Biology, among others)
    o Business (in the Eller College, with departments of Accounting, Management, Entrepreneurship, and Management Information Systems)
    o Southwest/Border studies (Anthropology, Folklore, English, Spanish, American Indian Studies, and Ethnobotany, among others)
    o Rhetoric (in the Department of English with connections to Literature, Creative Writing, Applied Linguistics, and the Writing Program, and to the fields of Communication,

Education, Information Science, and Performance Studies, among others)

- The state's appropriation in support of UA and its other universities has been steadily reduced, beginning in the 1990s. In recent years Arizona has led the nation in cuts to higher-education funding. At UA the state's contribution has declined over 50 percent to about 11 percent of UA's budget. Grant funding for Big Science is also being reduced nationally. Tuition at UA has more than doubled over this period. The Arizona Constitution continues to require that higher education be "as nearly free as possible."

- Ongoing design and construction projects at UA include Bioscience Research Laboratories, a new Environment and Natural Resources building on 6th Street, bicycle and pedestrian improvements, and upgrades to the McKale Memorial Center basketball arena. Significant upgrades were completed last year to Arizona Stadium, also known as the Lowell-Stevens Football Facility. On Speedway adjoining the campus, high-rise buildings for student housing are being privately developed.

- In 2013, the Laboratory of Tree-Ring Research that had been housed for decades beneath the west stands of the football stadium, was moved a block west to the new Bryant Bannister Tree Ring Building, one of a number of significant facilities and programs at UA made possible by gifts from Agnese Haury, the widow of UA anthropologist Emil Haury.

- The College of Science at UA has joined with the

Tucson Chamber of Commerce to encourage tourism by representing Tucson as "Science City."

2014

Pima Community College, which began offering classes in 1969, is the 18th-largest employer in Tucson, at 2,177. It now has six campuses in Tucson, four education centers, and several adult education learning centers. In 2005–2006 its enrollment had been 75,000, but it then experienced accounting and accreditation troubles, and in 2014, its enrollment was at 56,000, a decline of 25 percent. Pima Community College has also suffered declines in state funding, with the legislature threatening a zero budget allocation in 2015.

2014

Total expenditures on "Higher Education" in Tucson (including Pima Community College and other colleges) are $2,344,895,000. Total number of employees in this sector are 15,130.

2014

TUSD enrolls over 49,000 students, operates 89 schools, and is the #6 employer in Tucson at 6,525, with a budget of $313,200,000, nearly $3 million less than last year. At its peak, TUSD operated 120 schools with an enrollment of 63,000. The District is trying to sell or find uses for the schools it has had to close. Under the desegregation order, TUSD is still receiving $64 million a year in desegregation funds from the federal government. Arizona enrolls more than a million students in its public schools, with about 184,400 students attending a charter school last year. Most charter schools do not seem to be outperforming public schools, but one of them, Basis Tucson North (one of 14 Basis schools established in Arizona starting in 1998), appears on *U.S. News and World Reports'* list of the five best high schools in the nation. A number of parochial and private schools continue to offer these options in Tucson. Total employees in "Education" are 21,000.

2014

In the "Military and Defense" sector, Raytheon Missile Systems, with 9,933 employees, is the #2 employer (the U.S. Army Intelligence Center at Fort Huachuca is #8 with 5,717). Davis-Monthan Air Force Base, with 8,933 employees, is the #4 employer in Tucson. The 309th Aircraft Maintenance and Regeneration Group at Davis-Monthan is the #73 employer with 652. Total employees are 28,792, a little less than double that of the higher-education sector.

2014

The continuation of Davis-Monthan is threatened because of the Base Realignment and Closure decisions that began in 1989 with the end of the Cold War. Retirement of the A-10 close air-support fighter based at Davis-Monthan has been considered. The Davis-Monthan 50 has been joined by the Tucson Metro Chamber of Commerce and the Southern Arizona Leadership Council to form the Southern Arizona Defense Alliance. Base supporters consider hiring a Washington lobbyist. The Chamber of Commerce and Raytheon have also launched social programs to support airmen at the base departing on or returning from deployments. A group called Tucson Forward has opposed basing the new F-35 at Davis-Monthan, primarily because of its remarkable noise.

2014

Tucson International Airport continues to host the 162nd Fighter Wing of the Air National Guard, the largest Air National Guard wing in the U.S., now flying the F-16 Fighting Falcon. During its 56-year history at the airport, the Air National Guard has also operated the F-86 Sabre, F-100 Super Sabre, F-102 Delta Dagger, and the A-7 Corsair II. Not counting students or transient flight crews, the installation now employs more than 1,700 people, over 1,100 of whom are full-time Active Guard and Reserve and Air Reserve Technician personnel, and the remainder traditional part-time Air National Guardsmen.

2014

The state of Arizona is the #3 employer in Tucson with 9,439, Pima County is #5 with 7,328, the City of Tucson is #11 with 4,845, the Tohono O'odham Nation is #12 with 4,250, and the U.S. Border Patrol is #13 with 4,135. Total of "Government Employees" is 38,921, more than in any other sector.

2014

Health Care employs 25,451; Call Centers, Business Services and Staffing 10,215; Mining 7,966 (Freeport McMoRan is at #9); Nonprofits and Community Services 6,739. The nine Tucson resorts listed employ 3,405, with

Canyon Ranch having the most at 682 (#69). Construction and Contracting employs 1,616, Agriculture 1,252.

2014

Twenty-three retailers are listed in the *Arizona Daily Star*'s list of Tucson's top 200 employers, with a total of 22,704 employees. Walmart is the #10 employer in Tucson, with 5,200 people, more than twice as many as the next retailer, Fry's Food Stores, which is #20. All the retailers are part of national chains, except Bashas', an Arizona grocery store business started by Lebanese immigrants Ike and Eddie Basha in 1932 in a small town between Phoenix and Tucson, now with 130 stores. The only other local retailer in the top 23 is Gadabout SalonSpas, started in Tucson in 1979, now having 11 locations in Tucson.

2014

The 15 restaurants listed in the top 200 employers (two are beverage distributors) employ a total of 4,885 people. The largest employer is Darden, at #48 with 936 employees. Only four of the restaurant operations listed in the top 200 are locally owned. The others are national franchises. The highest-ranked local restaurant employer is the corporate parent of eegee's at #69. The next local restaurant employer listed is the Flores Family (El Charro, Chonitas, Sir Vezas) at #163. Tucson has many good local restaurants, however. Some are "ethnic" (Ethiopian, Greek, Indian, Italian, Japanese, Korean, Mexican, Spanish, Vietnamese, among many other cultures represented) and some are creatively local (Downtown Kitchen, Five Points, Feast, Kingfisher, Mother Hubbard's). Some, like El Corral and McMahon's (both "steak places") and Blue Willow are steady standbys. Food trucks have become an important presence in Tucson in recent years, increasing in numbers and in the range and quality of food offered.

2014

Tucson is nominated this year to become the first Global City of Gastronomy in North America as recognized by the United Nations Educational, Scientific and Cultural Organization. Criteria for this designation are a "vibrant gastronomy community with numerous traditional restaurants and/or chefs," "endogenous ingredients used in traditional cooking," "local know-how," "traditional food markets and traditional food industry," "tradition of hosting gastronomic festivals," "respect for the environment and promotion of sustainable local products," and "nurturing of public appreciation, promotion of nutrition in educational institutions and inclusion of biodiversity conservation programmes in cooking schools curricula."

2014

Tucson Water moves about 94 million gallons of water a day across 390 square miles, 4600 miles of water mains, 230 wells, and 220,000 water meters. Tucson's annual water demand is about 100,000 acre-feet (326 billion gallons), the same as in 1989, even though the city has 200,000 more people: Conservation measures seem to have had an effect. The city's current allotment from the Central Arizona Project is 144,000 acre-feet a year, the largest municipal and industrial allocation on the system. Tucson Water is able to "bank" and recharge the surplus of 44,000 acre-feet and estimates that it has by now banked almost 500,000 acre-feet of water that might be drawn on later. The city is also using now about 35 acre-feet per year of recycled water, at present only for parks and golf courses, not for residences. The water table is now rising, especially in the recharge areas, up 50 feet from its lowest point, but still nowhere near where it was at statehood. Allocations of CAP water will be reduced, however, if the water level in Lake Mead, the largest reservoir in the United States by volume and now at 1,082 feet above sea level (37 percent of capacity) and declining, ends the year below 1,075 feet. If the level in Lake Mead drops below 1,000 feet, generation of hydroelectric power at Hoover Dam will cease as well. Power from the dam is used by Arizona (18.95 percent), Nevada (25.14 percent), and California (74.86 percent).

2014

A new control tower is to be built at Tucson International Airport. Passenger traffic, with 1.6 million passengers "enplaned" and about the same number "deplaned," is down about 200,000 from 2010. Air freight "enplaned" has risen by two million pounds from 2010 to almost 30 million pounds. Air freight "deplaned" has declined by five million pounds to 33 million pounds since 2010.

2014

The Union Pacific Railroad, which carries freight east and west through Tucson and across southern Arizona, with spurs north to Phoenix and south to Nogales, reports 27,946 rail cars originating in Arizona (an increase of 56 percent since 2010) and 111,734 rail cars terminating in Arizona (an increase of 35 percent since 2010). Union Pacific reports its capital investment in Arizona from 2010 to 2014 to be more than $437 million. Tucson is Union Pacific's principal terminal in Arizona.

2014

Three Amtrak trains a week run out of the renovated depot in what is now the Tucson Warehouse Arts District (five passenger trains a day ran in 1925). The Sunset Limited and Texas Eagle offer service from Los Angeles through Tucson eastbound to New Orleans or to Chicago. The Sunset Limited's average time from Los Angeles to New Orleans is 48 hours, with 20 stops. Texas Eagle's average time from Los Angeles to Chicago, including stops, is 68 hours 45 minutes.

2014 July 25

The Sun Link (Tucson Modern Streetcar) route opens. It connects midtown and downtown to Tucson's Birthplace, with other routes planned for the future. New businesses open along the route. Will downtown revitalization take hold this time?

2014

The Tucson Convention Center, constructed downtown in a large part of Barrio Viejo during the urban renewal of the 1970s, has recently been losing about $3.5 million a year even though it had gotten a $7.8 million makeover through Rio Nuevo. As a way of trimming losses, the city is now exploring turning it over to a private management group, something it had tried a couple of years ago with the municipal golf courses, apparently without success. Tucson is not the only city in this fix. Phoenix and Las Vegas are also losing money on their convention centers.

2014

Tucson Electric Power's parent company, Unisource, is purchased this year by Fortis Inc., a Canadian gas and electric utility holding company. Fortis will have to abide by the state of Arizona's renewable-energy standards which require state-regulated utilities to boost their share of renewable generation to 15 percent of their retail power sales by 2025. To help meet this obligation, Tucson Electric Power has asked the Arizona Corporation Commission to allow it to offer to install solar panels for its customers without upfront charges if customers will agree to pay a fixed monthly rate for 25 years that is based on their historical usage.

2014

During the American era, Tucson has always had a jail. The city got its first state prison in 1979 when the Arizona State Prison Complex opened on Wilmot southeast of Tucson with 384 nonviolent first-offender inmates. That complex now has an inmate capacity of approximately 4,358—an 11-fold increase in 35 years—in seven housing units and three special housing units, at security levels 2, 3, 4, and 5, with 5 being "the highest level of risk or need" in the prison system. A federal prison has been built next door. The first prison in the Arizona Territory opened in Yuma in 1876 with seven inmates, and what would be the first prison in the state opened in Florence in 1908, both prisons having been built with inmate labor. In 1912, Fort Grant, near the site of the Camp Grant massacre, had been made a facility for "wayward youth" (a refrain when the author was at Tucson High: "Keep that up, you'll end up in Fort Grant"). In 1973, it became a prison for adult males. The Arizona Department of Corrections now supervises 10 large prison complexes like Tucson's and five private prisons, incarcerating over 34,000 people.

2014

Birding has become an important activity in Tucson. The Tucson Audubon Society, with offices in the historic YWCA Building, is actively supporting birding with projects in the region such as in the Atturbury Wash that runs through the Fred Enke Golf Course, the Paton Center for Hummingbirds on the outskirts of Patagonia, the Esperanza Ranch conservation easement in northern Santa Cruz County, the Barrio Kroeger Lane project in Barrio Viejo, and in the Simpson/Martin Farms restoration project on the Santa Cruz downstream of Marana.

2014

Downtown just east of the Santa Cruz, the house built on Granada Street in the late 1800s by Leopoldo Carrillo is being restored. Now owned by the Arizona Historical Society, it is known as the Sosa-Carrillo-Fremont House.

2014

The Loop, a bike trail and shared-use path around Tucson being built collaboratively by the City of Tucson and the Pima Association of Governments, is now 85 percent complete. When finished, it will comprise 131 miles of paved path. It follows, for the most part, the Santa Cruz River and its tributaries, including the Rillito.

2014

Upstream of Tucson on the Santa Cruz, the Green Valley Pecan Company, 7,000 acres on the old Continental Farms site south of Tucson, still operated in 2014 by the Walden family, is said to be the largest irrigated integrated pecan orchard in the world. Water must be shared with the residents and golf courses of Green Valley and Continental, with ASARCO and Phelps Dodge mines across Interstate 19 to the west, and with Tucson downstream.

2014

Downstream from Tucson on the Santa Cruz, near I-10 and Twin Peaks Road, at the site of a planned outlet mall, another significant Hohokam site is excavated.

2014

On April 10, another automated wildlife photograph is taken of a jaguar on the east side of the Santa Rita Mountains. Debate continues about whether the U.S. Forest Service should permit the Augusta Resource Corporation to dig its new open-pit Rosemont Copper Mine on the eastern flank of the Santa Rita Mountains not far from Sonoita, in part of the jaguar's apparent habitat. Residents of Sonoita are also worried about the effect of the mine, which will be in view west of one of Arizona's most scenic roads, on tourism and the town's water supply. Augusta claims that the mine would be the third-largest copper mine in the country, have a life span of 21 years, and provide more than 2,900 jobs.

9
To Be Continued

THAT'S THE STORY of the place called Tucson, a version of it, not the definitive account, and not the end of the story either.

What does the future hold? Let's see: In this place now called Tucson the population grew in the time of the Hohokam, then declined, then started growing again (though not the Indian population) with the arrival of the Spanish, then declined again. In the century that followed the arrival of the Americans, it increased steadily, especially after the arrival of the railroad, and even more after World War II. In recent years, growth has slowed, but the census says Tucson's population is still increasing by about 160 people a month.

Increase is not necessarily improvement, of course. Growth that is mere increase creates only growths, not a fuller realization. On the other hand, not to be growing in some way is probably not to be fully alive.

We may not always know where our own actions stand on this scale, but we do know, I hope, where we should try to stand as the drama that is Tucson continues to unfold.

Thanks again to those who came before in this story and in the telling of it.

Thanks in advance to those readers who will correct and expand and enliven this account by visiting the website for this book and putting in their oar.

Acknowledgments and Thanks

SOME OF THE people who contributed to this account, sometimes without knowing that's what they were doing, are Andrew Agnew and Bradley Fletcher (TUSD), Susan Aiken and the late Chris Carroll, Colette Altaffer, Charles Ares, Jeffrey Banister, Fred Boice, Dianne Bret Harte, Rachel Buck, Roger Carpenter, John and Georgiann Carroll, John Carter, Gene Caywood, Ruth Ann and Phil Cline, Dick Cota-Robles, Libby Coyner (Arizona State Archives), Sally Day, Patti Doar, William Doelle (Archaeology Southwest), Johanna Eubank, Larry Evers, Eileen and Andy Garrish, Dave Giles, Phil and Anne-Marie Hall, Greg Hansen, Steve Hazen, Ann Hughart, Neel Hall, Michelle Henry (Pima Community College), Jennifer Jenkins, Gloria Kalil, Sharon Kha, Bonnie Kirk, Jay Kittle, Fred Knipe, Steve Kozachik, Doug Kreutz,

David Leighton, Stan Maliszewski, Lucy Masterman, Cynthia Miller, Martha Ortiz, Sister Ann Patrick, Ernesto Portillo Jr., Corky Poster, Alice Roe, Don Rollings, Richard Sand, Ken Scoville, Charles Scruggs, Richard Shelton, Ben Smith, Evren Sonmez, Katie Sylvester, Judy Temple, Ed Updegraff, Javier Varela, Bob Vint, Martha Warnock, Rick Wiley, Bill Woodin, the members of the THS Class of 1959, still carrying on for Tucson High, and the good people of the Arizona Historical Society Archives, especially Laura Hoff, Caitlin Lampman, and Lizeth Zepeda; and University of Arizona Special Collections, especially Bob Diaz and Leslie Sult.

Special thanks to Alex Smith, JD, MA, Geographical Information Science and Technology, University of Arizona, who as an unpaid graduate student took the idea of a collection of maps that showed the evolution of mapping styles after Kino and ran with it.

Some of the organizations whose work supports local place-making:

- Archaeology Southwest with its *Archaeology Southwest Magazine*, its blog "Preservation Archaeology," and its Archaeology Cafe
- Arizona Archaeological and Historical Society with its monthly newsletter *Glyphs* and its quarterly journal *Kiva* (founded 1916)
- Arizona Historical Society (founded 1864) and its *Journal of Arizona History*
- Arizona State Museum with its Office of Ethnohistorical Research and Documentary Relations of the Southwest project supporting research in the written record that began with the arrival of the Spanish in the 1530s

- Climate Assessment for the Southwest (CLIMAS) and its various publications, established in 1998 under the auspices of the National Oceanic and Atmospheric Administration and housed at the Institute for the Environment
- Friends of Tucson's Birthplace
- Hispanic Chamber of Commerce
- Jewish History Museum
- Living Streets Alliance
- Los Descendientes del Presidio de Tucson
- Patronato San Xavier
- Santa Cruz Valley Heritage Alliance
- Southern Arizona Home Builders Association
- Southwestern Mission Research Center (established 1965) and its quarterly newsletter/magazine *Revista*
- Southwest Folklife Alliance, housed in the Southwest Center, University of Arizona
- Tubac Presidio State Historic Park
- Tucson Chinese Cultural Center
- Tucson Corral of the Westerners (established 1960) and its journal *Smoke Signal*
- Tucson Historic Preservation Foundation
- Tumacácori National Historical Park

Groups and institutes at the University of Arizona whose work and publications frequently focus on local place-making:

- Arid Lands Resources Graduate Interdisciplinary Program
- Bureau of Applied Anthropology
- Institute for the Environment, especially its Arts and Environment Network with its *Proximities* blog
- Latin American Studies
- Mexican-American Studies
- School of Geography and Development
- Southwest Center with its *Journal of the Southwest* and other publications, including media programs
- Udall Center for Studies in Public Policy (established 1987)
- University of Arizona Press, founded in 1959, publishing 55 books annually with 1,000 currently in print
- Water Resources Research Council with newsletters, maps, pamphlets, and other publications

Special acknowledgment to Joe Wilder, director of the Southwest Center at the University of Arizona, editor of the *Journal of the Southwest* (where the first version of this work appeared, 58:3 Autumn 2016), and sponsor of many significant projects about the region, who saw the potential in this project and helped me see it; to Ray Thompson, past head of the University of Arizona's Department of Anthropology and past director of the Arizona State Museum, who "got" it and in many ways helped me get it right; to the late Bernard Fontana, one of Tucson's most significant place-makers, who generously helped me fill in some gaps and avoid a number of embarrassments; and to Tilly, without whom so much not. All did their best to rescue me from error. The errors that remain are mine.

Selected Documents and Stories by Those Who Came Before

Arizona: Good Roads Association Illustrated Road Maps and Tour Book. Originally compiled and published in 1913 by Arizona Good Roads Association, Prescott, AZ, reprinted 1987 by *Arizona Highways* magazine.

Ball, Phyllis. *A Photographic History of the University of Arizona, 1885–1985* (privately printed, 1986, distributed by University of Arizona Press).

Barnes, Aloma J. *Dunbar: the Neighborhood, the School, and the People 1940-1965.* Tucson: Wheatmark, 2016

Barrow, William C. *Historical Tucson.* Cleveland State University Institutional Repository, Michael Schwartz Library, September 2014 (a republication of articles that appeared originally in *The Saguaro* and *The Desert Leaf* in Tucson in 1986–1987), http://engagedscholarship.csuohio.edu/cgi/viewcontent.cgi?article=1128&context=msl_facpub.

Bolton, Herbert Eugene. *Rim of Christendom: A Biography of Eusebio Francisco Kino, Pacific Coast Pioneer.* New York: Macmillan Company, 1936.

Borderman: Memoirs of Federico José Ronstadt, edited by F. Ronstadt. Tucson: University of Arizona Press, 2003.

Bourke, John Gregory. *On the Border with Crook.* New York: Charles Scribner's Sons, 1892.

Bret Harte, John. *Tucson: Portrait of a Desert Pueblo.* Woodland Hills, CA: Windsor Publications, 1980.

Brophy, Blake. "Tucson's Arizona Inn: The Continuum of Style," *Journal of Arizona History,* autumn 1983, 255–282.

Browne J. Ross. *A Tour through Arizona, 1864, or Adventures in the Apache Country.* Tucson: Arizona Silhouettes, 1950.

Bufkin, Don. "From Mud Village to Modern Metropolis," *Journal of Arizona History* 22, spring 1981, 63–98.

Cabo, Tomás Serrano. *Cronicas: Alianza Hispano Americana.* Tucson: Arizona Historical Society, 1929.

Caywood, W. Eugene. *A History of Tucson Transportation Beginnings circa 1880: The Arrival of the Railroad, Beginnings of Transit in Tucson,* Tucson–Pima County Historical Commission, 2005, a reprinting of "A History of Tucson Transportation," 1980.

Chanin, Abraham S. *Cholent & Chorizo.* Tucson: Midbar Press, 1995.

Cooper, James F. *TUSD District History: First Hundred Years,* edited by John H. Fahr. Tucson, 1967.

Czaplicki, Jon S., James D. Mayberry, James E. Ayres. *An Archaeological Assessment of the Middle Santa Cruz River Basin, Rillito to Green Valley, Arizona, for the Proposed Tucson Aqueduct Phase B, Central Arizona Project.* Archaeological series, Tucson Arizona, no. 164. [Tucson, AZ?] The Division; Springfield, VA.: available from the National Technical Information Service, 1983.

Devine, David. *Tucson: A History of the Old Pueblo from the 1854 Gadsden Purchase*. Jefferson, NC: McFarland Publishers, 2015.

Dobyns, Henry. *Spanish Colonial Tucson*. Tucson: University of Arizona Press, 1976.

"The Downfall of Downtown," *Tucson Weekly*, March 6, 1997.

Drachman, Roy P. *From Cowtown to Desert Metropolis: Ninety Years of Arizona Memories*. San Francisco: Whitewing Press, 1999.

Elliot, Bob, and Eric Money. *Tucson: A Basketball Town*. Tucson: Wheatmark, 2014.

Ferg, Alan. "The Petroglyphs of Tumamoc Hill," *Kiva* 45:1/2 1979, 95–118.

Fontana, Bernard. "The Westernmost Skirmish of the Civil War," *Arizona Highways* 63:1, January 1987, 26–29 (drawings by Brian Calkins).

---------. *A Guide to Contemporary Southwest Indians*. Tucson: Southwest Parks and Monuments Association, 1994.

---------. "Biography of a Desert Church: The Story of Mission San Xavier del Bac." *Smoke Signal* no. 3, 1961. Tucson: Tucson Corral of the Westerners, 1996 (revised edition).

---------. *San Xavier del Bac: Portrait of a Desert Church*. Tucson: Southwestern Mission Research Center, 2015.

---------. *A Gift of Angels: The Art of Mission San Xavier del Bac* (photographs by Edward McCain) Tucson: University of Arizona Press, 2010

Frontier Tucson: Hispanic Contributions. Tucson: Arizona Historical Society, 1987.

Glinski, James, with Gene Magee's vintage photographs.

Above Tucson: Then and Now. Tucson: JTG Enterprise, 1995. http://www.abovetucson.com/

Gonzalez, Manuel. "Mariano G. Samaniego," *Journal of Arizona History* 31:2, summer 1990, 141–160.

Grace, Ruthann. "Don Pedro Pellón: Tucson's Pioneer Actor and Activist, *Journal of Arizona History,* 57:2, summer 2016, 153-196

Haney, John A., and Cirino G. Scavone. "Cars Stop Here," *Smoke Signal* no. 23. Tucson: Tucson Corral of the Westerners, spring 1971.

Haury, Emil W. *Prehistory of the American Southwest.* Tucson: University of Arizona Press, 1986.

Henry, Bonny. "Another Tucson." Tucson: *Arizona Daily Star,* 1992.

Hillary, Debra L. *A Legal and Political History of South Tucson, 1935–1940.* Tucson: privately printed, 1975 (in holdings of the Arizona Historical Society).

Hoffman, Paul Dennis. "Tucson School District #1, 1941–1978: A Study in Relationships." PhD dissertation, University of Arizona, 1982.

Images of America: Early Tucson. Anne I. Woosley and the Arizona Historical Society. Charleston, SC: Arcadia Publishing, 2008.

Jenkins, Jennifer. *Celluloid Pueblo: Western Ways Films and the Invention of the Postwar Southwest.* Tucson: University of Arizona Press, 2016.

Jim and Loma Griffith Arizona-Sonora Folklore Archives, 2013, http://www.griffitharchives.org/.

John Spring's Arizona. Edited by A. M. Gustafson. Tucson: University of Arizona Press, 1966.

Jones, Oakah L. *Los Paisanos: Spanish Settlers on the Northern Frontier of New Spain.* Norman: University of Oklahoma Press, 1979.

Kalt, William D., III. *Tucson Was a Railroad Town: The Days of Steam in the Big burg on the Main Line.* Mountlake Terrace, WA: VTD Rail Publishing, 2007.

Kessell, John L. *Spain in the Southwest: A Narrative History of Colonial New Mexico, Arizona, Texas, and California.* Norman: University of Oklahoma Press, 2002

Kino, Eusebio Francisco. *Crónica de la Pimería Alta: Favores Celestiales.* Hermosillo: Gobierno del Estado de Sonora, 1985

Kühn, Berndt. *Chronicles of War: Apache and Yavapai Resistance in the Southwestern United States and Northern Mexico, 1821–1937.* Tucson: Arizona Historical Society, 2014.

Lamberton, Ken. *Dry River: Stories of Life, Death, and Redemption on the Santa Cruz.* Tucson: University of Arizona Press, 2014.

Levstik, Jennifer. "Tucson Health Seekers: Design, Planning and Architecture in Tucson for the Treatment of Tuberculosis." National Register of Historic Places Multiple Properties Documentation Form. Tucson Historic Preservation Foundation, August 2012.

Logan, Michael F. *The Lessening Stream: An Environmental History of the Santa Cruz River.* Tucson, AZ: University of Arizona Press, 2002.

Lyons, Bettina. *Zeckendorfs and Steinfelds: Merchant Princes of the American Southwest.* Tucson: Arizona Historical Society, 2008. See also Steinfeld story by Bettina Lyons in Southwest Jewish Archives, http://parentseyes.arizona.edu/mrsteinfeld/.

Martin, Douglas D. *The Lamp in the Desert: The Story of the University of Arizona.* Tucson: University of Arizona Press, 1960.

McCarty, Kieran. *Desert Documentary.* Tucson: Arizona Historical Society, 1976.

Miller, Kristie. *Isabella Greenway: An Enterprising Woman*. Tucson: University of Arizona Press, 2004.

Otero, Lydia. *La Calle: Spatial Conflicts and Urban Renewal in a Southwest City*. Tucson: University of Arizona Press, 2010.

Nequette, Anne M. and R. Brooks Jeffery. *A Guide to Tucson Architecture*. Tucson: University of Arizona Press, 2002

Painter, Muriel Thayer. *With Good Heart: Yaqui Beliefs and Ceremonies in Pascua Village*. Tucson: University of Arizona Press, 1986.

Poltzer, Charles W., S.J. *Kino, a Legacy: His Life, His Works, His Missions, His Monuments*. Tucson: Jesuit Fathers of Southern Arizona, 1998.

Potter School Yearbook, 1949. Tucson: Arizona Historical Society.

Reinhold, Ruth M. *Sky Pioneering: Arizona in Aviation History*. Tucson: University of Arizona Press, 1982.

Santiago, Dawn Moore. "The Owls Club of Tucson," *Journal of Arizona History*, 33:3, autumn 1992, 241–268.

Scavone, Cirino G., and W. Eugene Caywoo. "Please Step to the Rear," *Smoke Signal* no. 32. Tucson: Tucson Corral of the Westerners, winter 1975.

Segesser, Philipp. *A Jesuit Missionary in Eighteenth-Century Sonora: The Family Correspondence of Philipp Segesser*. Edited by Raymond H. Thompson. Albuquerque: University of New Mexico Press, 2014.

Seymour, Deni J. *A Fateful Day in 1698: the Remarkable Sobaipuri-O'odham Victory over the Apaches and Their Allies*. Salt Lake City: University of Utah Press, 2014

Sheridan, Thomas. *Los Tucsonenses*. Tucson, AZ: University of Arizona Press, 1986.

---------. *Arizona: A History*. Tucson: University of Arizona Press, 1995.

---------. *Landscapes of Fraud: Mission Tumacácori, the Baca Float,* and the Betrayal of the O'odham. Tucson: University of Arizona Press, 2006.

Sloan, Eleanor B. "Seventy-Five Years of the Arizona Pioneers Historical Society, 1884–1959," *Journal of Arizona History* 1:1, spring 1959, 66–70.

Sonnischen, C. L. *Tucson: The Life and Times of an American City.* Norman: University of Oklahoma Press, 1982.

Spicer, Edward H. *Cycles of Conquest: The Impact of Spain, Mexico, and the United States on the Indians of the Southwest, 1533–1960.* Tucson: University of Arizona Press, 1962.

———. *A Short History of the Indians of the United States.* New York: Van Nostrand Reinhold, 1969.

———. *The Yaquis: A Cultural History.* Tucson: University of Arizona Press, 1980.

Stanley, Jerry. *Frontier Merchants: Lionel and Barron Jacobs and the Jewish Pioneers Who Settled the West.* New York: Crown Publishers, 1998.

St. Augustine's, 1964 (holdings of the Arizona Historical Society).

Stiffler, Ethel G. *Letters from Tucson, 1925–1927*, 2nd edition. Edited by Roger Carpenter (self-published 2014 [1st edition published 2006]).

———. *Letters from Tucson, 1933–1942.* Edited by Roger Carpenter (self-published 2009).

Summerhayes, Martha. *Vanished Arizona: Recollections of the Army Life of a New England Woman.* Lincoln: University of Nebraska Press, 1979.

Tucson, "The Old Pueblo": A Chronology. Edited by James E. Officer. Tucson: Tucson–Pima County Historical Commission, 1979.

Voices of El Presidio: Personal Tucson Histories. Edited by David Burckhalter. Tucson: Southwest Center, University of Arizona, 2004.

Wagoner, Jay J. *Arizona Territory, 1863–1912: A Political History.* Tucson: University of Arizona Press, 1970.

Webb, Robert H., Julio L. Betancourt, R. Roy Johnson, and Raymond M. Turner. *Requiem for the Santa Cruz: An Environmental History of an Arizona River.* Tucson: University of Arizona Press, 2014 (forward by Bernard Fontana).

Whiskey, Six-Guns & Red-Light Ladies: George Hand's Saloon Diary, Tucson, 1875–1878. Edited by Neil Carmony. Silver City, NM: High Lonesome Books, 1994 (manuscript in holdings of the Arizona Historical Society, Tucson)

Wright, Harold Bell. "Why I did not die," *The American Magazine* (June), 1924, 13-15, 82-90.

Resources on the Web

MUCH CAN BE found on the web but material residing there can sometimes disappear. With apologies in advance for any dead or superseded links and sites.:

Above Tucson: Then and Now (1995), website for the book of aerial photographs:
    http://www.abovetucson.com/

Applications by Tucson sites for Historic District status:
    http://www.tucsonaz.gov/preservation/historicdistricts

    Pending application for Broadway Historic District
    http://www.tucsonaz.gov/sites/default/files/hcd/THPO/ths_map_fp_sm.pdfhttp://www.tucsonaz.gov/files/projects/broadway/BwayHistoric_Final_Vol1_rev.pdf

Application of Binghampton Rural Historic Landscape (2003)
http://pdfhost.focus.nps.gov/docs/NRHP/Text/03000316.pdf

Arizona Archives Online (free public access to descriptions of archival collections in Arizona repositories, searchable):
http://www.azarchivesonline.org/xtf/view?docId=ead/uoa/UAAZ505.xml

Arizona Daily Star Top 200 Trend Tracker:
http://dynamic.azstarnet.com/star200/index.php

Arizona Geological Society mapping of the Tucson Basin:
http://data.azgs.az.gov/geologic-map-of-arizona/
http://azgeology.azgs.az.gov/article/earth-science/2014/05/statemap-mapping-program-arizona-2014-update

The Arizona Historical Society's description of its collection of the Tucson photographs by members of the Buehman family, 1875–c. 1951:
http://www.arizonahistoricalsociety.org/wp-content/upLoads/library_Buehman-Family.pdf

The Arizona Historical Society's description of its collection of the drawings and photographs of buildings designed in Tucson by Roy and Lew Place, 1916–1976:
http://www.arizonahistoricalsociety.org/wp-content/upLoads/library_Place-Architects.pdf

The Arizona Memory Project is "open to any Arizona cultural institution that is interested in making their digital holdings available online." Portions of hundreds of collections:
> http://azmemory.azlibrary.gov/cdm/ref/collection/ahstuc/id/72

Central Arizona Project:
> http://www.law.arizona.edu/library/Pathfinders/rstreat/pathdesc.html

Chamber of Commerce of Tucson, Quick Facts:
> http://tucsonchamber.org/community/relocate-to-tucson/community-profiles/

City of Tucson:
> City of Tucson 2013 Comprehensive Annual Financial Report" (PDF)

City of Tucson GIS Map:
> https://maps2.tucsonaz.gov/Html5Viewer/?viewer=maptucson

> This is an extraordinary resource, with layers offering all kinds of historical and current information.

Climate Assessment for the Southwest (CLIMAS)
> http://www.climas.arizona.edu/

Coronado's route in Nugent Brasher's detailed and field-tested argument:
> http://chichilticale.com/latest.htm

Documentary Relations of the Southwest (documents of Spanish Colonial History, 1530–1821):
 http://uair.library.arizona.edu/item/79579 or http://www.statemuseum.arizona.edu/oer/

Early mines and mining:
 http://southwest.library.arizona.edu/hav1/body.1_div.17.html

Early Tucson architects:
 https://preservetucson.org/basic-page/iconic-tucson-architects

El Fronterizo newspaper digitized:
 http://chroniclingamerica.loc.gov/lccn/sn95070521/

Friends of Tucson's Birthplace:
 http://www.tucsonsbirthplace.org/tucsons-birthplace/

Graduate Education at the University of Arizona:
 http://grad.arizona.edu/legacy/about/history

How did Himmel Park get its name?
 http://samhughes.org/how-did-himmel-park-get-its-name.html

"In the Footsteps of Esteban: African Americans in Tucson":
 http://parentseyes.arizona.edu/esteban/neighborhoods.html

Jewish Museum of the American West:
 http://www.jmaw.org/philip-drachman-pioneer-jewish/

Marist Brothers School:
https://preservetucson.org/projects/marist-college

Marshall Foundation website:
http://www.marshallfoundation.com/remarkable.html

Masons in Arizona:
http://www.epesrandolphlodge32.org/History.html

Patronato Mission San Xavier del Bac:
http://www.patronatosanxavier.org/preservation/scholars/

Pima Community College
https://www.pima.edu/Pima County Assessor's Office (parcel info):
http://www.asr.pima.gov/links/frm_Parcel.aspx?parcel=12306070A&taxyear=2016

Pima County Recorder's Map:
https://pimamaps.pima.gov/Silverlightviewer/Viewer.html?ViewerConfig=https://pimamaps.pima.gov/Geocortex/Essentials/REST/sites/mainsite/viewers/mainmap/virtualdirectory/config/viewer.xml&showAdvancedTools=False&showDataFrame=True&showOverviewMap=True&extent=&pmtype=pimamapsmain&layername=Parcels&fieldname=parcel&matchvalue=123-01017E&attributeSearch=Parcels,parcel,12301017E

Presidio excavation in 1998, Homer Thiel's account:
http://government.tucsonaz.gov/info/search-el-presidio-de-tucson

The Saguaro-Juniper Corporation's summary of the history of the Eastern Sobaipuri in Kino's time:
   http://www.saguaro-juniper.com/i_and_i/history/early_history/fr_kino_visits.html

Spanish Colonial Tucson:
   http://southwest.library.arizona.edu/spct/body.1_div.8.html "

"Street Smarts" series by David Leighton in the *Arizona Daily Star*. For example:
   http://tucson.com/news/local/street-smarts-adventurous-life-led-oury-here/article_8e98a574-0a94-5a07-9fb3-94dc907a5fbf.html
   http://tucson.com/news/local/street-smarts-woman-who-wrote-of-tucson-well-i-hardly/article_1887ad66-9cb1-5830-be34-ea2caa21be1d.html
   http://tucson.com/news/local/street-smarts-feldman-brought-family-to-tucson-after-s-economic/article_4451d045-997a-5c77-a892-5ef7f44ba36d.html
   http://tucson.com/news/local/street-smarts-foothills-street-name-honors-one-of-tucson-s/article_a334f1fe-28cb-5c85-a982-6277e6353622.html
   http://azstarnet.com/news/local/street-smarts-kramer-ave-named-for-winter-visitor-who-helped/article_83577fb0-db6d-5bee-a64a-e5a35dd52130.html
   http://tucson.com/news/local/street-smarts-hill-road-honor-mexican-military-commander/article_32411b25-2160-5ddd-bf3b-69697c1415d1.html

Surveying in Arizona Territory (Books of the Southwest, University of Arizona Library):
http://southwest.library.arizona.edu/hav6/body.1_div.15.html

Trichlorethylene (TCE) pollution in Tucson water:
http://www.library.pima.gov/blogs/post/trichlorethylene-tce-pollution-in-tucson-water/

Tucson Indian School:
http://tucson.com/news/blogs/streetsmarts/streetsmarts-tucson-indian-school-taught-hoeing-sewing/article_23d6699b-d9e8-5f9e-92fa-e3ec86f58f45.html

Tucson Meet Yourself:
http://www.tucsonmeetyourself.org/

Tucson Origins archaeology:
http://www.archaeologysouthwest.org/what-we-do/investigations/to/

Tucson Water Department
https://www.tucsonaz.gov/water

Tumamoc Ecological Reservation
http://tumamoc.arizona.edu/

University of Arizona Campus Arboretum:
http://arboretum.arizona.edu/history

University of Arizona Planning, Design, and Construction Division (historic preservation pages):
http://pdc.arizona.edu/planning/historic/default.aspx

University of Arizona Water Resources Research Center
https://wrrc.arizona.edu/

Web de Anza from the University of Oregon, with "primary source documents and multimedia resources covering Juan Bautista de Anza's two overland expeditions" from southern Arizona to northern California in 1775–1776:
http://anza.uoregon.edu/

Made in the USA
Coppell, TX
24 October 2019